the FRENCH PLAY

the FRENCH PLAY

Exploring Theatre "Re-creatively" with Foreign Language Students

by Les Essif

© 2006 Les Essif
Published by the University of Calgary Press
2500 University Drive NW
Calgary, Alberta, Canada T2N 1N4
www.uofcpress.com

Library and Archives Canada Cataloguing in Publication

Essif, Les

    The French play : exploring theatre "re-creatively" with foreign language students / Les Essif.

Includes bibliographical references.
ISBN-13: 978-1-55238-213-4
ISBN-10: 1-55238-213-3

    1. College theater—Study and teaching (Higher) 2. French drama—Study and teaching (Higher) 3. Theater—Production and direction—Study and teaching (Higher) 4. French language—Study and teaching (Higher)—English speakers. I. Title.

PN2075.E77 2006   792.02'807   C2006-903983-6

No part of this publication may be reproduced, stored in a retrieval system or transmitted, in any form or by any means, without the prior written consent of the publisher or a licence from The Canadian Copyright Licensing Agency (Access Copyright). For an Access Copyright licence, visit www.accesscopyright.ca or call toll free to 1-800-893-5777. We acknowledge the financial support of the Government of Canada, through the Book Publishing Industry Development Program (BPIDP), and the Alberta Foundation for the Arts for our publishing activities. We acknowledge the support of the Canada Council for the Arts for our publishing program.

Cover design, page design and typesetting by Mieka West

Cover Photo by Kenton Yeager. THE CHAIRS by Eugene Ionesco at Round House Theatre, Silver Spring, Maryland (Blake Robison, Producing Artistic Director). Direction and Scenic Design by Alain Timar. Lighting Design by Kenton Yeager. Costume Design by Denise Umland. Featuring Marcus Kidd and Jessica Brown-White.

  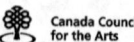 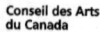

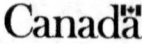

For Debbie, my soul mate
Here's to being together almost since the dawn of time and to continuing our journey with our happy, witty, utterly unique children, Davenne and Amien.

List of Illustrations   xiii
Acknowledgments   xv
Introduction   1

   The Pedagogy of Performance by and
      for Students of Foreign Language   7
   The Creativity-Complexity Matrix by Re-
      creative Design   10

   Theories 1: Performance and
      Re-creative Language Learning   13
   Theories 2: The Spect-actorial
      View of Performance   15
   Theories 3: Teaching Literary-Dramatic
      Texts as Culture-in-Process   19
   Theories 4: Regenerating the Creative
      Principle of the Text   25

Prologue: Advance Preparation
for the Project   31

   Selecting the Play   31
   Selecting the Rehearsal and
      Performance Spaces   35
   Recruiting the Students   37

1 Day One – You're On! 39

    1.1 Discussing the Syllabus and the Project: Organizing the Class Sessions and Semester, and Setting the Rehearsal Schedule 40
    1.2 Setting a Creative-Critical-Performative Tone for the Project 44
    1.3 The Introductory Re-creative Exercise 46
    1.4 Assessment of the Re-creative Exercise 53
    1.5 Homework 55

2 The First Six Weeks of Performance Awareness and Textual Analysis 57

    2.1 Creating a Performance Space, Challenging Habit, Trusting the Teacher-Director 57
    2.2 Questions 58
    2.3 Class Roster 58
    2.4 Recap 59
    2.5 Warm-Up Exercises 59
    2.6 Interactive Dramatic Games 63
    2.7 La Petite Mise-en-Scene (The Short Sketch) 64
    2.8 Textual Analysis 65
    2.9 A Performative Approach to the Text 67
    2.10 Guidelines for Performative-Textual Analysis 69
    2.11 The Journal 72
    2.12 Schedule of Re-creative Sketches (Petites Mises-en-Scènes) for Each Class 74
    2.13 Inducing a Semiotic Understanding of the Performance Work Vive la Différence! 76

2.14 The Discovery of Semiotics through
   Recreation and Re-creation   78
2.15 Introducing the "Systems" of Style,
   Costume, Prop, and Music, and the
   Styles of Jeanne d'Arc   79
2.16 Day Three and Beyond   90

3 The Collaborative Re-Creation
   of the Original Text   93

   3.1 The "How To" Guidelines for the
       Comprehensive Re-creational
       Assignment   93
   3.2 D-Day: Pieces Come Together and
       the Full Story Takes Shape   97
   3.3 Collaborative Examination of the
       Re-created Texts   99
   3.4 My Weekend from Hell!   99
   3.5 Discussing the Text and Giving
       It and Ourselves a Name   103
   3.6 Casting: The Anti-(Lone)Star
       System, or, Every Star Has a Prominent
       Place in the Constellation   105

4 Co-operatively and Re-creatively Rehearsing,
   Revising, Refining, and Promoting the
   Performance   109

   4.1 Early Rehearsals   110
   4.2 Blocking the Text   111
   4.3 Memorizing Text and Individual
       Work with Voice-Accent Intonation-
       Expression   113
   4.4 The Journal   114
   4.5 The Week before Spring Break 114
   4.6 After the Break: Discovering and
       Claiming Our Space   116

    4.7 The Material Genesis of the Play: Set,
        Costumes, Props, Sound, and Light   118
    4.8 Collaborative, Co-operative Duties:
        Stage Management and Promotion   122
    4.9 Poster and Program Design   127
    4.10 Financing the Production and
        Ticket Sales   128
    4.11 Activist Promotion: "Storming"
        the Foreign-Language Classrooms   129
    4.12 The Final Rehearsal Phase   131

5   The Opening Show: C'est fini! ...
   Ce n'est pas fini!   133

    5.1 Inevitable Doubts and Problems   134
    5.2 Rehearsing the Audience   135
    5.3 Audience Feedback: The Survey   139
    5.4 Photographing and Videotaping
        the Process and the Performance   140
    5.5 On the Road: Another Space,
        Another Audience   143

6   Post-Performance Student Evaluation of the
   Performance and the Project   147

7   The Analytical-Subjunctive Art of Combining
   Texts and Con-fusing Character Identities   151

    7.1 Regeneration through Combination   152
    7.2 Reinterpreting the Absurdity of Cruelty
        through the Con-fusion of Character
        Identities in Ionesco's Macbett   163

7.3 Taking Combination and Con-fusion to Another Level: "Dom Juan, Ubu, Hamm: Quelque chose suit son cours" ("Dom Juan, Ubu, Hamm: Something Is Taking Its Course")   171

Conclusion   179

Appendices   185

  Appendix A: Sample Course Description and Syllabus   185
  Appendix B: Sample Interactive Dramatic Games and Exercises   191
  Appendix C: Sample Study and Performance Guide for a Critical-Creative-Performative Approach to Ubu Roi   201
  Appendix D: Pavis's Questionnaire   204
  Appendix E: Textual Re-creation: Guidelines for Ubu 2000   208
  Appendix F: Sample Excerpts and Materials from Rewritten Plays   213
  Appendix G: Sample Promotional Materials and Methods   230
  Appendix H: Audience Survey   235
  Appendix I: Instructions for Final Undergraduate and Graduate Written Assignments   236

Works Cited   239
Notes   243

List of Illustrations

Fig. 1.	"Jeanne d'Arc." The narrative introduction.	82
Fig. 2.	"Jeanne d'Arc." Joan as a child.	83
Fig. 3.	"Jeanne d'Arc." Joan with Captain Beaudricourt.	84
Fig. 4.	"Jeanne d'Arc." Joan with King Charles.	84
Fig. 5.	"Jeanne d'Arc." Joan at the Battle of Orléans.	84
Fig. 6.	"Jeanne d'Arc." King Charles's coronation.	84
Fig. 7.	"Jeanne d'Arc." Joan's Trial.	84
Fig. 8.	"Jeanne d'Arc." Joan at the stake.	85
Fig. 9.	"Père Ubu," act 1, scene 1: "I'll clobber you, Mère Ubu!"	217
Fig. 10.	"Père Ubu," act 1, scene 1: "I'd like to place your butt on a throne!"	217
Fig. 11.	"Père Ubu," act 1 scene 1: Mère Ubu appeals to Pa's superior instincts.	217
Fig. 12.	"Père Ubu," act 4, scene 2. The battle scene: Soldiers dance in the aisles, ballet-style, to Tchaikovsky's "Dance of the Sugar Plum Fairy."	120
Fig. 13.	"Père Ubu." The Grande Finale.	137
Fig. 14.	"Père Ubu." Actors direct the audience in singing "The Debraining Song."	221
Fig. 15.	"Ubu Roi déformé." "Exercices" meets "Ubu Roi."	156
Fig. 16.	"Dom Juan-Cyrano." "Dom Juan" meets "Cyrano."	162
Fig. 17.	"Macbett." Witches and Limonadier plot the story.	166
Fig. 18.	"Macbett." Macbett and Banco declaim in tandem.	168
Fig. 19.	"Macbett." Witch-Babe revealed.	168
Fig. 20.	"Macbett." Witch/Lady Duncan and Limonadier behind the marionettes.	168
Fig. 21.	"Macbett." Macol-Marionette, emperor of all emperors.	170
Fig. 22.	"Dom Juan, Ubu, Hamm." A "chance" meeting of legendary theatrical figures.	176

Acknowledgments

This book is in many ways the result of collaboration with a great many generous, talented, and perceptive individuals, including students, colleagues, and the faculties and staffs of high schools, middle schools, community colleges, and my own university. I'm bound to overlook the names of some people who were helpful along the way.

Thanks to the colleagues, the journal editors, and the reviewers who have read and commented on the drafts of my previously published articles that I have rewoven into the chapters of this book. Special thanks to Elizabeth Welles and David Goldberg, to the excellent editorial staff of the *ADFL Bulletin*, to Stacy Wolf of *Theatre Topics*, and to Maria Stadter Fox and Dolly Young.

I'm much obliged to Patrice Pavis for all his insightful ideas and explanations, and for his permission to modify and reproduce his performance questionnaire.

John Romeiser, my first department head at the University of Tennessee, was exceptionally supportive of my work and he helped clear the way for the continuation of my performance projects. My current department head, Jeff Mellor, has made life at the office a great deal more bearable, and he and Frank Harris, associate vice chancellor of research, were instrumental in creating a source of funding for this book project.

My university's theatre department faculty and staff were invaluable, of course. Bonnie Gould was always there for me and I'd like to think that at least some of her passion for the theatre has rubbed off on me. Laura Sims, the UT Clarence Brown Theater production manager, always did her best to accommodate my performance projects. Kenton Yeager went far beyond the call of duty with his time and talent. Many of the photo illustrations in this book were processed from low-tech video recordings of the productions. Kenton took the time to single-handedly rescue many of these images from the obscurity in which they lay. And he offered valuable advice on their form and content.

I am much obliged to my colleagues in the UTK Center for Telecommunications and Video for their generous support. Supervisors William Terry and Brad Prosise organized on-campus video shoots for my plays, and some excellent cameramen, Robert Hill and Brad Lyle among them, did a superb job with the filming.

My department staff, especially Viviane Manigat and Lisa Pass, graciously accepted the burden that many of my projects added to their already busy workload. My colleague Florence Abad-Turner stepped in at the last minute to help with the proofreading of the French in the book's appendices.

Saralee Peccolo-Taylor of Powell High School greatly expanded outreach opportunities for our productions, thanks to her invaluable help with organizing the production of our plays at her school and with promoting our plays to her colleagues at other schools. Thanks to high school French faculty members Korey Dugger, Diane Changas, and Patricia Harris, and to Jim Frank and Catherine Smith of Cleveland State Community College for their organizational efforts.

Almost since the beginning of my commitment to exploring re-creative foreign-language theatre, the Theatre in Academe Symposium at Washington and Lee University (Lexington, VA) has been both the forum for the presentation of my work in performance pedagogy and a scholarly-artistic-instructional laboratory where I can see and hear about other fascinating experiences in the field. Thanks to the many inspired presenters and participants who have left their mark on my work, most especially to the symposium's vital founder and dynamic director, Domnica Radulescu. Long may she reign!

All those talented, creative, and dedicated students who made my projects and productions possible have also contributed in various ways to the growth and improvement of my re-creative approach. A special *chapeau bas* to Pat McCoy for her creative and collaborative contributions.

My thanks to the savvy and considerate editorial and administrative staff at the University of Calgary Press: John King, Karen Buttner, Kellie Moynihan, and Joyce Hildebrand. It has been a pleasure to work with all of them and Joyce's meticulous copy-editing has considerably enhanced the quality of this work.

ACKNOWLEDGMENTS xvii

Finally, I can't help but wonder how much my theatrical work would have suffered without the continuing support, inspiration, and helping hands of my wife, Deborah, our daughter, Davenne, and our son, Amien – artists, designers, and critics all!

Early versions of portions of this book have previously appeared in the following published forms: "Way off Broadway and Way out of the Classroom: American Students De-, Re-, and Per-forming the French Dramatic Text." *ADFL Bulletin* 27.1 (Fall 1995); "Teaching Literary-Dramatic Texts as Culture-in-Process in the Foreign Language Theater Practicum: The Strategy of Combining Texts." *ADFL Bulletin* 29.3 (Spring 1998); "(Re-)creating the Critique: In(tro)ducing the Semiotics of Theatre in the Foreign-Language Performance Project." *Theatre Topics* 12.2 (September 2002); and "A Workshop on the *Re-Creative* Approach to Performing and Teaching Theatre: The Example of Jarry's *King Ubu*." *The Theater of Teaching and the Lessons of Theater*. Ed. Maria Stadter Fox and Domnica Radulescu. New York: Lexington Books, 2005.

Part of the research for this book was made possible thanks to two Practitioner Research on Teaching Awards and one Professional Development Award from the University of Tennessee, Knoxville. Financial assistance for the production of the book was also provided by the Department of Modern Foreign Languages (Jeff Mellor, Head) and by the University's EPPE Fund.

Introduction

> Art re-creates the creative principle of things created.
> Everyone can do theatre, even actors.
> One can do theatre anywhere, even in a theatre. –*Augusto Boal*

Theatre as an art form is a survivor. In the greater community of consumers of culture, theatre has survived the accessibility, the convenience, and the technological success of the televisual, cinematic, and otherwise hyper-industrialized production of stories and images. In the academic community, a growing number of teachers and scholars treat theatre as a distinctly unique and complex academic subject. But much of the interest of both the community of spectators and the critically oriented academics has shifted from theatre as a literary form – theatre as word – to theatre as (either a potential or actual) performance: that is, to *theatre as the presentation of a transformation*.[1] The transformation takes place on a "stage" (any designated playing space) where the dramatic text's verbal system of meaning becomes the subject of – as it is subjected to – a veritable cauldron of interdependent, overlapping sign systems, including live bodies and voices, costumes, sets, props, sound, and possibly lighting. In view of our growing awareness and orchestration of the transformation process, theatre is more alive than ever, and thanks to the equally expanding interest in active and interactive foreign language pedagogy that has paralleled the shift from page to stage, theatrical performance has the potential to revolutionize foreign-language instructional methodology.

So why is this (to my knowledge) the first book available to guide foreign language educators through the multifaceted process leading to the production of a foreign language play with their students? Frankly and simply put, it is because precious few foreign language educators specialize in the practice and art of play production per se. Primarily trained as specialists of language, literature, or culture, they do not feel sufficiently qualified to speak, act, or write as practitioners of theatre. Consequently, there are plenty of books available that serve as guides to play production in general. But these books tend to have two shortcomings: they deal with plays written in the director's and the student-actors' native tongue, ignoring any demand to reproduce an untranslated text that is far removed linguistically and culturally from the immediate reality of the actors and the majority of the spectators; and they tend to focus on the artistic merit of the finished product, ignoring the instructional merit of the process.[2] On the foreign language side, we find journal articles that report on a given instructor's experience in producing a foreign language play and others that address certain dramatic strategies, techniques, and exercises in foreign language performance. But these endeavours do not do what this book does: that is, guide the foreign language teacher step-by-step through the entire process of play production and beyond, from the decision to mount a play, through the closing curtain and the final day of class, and finally to the completion by the student of a critical assessment of the project.

In addition to its use as a detailed instructional guide, this book introduces a *re-creative* approach to theatre production and it outlines the many instructional benefits that derive from this type of approach. My re-creative strategies include 1) the collective-collaborative rewriting of the original dramatic text, where the teacher-director collaborates with students not only to theatricalize the original text but also to contemporize, vulgarize, compress, and yes, even personalize it; 2) the combining of the performance of one text, such as Molière's *Dom Juan*, with selections from another text, such as Rostand's *Cyrano*; and 3) the sharing of the major roles among several of the student-actors, with the dual objective of according all students a significant acting contribution while providing them and the audience with alternative interpretive models for comparison and critical evaluation. This approach stimulates artistically and intellectually the actors as well as an audience comprising individuals with a wide range of competence in the foreign language, from beginning learners to native speakers.

While the chapters that follow emphasize my re-creative approach to foreign-language theatrical production in French, their use is certainly not limited to instructors of French. On the contrary, my strategies, practices, and exercises – textual as well as presentational, critical as well as artistic – are sufficiently innovative to be of interest to teachers of all

INTRODUCTION

foreign languages, teachers of English, English-as-a-second-language, and theatre, and to many other readers with an interest in theatre. While the texts and performances discussed in this book are almost exclusively from the French canon, almost all of these are either well-known classics (*Cyrano, Dom Juan, Candide*) or stories of legendary figures (Macbeth, Joan of Arc) whose structures and themes are especially familiar to colleagues and students working in all other foreign languages and in English. The text of reference that I use, *Ubu Roi*, perhaps less familiar than the other works, remains nonetheless a seminal work of the Western canon, and it is easily and thoroughly explained. My theories, strategies, and approach, as well as much of my production program and many of my exercises, will easily apply to all types of drama in any other foreign language. (Why not Tirso de Molina's *El Burlador de Sevilla* [The Seducer of Seville] or Goethe's *Faust*, for instance?) And chapter 7 provides a (re-)creative comparative study of Shakespeare's *Macbeth* and Ionesco's rewritten version of the story, *Macbett*, along with a rather detailed account of how my students and I re-creatively combined elements of the two texts. So I see no reason why colleagues working in other languages would not feel reasonably "at home" with this book.

For those educators, practitioners, or readers who are not particularly interested in re-creating the text, this book offers guidance and insight for a broad range of performance tasks and responsibilities and will allow the reader/practitioner to adopt my approach to varying degrees. In short, this book contains an array of new strategies for planning, producing, and analyzing theatre, covering such diverse yet essential topics as exercises to produce a total corporeal expression of the foreign language, reading drama from a performative point of view, performance semiotics, organization of rehearsal schedules, the collaborative-collective assignment of roles, outreach to other academic institutions and to the community at large, taking the play on tour, and the evaluation of the student-actors' work.

This book is about theatrical performance motivated by a text, a story; it is about this type of (play) performance at its most creative; and it is about the instructional and artistic benefits of a re-creative approach to theatre. In response to the three primary goals that motivated me to write this book, the book's contents provides the following: 1) a comprehensive and straightforward guide for the highly diversified, complex task of producing a foreign-language play with students who on the whole have relatively little experience with theatre; 2) a critical-theoretical framework that outlines in detail my re-creative approach to the task; and 3) a reference source for new and effective performative methods to interpret, analyze, and perform not only all sorts of dramatic texts but narrative texts as well. In sum, I expect my guidelines and strategies to motivate many more academics, professionals, and non-professionals to explore theatre as both an instructional tool and a multifaceted, multilayered source of meaning production.

WHO AM I TO WRITE THIS BOOK?

Having presented a rationale for the book and a summary of its form and content, let me attempt to establish my qualifications for writing it. First, I had a rather unique experience as a student doing performance projects in foreign languages. As an undergraduate in the late seventies, and then as a graduate student in the early eighties, I studied Spanish, French, and Portuguese at advanced levels, and in all these languages I took upper-division courses that exposed me to various amounts of performance projects. After one year of doctoral work in Spanish, I decided to change course. Largely due to my developing interest in the avant-garde types of drama and performance issuing primarily from French and francophone culture, I decided to drop Spanish and pursue graduate studies in French. My wife and I moved to France for two years. In 1985, I enrolled in a Diplôme d'Etudes Approfondies (advanced, doctoral level) program of studies at the Institut d'Etudes Théâtrales in Paris, where I studied theatre, drama, and performance from a number of different angles and with some of the most influential scholars, writers, and practitioners of theatre in France, among them Anne Ubersfeld, Patrice Pavis, and Michel Vinaver. I participated in a number of workshops on the pedagogy of dramatic games (*jeux dramatiques et pédagogie*) with Richard Monod and Jean-Pierre Ryngaert, and in a number of small group discussions with innovative theatrical troupes and theatre directors, such as Ariane Mnouchkine and actors from her Théâtre du Soleil, Patrice Chéreau, and Antoine Vitez. With fellow students from the institute representing a range of national cultures, I helped form what we thought of as an

INTRODUCTION 5

international theatre company. We did mostly dramatic readings, but we also began a more ambitious project: planning and rehearsing a multi-cultural production of *Candide*, which unfortunately never got too far off the ground – that is, out of my apartment and onto a stage. While most of my academic work in Paris related to the theory and analysis of drama and performance, the practitioner activities and pedagogical workshops contributed to my understanding of the production side of theatre.

When my wife and I returned to the U.S. in 1987, I spent a couple of years completing my PhD at Brown, where I experimented with the use of performance and production with my students. I continued my theatrical ventures with my French students of English when I held my first post-doc position in 1990-91 at the University of Burgundy in Dijon, France. But the real watershed in my approach to doing theatre with students of foreign language came when, as an assistant professor of French, I was assigned to do the French theatre practicum at the University of Louisville in 1993. About twenty students were originally enrolled in the course, and I wound up with eighteen. I was determined to make this course a comprehensive introduction to theatrical art in general and French play production in particular. I also assumed that all my students were interested in some way or another in having a genuine acting role in a French play, even though many of them had never seen a live play and their only experience with performance was purely vicarious – that is, it was mediated by electronically generated illusions projected on screens, large and small. Consequently, I decided to consolidate all my knowledge of theatre, my instructional discoveries, and my somewhat audacious ideas about performance to design for these students a truly unique and comprehensive, critical and artistic encounter with the wonders of theatrical art, and a project in which all eighteen students could have a real stage experience.

Below I will elaborate on the theoretical and conceptual principles that inspire and inform the new approach to foreign-language theatrical production that I began to develop consciously and carefully with my Louisville project and students. But, for now, let me say that the project was successful enough for me to continue researching and fine tuning my approach to this practice and to begin to write on various aspects of it. For the past twelve years, I have not only continued to practice the re-creative staging of foreign-language plays but have also laid the groundwork for this book, publishing articles and presenting workshops, papers, and lectures on my ideas and my work. Seeking to do justice to this book project, I was not content to rest on the laurels of student praise and laudatory student evaluations, or the compliments from colleagues in foreign-language studies and theatre studies. (Professional protocol among academics is not always a reliable barometer for achievement.) I have made a habit of providing my audiences with confidential surveys concerning their reception of my performance projects. In addition, the feedback I have had from editorial boards, readers of my papers, and those who have attended my lectures and workshops has helped me to improve my methods and my writing and to place my work into a broader perspective. I am convinced my approach is sufficiently innovative and productive to warrant passing it on to a variety of scholars and practitioners in other disciplines who do drama and theatre with their students, disciplines such as theatre, English, and English-as-a-second-language.

Let me say a word about the incorporation of theory in this book. The theoretical underpinnings of my views of theatrical art and pedagogy in general, and of my re-creative approach and strategies in particular, are most evident in this introduction, chapter 7, and the book's conclusion. Interspersed throughout the primarily utilitarian chapters of the book, the reader will also discover an array of additional critical and analytical explanations and references, such as those dealing with a performative method of reading drama and those dealing with performance semiotics in chapter 2. The theory and analysis of both text and performance should be of interest to many readers, especially those scholars, teachers, and directors who seek a clearer rationale for performance, for the transposition of text to stage, and for the pedagogy of performance. However, I also realize that many other readers might prefer to concentrate on the book's use as a step-by-step guide for producing a play, especially a foreign-language play. These readers will find that while all chapters contain some reference to drama and performance theory and criticism, the prologue and chapters 1 through 6 will easily stand on their own for the purposes of play production.

THE PEDAGOGY OF PERFORMANCE *BY* AND *FOR* STUDENTS OF FOREIGN LANGUAGE

Theatrical performance comes in a variety of shapes, sizes, and qualities at a wide range of educational institutions, from high schools to college campuses, large and small. Students participate not only in the usually high-budget productions destined for the university theatre department's main stage, but also in less elaborate productions that are components of drama courses in the programs of English, classics, and theatre departments. Play productions also happen in foreign-language programs. All these productions are supposed to have two primary objectives benefiting two different groups of individuals in two essentially different ways. The first objective is instructional, and it benefits student-actors by developing their knowledge of what drama is all about and their skill to perform a given dramatic work. The second objective is artistic – though, as Horace pointed out a couple of millennia ago, art should always instruct. Theatrical art is supposed to benefit the audience. Our understanding of and approaches to both art and instruction have come a long way in the last half-century: they have become both more creative and more complex. Artistically and even instructionally, foreign-language play production by students is often considered the "low end" of campus performance. The student-actors as well as the audience that views their work are too often not as convinced as they should be of the creativity and the complexity of their art, and the students are probably not very clear about the instruction they've received. This must change.

As teachers of foreign language and culture, we do not all have the same objectives in integrating drama and performance into our courses. Some of us treat the written dramatic text as a literary genre and do little to distinguish it from the more comprehensive act of production that this text implies. Many of us go no further than to encourage our students to "act" like native speakers of the foreign language. Others do dramatic readings of texts in which they "dramatically" place a piece of foreign literature in a concrete, historically and culturally specific, foreign context. When we go so far as to direct the students in the performance of a text before an audience, we feel we have exploited the theatrical approach for all it is worth. The fact is that, in most foreign-language curricula, most of us use theatrical performance with the same primary objective that we use dramatic games and dramatic readings: to enhance language learning. In writing about their experiences with integrating drama into a given foreign-language curriculum, many educators emphasize linguistic precision, preferring to refer to themselves as "word professionals."[3] For "word professionals," the drama effect amounts to providing a stimulus, creating a concrete context for the foreign word (the "paper" characters become flesh and blood) and encouraging the students to develop a more holistic form of expression through the use of their body and emotional apparatus. To their credit, these same "word professionals" are largely responsible for introducing into the foreign-language curriculum the theatre practicum, a course that usually includes the following steps: the selection of a prewritten dramatic text, the assignment of roles and ancillary duties, and the attainment of the best possible *mise-en-scène* (combination of language with image and action) of the foreign-language text. While the course itself represents a step in the right direction, I would contend that when we as professionals focus too closely on the speech component of the project, both the real instruction to the students and the *mise-en-scène* will suffer. The ultimate effect the project produces on the student-actors as well as on the audience will not reach a sufficient level of aesthetic, cultural, and critical awareness. To be sure, despite the emphasis on the purely verbal component of culture, the traditional, language-based approach to the theatre practicum can help not only language acquisition but also cultural awareness. If the teacher is tenacious and organized enough, the process will prove effective as a language-learning tool, especially since the greatest energy is spent on the memorization and recitation of foreign text. However, my focus in this type of course has never been on the language content per se, but rather on the theatrical context, on the material and spatial imagery (first visual, then aural) through which a story is told, and on immersing the students as completely as possible in creative performance technique. I try to make the student-actors feel that the role of the foreign language is merely instrumental to the theatrical context of the performance project, a uniquely comprehensive kind of context.

    I will return to the topic of language acquisition later in this chapter, but let me say for now that foreign-language theatre production can mean so much more for the student-actors and the audience if we step back from the obsessive focus on reproducing the language of a fixed text and begin to realize that theatrical art comes to life through the added contextualization of the language, and it begins to breathe more freely and deeply as it bridges the gaps between language, literature, and culture, the three primary subfields within our language programs. By emphasizing the material, spatial, psychosomatic, and gestural performance of the language and around the language, we can elevate our play projects to the level of *real* theatre; only then can we properly attend to two other very important dimensions of theatrical production by students, the critical and the artistic, which are enlightening, enriching, and otherwise instructive for the acting participants and the spectators alike. The project can and should provide critical insight (for actors and spectators) into textual and artistic construction, and, well beyond the more or less cosmetic application of the accouterment of theatre, such as costumes, props, music, and human gestures, it can lead to an innovative, original art form.

In an essay that does not emphasize verbal language acquisition, Margaret A. Haggstrom rightly argues that a "performative approach" to the study of theatre in the foreign-language classroom will help students become "critical and independent readers of the wide range of literary texts" (8-9) precisely because this approach transcends conventional language: "Since students can approach the theatre from the inside, as actors, rather than from the outside, as observers, the literary text does not remain simply words on a page, but actively and directly engages the student-actor both mentally and physically" (9).

But the accurate verbalizing of the words on the page does not fulfill the performative objective. Haggstrom adds that the students must get "actively involved" in the "interpretive and communicative decisions" of the creative process (9). This is a good start toward a performative approach to the study of theatre, an approach I will develop in detail in the course of this book. For now, let me say that the more actively involved the students become in the performance project, the greater understanding they will have of the concepts of text and performance taken to their highest level. I further believe that one can get the actors totally involved by increasing the potential for their creativity in producing the cultural artefact.[4]

THE CREATIVITY-COMPLEXITY MATRIX
BY RE-CREATIVE DESIGN

The creativity-complexity matrix underpins my focus on performance. Theatrical performance is both more and less profound than any of us believe it to be. "More" because, as the presentation of a transformation, it is always more than either the imitation or interpretation of a dramatic text, more than verbal language, and "less" in the sense that, as members of a human cultural community, we are all naturally endowed as performers, and we regularly perform culture using more than just verbal language. All the more reason that no matter how little formal experience students and instructor might have, they are entitled to approach the performance project as a bona fide creative work that they intend to perform/transform *au max* ("to the max"). My theatre projects represent some of the most creative, complex work that most, if not all, of the students and I have ever accomplished in any capacity. But the theatrical projects I am talking about are special in that I have designed them to exact creativity from the performers through a re-creative complexity in the composition of the performance text.

What does it mean to transpose a theatre text to the stage? More precisely, on the one hand, what does this act teach us about the nature and value of art, and, on the other, what does it produce in the form of art? I believe that much can be felt, learned, and produced if, instead of simply mounting, presenting, or creating the text, we deliberately set out to substantially *re-create* it.

I work with my students to produce exceptionally free adaptations of written texts from the French canon, collaborating with them to "re-create" the original written texts by compressing, contemporizing, vulgarizing, and yes, even personalizing them. This process is an unabashed negotiation of the story's images, actions, and language, a process that produces relevant meanings for our historical period and "local" (sub)culture: that is, a social community that falls somewhere in the realm of mostly middle-class and contemporary public university students.

To be sure, since all *mises-en-scènes* must rely on material interpretation (a transposition to the stage), they all are to some extent re-creative. Mine are nonetheless more self-consciously and deliberately so, for artistic as well as instructional purposes. By heavy-handedly manipulating these texts, my student-actors and (we hope) the spectators who eventually see the plays develop unique responses and learn new things about the ways in which all texts work, about the complex relationships of these texts with what we call "reality," and, in the specific case of the dramatic text, about the passage from text to stage. They also learn something about themselves and their personal relationship to art.

As far as art goes, over the years my re-creative work with students has produced unique theatrical images and effects that could not have found their way to the stage through any conventional approach to play production. In a 1995 production, for instance, we brought Molière's "classical" seventeenth-century womanizer Dom Juan together with Rostand's neo-romantic nineteenth-century Cyrano, the epitome of the one-woman man, "drawing" (literally) ironic parallels largely through theatrical imagery as well as textual revision. In a 1996 re-creation of Voltaire's (quite theatrical) novel *Candide*, we used forty-eight cues for an exceptionally wide variety of musical pieces to evoke thematic variations throughout the odyssey of Candide's wanderings and experiences, marking his progress toward intellectual and emotional maturity. In a 1997 re-created version of Jean Anouilh's Joan of Arc story (*L'Alouette*), we determined six distinct phases of Joan's short and tragic life, with a different actress representing and interpreting each of those phases, ending with a nine-year-old girl in a black body suit. A year later, in re-creating Ionesco's (already "re-created") version of Shakespeare's *Macbeth* – Ionesco called it *Macbett* – we concentrated on the idea of "doubling," which Ionesco inscribes in his text by techniques such as having Banco repeat verbatim whole passages delivered by Macbett. We further pursued this challenge to facile psychological character identity through the use of costume layering, the visible manipulation of life-sized marionettes, and the constant switching of actors who manipulated these marionettes. I have also worked with my students to mount two separate and very different productions based originally and largely on Jarry's absurdist classic, *Ubu Roi*, the text I will use in this book as the basic model for my theatre practicum project.

How did my students produce these uniquely re-created versions of these classic texts? They first learned to take a re-creative approach to the stories of Dom Juan, Joan of Arc, or Pa Ubu through their involvement in what I call *petites mises-en-scènes*, performance sketches based on a scene or a fragment of the story taken from the respective texts. In fact, on the very first day of the course, I introduce the students to the text performatively and re-creatively with the first-day re-creative exercise that sets the standard for my approach to the performance project. The basic steps to this exercise are as follows: 1) we discuss the story of, say, Dom Juan, Joan, or Ubu; 2) we read an excerpt from the dramatic text, one that is easily contextualized, usually the first or one of the first scenes of the play; 3) the students then put aside their texts and collectively and collaboratively reinvent three or four short lines total for two or three of the principal characters (Dom Juan, Sganarelle, and Done Elvire; Joan and her father; Ma and Pa Ubu), lines that they consider key to conveying the meaning or the spirit of the scene; 4) once the class has decided and fine-tuned the abridged and condensed version of the scene, they have ten minutes to develop a sketch, based either closely or loosely on the original scene, using these exact lines; and 5) each group performs their version of the scene and, as a group, we critique, compare, and contrast each of these versions.

In the next chapter I outline in detail this re-creative exercise, which I use to introduce the text we plan to reproduce, but at this point the reader should have some idea of how this exercise orients the class performatively and re-creatively. Nevertheless, I think all practitioners of theatre will get the sense of how this exercise acts first as a process moving from familiarization to de-familiarization to re-familiarization and then as an important step toward understanding the potential of performance practices, and finally how it sensitizes students to de-constructing and re-constructing textual authority in the passage from the text to the stage. It should also become clear that teacher-practitioners can use this exercise with any part of any text. Many of my students have never set foot in a theatre; they work in a foreign language and their capacity to speak and understand French varies considerably. So, compared to students learning to perform in their own native language, they probably derive more benefit from an exercise that de-emphasizes the conceptual component of verbal language by employing it as a mere point of departure instead of an end in itself.

THEORIES 1:
PERFORMANCE AND RE-CREATIVE
LANGUAGE LEARNING

As I said at the beginning of this introduction, most of us do theatre with our students primarily as a way to get them to *perform* the foreign language rather than to simply recite it. We are largely concerned with and focused on the language-learning benefit of the project. So let me speak to this benefit by saying that, paradoxically, I think we can improve the language-learning capacity of the project by de-emphasizing the verbal language of the text and re-emphasizing the pluridimensional con-text in which the language is produced through the medium of performance: performatively.

In my performance projects, the French language learning succeeds because I direct the student-actors' attention not to French at all but to performance. I intend to make my students forget that this is a foreign-language course. Properly introduced, theatrical performance can become much more than a language-learning tool. As an essential step (or rite of passage), it can provide the framework to prepare and encourage non-native French speakers to enter into a culture in which they eventually become not francophones but highly competent ("near-native") communicators, with or without much of an accent. So I focus my method not so much on French language teaching through theatre as on theatre through French language. Even if the instructor's primary or sole objective is to improve her students' language skills, she would do well to place the emphasis on theatre for the following reason: as second-language acquisition research has indicated, students will acquire greater proficiency in a foreign language through an instructional approach based on a combination of subject-matter emphasis (also understood as content-based instruction) and the *parole* concept of language. Theatrical performance is the ideal vehicle for this combination.

According to Janet K. Swaffar, the 1980s gave birth to a multidimensional paradigm shift in foreign-language learning. On one hand, educators moved away from purely linguistic basic-language courses and toward an earlier introduction to subject matter emphasis, in which students learn substantive information through the target language instead of focusing on the grammar and vocabulary skills themselves. On the other hand, the language component of the curriculum shifted from the teaching of *langue* to a more learner-sensitive teaching of *parole*. Swaffar uses Saussure's *langue-parole* dichotomy to illustrate this shift. Wherein *langue* represents the language accessible to the entire speech community, *parole* represents the language used by a particular group for particular purposes (59). Thus, abandoning the idea that "teaching comprehensive linguistic rules would result in comprehensive second language skills" (*langue*), educators began to embrace "*authentic input-language creation*" as a goal (55). Instead of presenting replication of a "normed language" as a goal, the new *parole* paradigm would stress creativity within a functional, communicative context. Teachers would divert the curricular focus from the vocabulary and grammar in themselves to the students' imaginative (and, I will add, often original) use of them in concrete situations.

In fact, the parole concept goes hand-in-hand with subject-matter emphasis, especially when the subject matter is theatrical performance instead of, for instance, culture, literature, or business. This is because the performance side of theatre is – or was meant to be – based on a kind of *parole* concept, on a notion of focused, transformative, creative, holistic, communal language production. Through my experience with theatre I am convinced that performance, which has been used in some fashion by all foreign-language teachers, can inspire a far more fundamental and engaging *parole* situation (that is, an immediate, functional, and group-specific context for language) than other kinds of subject matter inspire; it has a special and absolutely crucial effect on the imaginations of foreign-language learners. If we reassign performance from its role as a mere technique into the content of meaning of the class, if we persuade the students that we are more concerned with their abilities to involve their bodies in a communicative context than with the purely linguistic knowledge of French, they will acquire an extralinguistic awareness of how to perform French, how to get their bodies to speak it, through the broad experimentation with the communication context.

One could detect an analogy here, contrasting the experiential, phenomenological dimension of performance, which I briefly outlined above, with the referential principle of semiotics, which I will develop in more detail in the next section of this introduction. The semiotician's preoccupation with the production of meaning corresponds to the foreign-language educator's preoccupation with systems (such as *langue*) that tend to transform meaning creation into a mathematical calculation. Systems must be received in a certain way to have not only meaning but also relevance as an act. Like the *langue* approach to language teaching, a too rigorously referential semiotic point of view would not be sufficiently receptive to idiosyncratic usage (*parole*) or re-creation, the non-normative manipulation of codes. *Langue* is an abstract ideal until it is produced by a body and a voice that are as unique as a snowflake. No two native speakers perform French exactly the same way; there is really no such thing as standard French. So why deny the freedom enjoyed by native speakers to foreign-language learners?

For a very long time, academic programs in foreign languages ignored or even suppressed the unique and "consummating" experience of performance. For the past ten to fifteen years, however, a variety of performance exercises have crept into more and more instructional methodologies of a range of intermediate to advanced French-language texts.[5] Still, it is not enough to ask students to perform a canonic text or create a sketch based on an everyday situation or an historical or literary event. While there is nothing wrong with this approach, we could go further in giving performance its due by creatively, or better, *re-creatively* structuring language, culture, and literature classes around performance, transforming the method into an experimental form of subject matter.

So much for language learning through performance. Now I will speak to the broader context of my particular re-creative approach to the reading and staging of the dramatic text.

THEORIES 2:
THE SPECT-ACTORIAL VIEW OF PERFORMANCE

Theatrical performance is essential to human culture, probably more essential than other symbolic acts, even than other forms of symbolic communication such as writing and discursive or purely narrative orality. Not just some but all human beings are born actors. Art (culture) is the quintessential response of humans to the mysterious reality that is their world (nature), and live mimetic performance is the quintessential art. Aristotle, the pragmatist, attested to this, and Plato, the idealist, was, of course, wary of it. Who among us has not done theatre, has not performed in some way, on stage or off, in one assigned or assumed role or another? Performance is the most primitive form of art we know, humans having produced it and engaged in it as soon as their basic needs for survival were met. Deriving from a mimetic effort to relate to other human individuals that probably paved the way for the symbolic verbal system of communication, a primitive form of performance was most likely our first language. So human performance goes hand-in-hand with human language, as it does with learning through self-instruction.

Performance is a mimetic act, and mimesis, we know, has been considered a first principle of both performance and education. Yet performance has its own intrinsic, autonomous value, which has more to do with fulfillment of human social consciousness than with imitation of nature, as Aristotle saw it. Cultural theorists like semiotician Erika Fischer-Lichte tell us that theatre is a "cultural system," and more than just one cultural system among others: it is a "cultural system *sui generis*, one that is significantly different from other cultural systems because of the special functions which it alone fulfills" (1). Fischer-Lichte goes on to point out theatre's special functions from a semiotic point of view, explaining that theatrical performance has a special way (a special circumstance, a special code) to generate meaning: the meaning production, the encoding act of the performers, is inextricably connected to the "reader" of the meaning (the decoder of the act, the spectator in the audience) (1-12). Despite her recognition of the uniqueness of theatre, and despite the primary role of semiotics in the critical evaluation and understanding of drama and performance, Fischer-Lichte's perspective has its limitations. Semioticians are generally more concerned with the referential than with the experiential, with what happens at the level of the interpretation of signs, the decoding, than with what occurs within the realm of the encoders.[6] For this reason, Fischer-Lichte does not recognize that the performance can exist without an audience: "The audience is in fact a constitutive part of theatre – without an audience there can be no performance" (7). Admittedly, this opinion seems to represent a consensus of contemporary theatre practitioners and scholars, not just the semioticians. But I would like to articulate a divergent point of view, one which I think goes further toward recognizing and establishing the complexity and uniqueness of theatrical art and which has profound consequences for the (learner-based) instructional value of theatre.

Theatrical performance is more than an act of representational meaning production for an audience; it is uniquely functional and communicative already at the level of the performers insofar as it is an encoding and enacting of cultural experience wherein the performers or encoders themselves function as readers – or, more appropriately, as "sensers" – of their own act. Anthropologist Victor Turner would evidently support this argument and disagree with the assertion that "without an audience there can be no performance." Regarding theatrical performance as a social ritual, Turner has a much more performer-centred point of view. In fact, for him, performance is a natural step toward the completion of an experience. Seeing "ritual essentially as *performance, enactment*," he says that, true to its etymology, performance (from the Old French *parfournir* 'to complete, carry out, or accomplish thoroughly') is the proper finale or consummation of any experience in life (79).[7] There is nothing gratuitous or "high culture" about performance; on the contrary, it is a vital step in the human attempt to create form. So not only is performance in our blood, but if we abstract it or suppress it from those developmental processes that define us as human, we are in some way not whole; we run the risk of not becoming fully developed. All great cultural "texts," from the Bible to American leadership (the allusion to the current political connection between these two texts was not intentional), inspire *mises-en-scènes* in the form of passion plays or *Saturday Night Live* comedy sketches. While the audience – the role we most often play – derives mostly a vicarious experience in the form of an entertainment, through their consummating act the performers themselves reap the lion's share of direct, consummate experience.

So, the meaning production of any given performance practice, including the rehearsals, is not limited to that which occurs between writer and reader or performer and spectator. As an educator I am primarily interested in the preliminary stage of meaning production negotiated by the actor as an active spectator of her own and the other actors' efforts toward creative communication. In rehearsal as well as in performance, when the group of actors on stage engage in dialogue and image creation, even before the intended audience comes into play, they produce meaning for themselves. Augusto Boal claims that the essence of theatre resides "in the human being observing itself.... Theatre – or theatricality – is this capacity, this human property which allows man to observe himself in action, in activity. The self-knowledge thus acquired allows him ... to imagine variations of his action, to study alternatives. Man can see himself in the act of seeing, in the act of acting" (*Rainbow* 4). "An actor, acting, taking action, he has learnt to be his own spectator" (*Rainbow* 13). I would add at least one other dimension to this act of communication. As Mikhail Bahktin's dialogic theory of language suggests for all acts of human expression, an actor first produces meaning for herself: that is, she doubles as her own interlocutor – her own "other" – communicating directly with herself. On the stage, however, in addition to this internal dialogue, she consciously and conscientiously produces meaning not only *with* other actors but *for* them as well. She communicates to and with other actors *and* she sees herself doing this. Finally, she produces meaning for either a virtual audience (in rehearsal) by means of her personal (self-to-self) and social (self-to-other-actors) awareness while communicating with this virtual and non-acting entity (the virtual audience), or with an actual audience, which, unlike the virtual audience, can and does respond. At any rate, Boal refers to this doubling of the role of actor into the role of spectator as the "*spect-actor* acting on the actor who acts" (*Rainbow* 13; my emphasis). There is reflexive communication between the actor and herself and between one actor and another. Even when she is alone on stage doing a monologue, the actor will see herself acting to/for a second degree, virtual, stage reality of an absent actor. This constitutes the triple dimension of performance communication: the actor performs for herself as well as for her partner(s) ... and her audience.

Let me complete this section by connecting the "spect-actorial" dimension of the actor to the critical, semiotic side of performance, a topic I will discuss in greater detail in chapter 2. The properly trained actor becomes critically conscious of her capacity to produce and control her meaning production, and, with a higher degree of experience, she becomes better able to forecast both her fellow actors' and the spectator's reception of the meaning she wishes to produce. An acutely and actively acquired sense of performance semiotics can only enhance the spect-actorial potential of our actors.

THEORIES 3:
TEACHING LITERARY-DRAMATIC
TEXTS AS CULTURE-IN-PROCESS

> One cannot stress this enough: there is no true meaning of a text. The author has no authority. Whatever he might have wanted to say, he wrote what he wrote. Once published, a text is like an apparatus that each of us uses in our own way and by our own means. It is not certain that the designer makes better use of it than others. – *Paul Valéry*

Could it be that, in our literature classes, especially foreign-language literature classes, we too often teach at a level which surpasses that of the understanding of a majority of our students? I do believe this is a problem in our profession, one we can begin to address if we teach literary texts not as finished works of art but as "culture-in-process," a principle at the core of my approach to the dramatic text within the context of the theatre practicum. My approach is based on a revisionist concept of the reception of literary texts that goes a long way toward shifting interpretive authority to the readers, according them full participation in the creative cultural process of textual construction. But the concept is consistent with theories of drama and performance that challenge purist principles of mimetic representation and advocate the perpetual, active renewal of classic texts.

Imagine, for example, a university student production of a foreign-language play, such as Molière's *Dom Juan* or Rostand's *Cyrano de Bergerac*, in which the student players have significantly abridged the original text and rewritten some of the language in order to make the play more comprehensible and accessible to themselves and their largely anglophone audience. Imagine that the principal roles in the play are not "owned" by one individual actor but shared by two or more of them. Imagine as well that both *Dom Juan* and *Cyrano* are being performed on the same stage space, not one after the other, but in the same one-hour-twenty-minute time-frame through the alternation of tableaux from each of the stories, an alternation that progressively blurs until the action and characters of the two works actually merge by the end of the performance. How do you think this would affect your perception of text? More to the point, since the student-actors collaborated in this integrated production, how do you think it affected their understanding of text as a historicized vehicle of authorial intention? Have they lost respect for the cultural monuments created by Molière and Rostand? Or have they gained new insight into their "readerly and writerly" participation in the textual process?

The literary text is a cultural process. As teachers of language, literature, and culture, we are used to teaching our students through the medium of some kind of text. Usually the text belongs to the canon, which means that generations of critics, scholars, and teachers have found the text to be a valuable tool for understanding our culture and ourselves. A problem arises, though, when we tend to translate the structures of time-proven texts as fixed and their ideas as truth. Through our complacency, the texts become closed within their own authority, one that usually remains mystically distant to the non-initiated student and consequently only approachable through the mediating authority of the teacher. Much of the problem stems not from our recognizing the text as a canonical vehicle of authorial intention but simply from its status as a text, a finished cultural product. Happily, the age of imperialism of the written text is waning, and philosophical, pedagogical, and cultural definitions of text have greatly evolved in the last several decades. Today, many scholars and teachers take for granted not only that a text can be something other than a written vehicle of expression – at base, we can define *text* as any network of relations rather than as the bounded pages of a book – but also that the "authority" of a text resides as much in its reception as in the text itself. The intellectual tyranny of the illusion of an objective (textual) truth is held at bay. This reflects an increasing abandonment of a conventional, historicist-objectivist approach to texts as fixed in history[8] and a new regard for textual criticism that Northrop Frye has referred to in terms of "presence":

> The critical principle involved is that the text is not the absence of a former presence but the place of the resurrection of the presence.... In this risen presence text and reader are equally involved. The reader is a whole of which the text is a part; the text is a whole of which the reader is a part – these contradictory movements keep passing into one another and back again. (994)

The "presence" of the reader undermines the possibility of a fixed creative message, structure, or meaning in the text, and it guarantees the reader's participation in the recurrent resurrection of the *process* of textual creation. Consequently, literature teachers today deal as much with textuality – the art of text production and the reader's role in this production – and intertextuality as they do with separate texts and their "original" authors.

Text is culture, culture is text, and both are creative processes. On the one hand, as Gérard Genette points out, all individual literary works are part of an intertextual process.[9] On the other hand, the reader has a cultural life that connects to the text through a kind of symbiosis of symbolisms. Like the culture a text reflects, the form, language, and content of the text are determined by a highly complex conjunction of forces, the most powerful of which is the "presence," the particular symbolic experience, of the reader. Primarily because of the importance of reception theory and the role that sociocultural context plays in reader response, we have elevated literary texts to a status of culture-in-process. Since culture-in-process is by nature always indeterminate, we apply to our reading of texts highly flexible structures of interpretation that tolerate difference as well as ambiguity, and even a little personalization.

According to her seminal work in foreign-language education, "Literary Texts in the Classroom," Claire Kramsch believes we should "sensitize the students to the process of literary creation" (358) and view the reading of literary texts as "an active construction process" involving text and reader: "Reading is the joint construction of a social reality between the reader and the text" (357). It is, as she describes it, a dialectical process between the author and the reader, where the authority related to the text is perhaps not eliminated but shifted to the side of the reader. Even many historicist-objectivist types of literature teachers might agree with Kramsch's stated goal, which is "to use the multiple perspective and life experiences of the readers to reach an understanding of the multifaceted world of the narrative" (361). Kramsch might only expect that the students understand, as best they can, the complex world of the fixed, objective text. But she erases any thought of textual authority when she speaks of "the negotiation of the meaning of the literary text" (357). Moreover, do we fully grasp the implications of how she envisions the interpretive situation when she speaks of "the privilege of the readers to interpret the text in a way that is meaningful to them" (361)? To be sure, Kramsch does not have in mind one individual reader, but groups of readers who, through class discussion, are entitled to "negotiate" textual meaning. Yet her distinct break with the history and objectivity of the text is a step in the direction of personalized, individualized interpretation.

So what is wrong with this direction? Only when we cling to some remnant notion of textual objectivity can we seriously criticize a sincere and motivated interpretation for being too personal. Under all circumstances, through reading, we transform the text with the sociocultural as well as personal baggage we bring to it and through which we see it and act on it. The *Dom Juan* originally created by Molière has a different meaning depending on whether the reader of the work is from the nineteenth or the twentieth century, the 1970s or the 2000s, man or woman, straight or gay, optimist or pessimist, young or old, and even depending on whether or not he or she has just imbibed a strong dose of caffeine. It is not that all readings of the textual character are equally valid or profound, but that a genius by the name of Molière was able to create a character and a story that could mean *something* (profound!) to such a great number of readers, crossing not only historical boundaries but also cultural and even personal tastes. Hence the canonic or classical status of the work: the true literary classic allows a large number and variety of readers from different generations to become more consciously involved in its *process*. I believe we could be more deliberate in our break with the illusion of textual objectivity and more active in our regard for this process. So deliberate and active, in fact, that we openly deal with the "risen presence" of reception as the discovery of an autonomous, re-generated text.

The major task of today's literature teacher is not to teach students to worship the canonic text as some kind of historical monument but to discover non-normative methods to reveal the text's cultural process by engaging it in open collaboration with the students. Kramsch finds that the "fundamental paradox of education" materializes in the teacher-student dichotomy: "Teachers have to impart a body of knowledge, but learners have to discover that knowledge for themselves in order to internalize it – how can teachers at the same time give it to them and make them discover it on their own?" (*Context* 6). As part of her strategy of negotiating meaning, she feels that "the only valid approach to teaching literary texts is to be ready to discover every one anew with every new

INTRODUCTION

group of students and to be surprised by their insights" ("Texts" 364). I take this advice quite seriously.

Textual engagement leads to discovery for the teacher as well as for the student. We should place the students in a position to discover *our* discovery, one that we too must genuinely experience because we truly believe in the text's openness and transformability. By both guiding and joining the students in generating a "risen presence" for the text, we can transport their attention from the apparent and superficial subject of the text to the deeper levels of its textuality and intertextuality – to what Roland Barthes has described as the "plurality" from which the text was made – and teach them something about literature and its cultural context instead of the details of just another book or of just another literary celebrity. The students will learn not simply something about the text's original production (that is, the world and the genius that produced it), but, more important, something about the text's continual reproduction: that is, about their own world, their own critical minds, and their critical participation in the text's regenerative process.

The foreign-language theatre practicum is an excellent way to train students to approach literary texts as a *regenerative process*. By nature, the dramatic text is explicitly designed to generate another text (its performance). But do we allow ourselves enough freedom in applying this process? The theatre practicum has been around for a long time in the modern language departments of American colleges and universities. Even many high school foreign-language programs have the potential to work with students to produce a foreign-language play. Usually introduced at the intermediate to advanced level of study, it often bridges the gap between language and literature studies through the added contextualization of the language offered by performance. As noted above, however, teachers often are not sufficiently motivated, confident, or informed to employ a bona fide performative approach to the course. Neither do they exploit the creative potential of the performance project for teaching textuality. Performance, with its text-to-stage transmutation, requires a conscious, complex adherence to the reading process. But readers should consider seriously what a "performative approach" would entail, a topic I address more specifically in chapter 2. Here I will take a first step toward defining this approach by situating it in the broader arenas of foreign language and textual authority. To expose the textuality of the foreign-language dramatic text through the performative approach, teachers must deal with two distinct receptive challenges for students, challenges that can be turned into pedagogical advantages.

First, the concept of text has a special status when presented to a reader from another culture and another language. The reader of the foreign-language text is always a nonintended reader. Molière could not have imagined perfectly the social, political, ideological, and personal temperament of each reader (or theatregoer) from his seventeenth-century bourgeois culture, let alone the makeup of the modern non-European reader. Conversely, modern non-French readers will never understand either Molière or his culture with the same assurance that they do contemporary authors and their own culture. It is not just history that separates our students from the original production of the written text but also some form of national culture and its language. The opportunity for "misreading" increases dramatically. The students' reception of the foreign text necessarily diverges from that of a member of the national culture. Yet, if the text is a genuine classic, if the student's reading ability in the language and the student's knowledge of literature are competent, and if the dialectical formula for the reading of the text as discussed above is valid, then foreign-language reception is valid, not only despite its divergence, but because of it as well. (If this were not the case, many of us teachers of foreign literature who are not native speakers would have little justification in writing critically about the texts we read.) What's more, in a class where text is taught as process, this divergence can be turned to advantage because the conscious employment of the foreign-language code (the grammar) tends to allow students a more playful and imaginative role in the creative (re-)production of texts.

The other challenge to reception concerns the performative aspect of the dramatic text, a text that does not present the same (tyrannical) illusion of completeness or wholeness that narrative texts do. Since the art of *mise-en-scène* came into its own in the late nineteenth century, we consciously write and read drama as a regenerative process whose reception implies the generation of another text, the *mise-en-scène*. As Anne Ubersfeld puts it, the dramatic text is characteristically full of "holes," more so than other literary texts (*Lire* 23). Because of the holes in the dramatic text, reader reception becomes both more complex and more dynamic. The holes left by the dramatist are there precisely for the *pro-*

INTRODUCTION

cess of performance. All readers of drama are in some way metteurs-en-scène, producing and spatializing stage, imagery, and gesture as well as text in their minds. When, to create meaning, the structure of the text openly calls for the collaboration of the reader to produce a graphic and personalized visualization of the transformation from page to stage, the shift in authority is enormous. A performative reading of the dramatic text is quite obviously an individualized cultural process, one that fills in the holes with corporal and vocal expression, movement, costuming, scenery, objects, lighting, and so on. Discovery is imminent. Since dramatic texts have a greater potential to make students aware of their active role as readers in the production and process of textual meaning, we would do well to introduce drama and performance at the earliest stages of literary studies. I design my re-creative strategies to turn students into willing and critical participants in textual process.

THEORIES 4:
REGENERATING THE CREATIVE
PRINCIPLE OF THE TEXT

Before leaving the realm of theory, let me round out the theoretical background for my approach with a look at theorists of theatre who, much like Kramsch and her approach to the literary text, regard both text and the symbolic act of performance not as finished cultural products but as ongoing cultural processes, and theorists who consequently consider individual and communal reception to be the primary determinant of the meaning of text.

Long before literary theorists began to break with their historicist-objectivist approaches to narrative texts, many of the great theorist-practitioners of theatre since Alfred Jarry in the late nineteenth century challenged the objective authority of the dramatic text. Gordon Craig, Jacques Copeau, Antonin Artaud, and Bertolt Brecht have provided a variety of arguments against the privileged status of the written text, advocating creating through *mise-en-scène* rather than simply reproducing or even reinterpreting the original text. To varying degrees, they also subscribed to a spect-actorial view of theatre, recognizing that theatre involves real human beings engaged in communication, that communication occurs among actors on the stage as well as between audience and actor, and that the performers of theatre have the potential to engage in a highly expressive form of "textual" communion. (For the purposes of the present discussion, I am, of course, particularly interested in communication at the level of the performers, which I consider the initial and primary level.) They understood that because of its active participation in cultural process, its explicit demand for communal re-production, and, I would add, the facsimile society its production process creates, theatre is the most socially oriented of the arts, and to a great extent its social dynamic depends on its capacity to transcend the static state of mimesis in order to pass into a process of poiesis.

For Victor Turner – who was concerned with the "ritual of performance," theatre at its most primitive cultural level – performance is a kind of ritual text whose primary task is not so much to reflect or to imitate culture as to produce it, to form a productive part of cultural process. The basic difference between poiesis and mimesis amounts to the difference between "making" (*poiesis*) and "faking" (*mimesis*) (93). Since culture is never fixed, it is never fully representative of itself, and, in a sense, never mimetic. So Turner explains the task of poiesis as one of "remaking cultural sense" (87). He further argues that the poiesis-mimesis dichotomy relates analogically to the grammatical categories of the subjunctive and indicative moods, because cultural renewal – that is, the passage from an older and possibly obsolete cultural form to a new one – is

a unidirectional move from the "*indicative*" mood of cultural process, through culture's "*subjunctive*" mood back to the "*indicative*" mood, though this recovered mood has now been tempered, even transformed by immersion in subjunctivity.... The subjunctive, according to Webster's Dictionary, is always concerned with "wish, desire, possibility, or hypothesis"; it is a world of "as if," ranging from scientific hypothesis to festive fantasy. It is "if it *were* so," not "it *is* so." The indicative prevails in the world of what in the West we call "actual fact." (82-83)[10]

Like all ritual process, performance is at its sociocultural best when it is in the subjunctive mood of poiesis, when it is active production rather than passive representation or interpretation. Creative tampering with cultural texts can lead to the productive tempering of obsolescent cultural forms.

This theory of ritual process is remarkably consistent with the sociodialectical approaches to theatre of socialist theorist-practitioners like Bertolt Brecht and Augusto Boal. In fact, the subjunctive "what if" mood of Brecht's plays has guaranteed their continued survival. The Marxists were aware of the political dangers of culture's indicative mood, of the world of "actual fact" and objective truth, which for them amounted to mere ideological illusion. Cultural process fosters social progress through the continued postulation of "What if it were (or were not) so?"; human individuals and their theatrical counterparts become an integral part of the evolving social con-text. To cut through ideological illusion, Brecht's epic theatre rejected conventional dramatic theatre's emphasis on "man as a fixed point" for "man as a process" (37); it sought to displace the emphasis from the dramatic character as a free individual to the situation (both dramatic and sociopolitical), a situation that the dramatist as well as the reader-spectator should regard as conditional rather than natural. Like Turner, Brecht was interested in sociocultural renewal by means of the creative manipulation of fixed cultural texts. Many of Brecht's theatrical works were, in fact, reworkings of the classics and the classical myths. He criticized traditional theatre's superficial, mimetic approach to the classics, an approach that was interested only in a "false greatness" of the original texts, a "surface greatness," and one that failed "to see the work afresh" and to "bring out the ideas originally contained in it" (272-73).

After Brecht, the Brazilian Augusto Boal decries our misreading of the Aristotelian concept of mimesis, which he prefers to read in a poietic light, translating the Aristotelian dictum "Art imitates nature" as "Art re-creates the creative principle of things created" (*Theatre of the Oppressed* 1; trans. modified). Determined to be re-creative in his theatrical projects, Boal was ever vigilant of the "limitations of copying" (164), and he writes of his experiences in mounting the masterpieces of the classical canon (Lope de Vega, Molière, Gogol) in twentieth-century Brazil, explaining how "the modification of the whole structure of the text was necessary in order to restore, centuries later, its original idea" (164).[11] Like Brecht, when Boal refers to "original idea," his main concern is to discover the idea's extracultural and extrahistorical force by reproducing an effect equal in intention, depth, and relevance to the original cultural effect of the text: that is, the original reader's response to the process of the text. The "original idea," deriving directly from the creative principle that inspired and forged the original written text, may be thoroughly disguised or obscured by the historico-cultural colouration of the text's form and content. Writers write and readers read (directors direct and actors act) through the inspiration of the creative principle underlying the forms, and we can only hope to recuperate that principle through the regenerative, subjunctive mood of culture. Questioning whether it is really possible for one historical period to read either literally or figuratively the text of an earlier period, Boal seeks to re-create a deep archaeological structure.

So a major objective of the socialist agenda is to find dialectical solutions for reconciling classical creative principles with, as Brecht put it, "the increasing difficulty of reproducing the present-day world" (274). Like Turner's and Brecht's arguments for an interventionist "what if?" approach to our performative production of culture and to our reception of cultural forms, Boal's revisionist search for the creative principle is entirely consistent with revisionist theories of text insofar as it illuminates the dialectical notion of mutual text production through reception. Turner, Brecht, and Boal realize that, beyond the original text, the creative principle appeals to the deep cultural consciousness of the reader, whose primary task is to renew the principle, and the culture of which it is part, by reproducing the present-day world through the medium of the text. My re-creative approach to theatre follows the spirit of these visionaries and their search to contribute to a subjunctive, poietic, creative meaning of life by rekindling the creative principle of text.

The chapters that follow have several overlapping objectives. In a linear fashion, they will guide the instructor step-by-step through the process required to successfully produce a foreign-language play with students. The journey through this play-production core is oriented by my re-creative perspective, one stocked with ideas and strategies to engage the participants performatively and analytically in their understanding of culture-in-process and a number of its artifices and artefacts, including not only the dramatic text and its transposition to the stage but also our awareness of body and mind. In order to illuminate the journey, to increase the clarity and expand the pleasures of its process and progress,

INTRODUCTION

and to render this volume more accessible and versatile for a variety of readers, I include an extensive set of appendices and a number of photo illustrations (of my productions) that provide concrete, detailed depictions of materials, activities, and constructions, as well as alternative paths toward achievement and enrichment. Allow me to apologize in advance, however, for the rather poor quality of the majority of the photo illustrations, which are in fact not photographs at all but shots that have been captured and reprocessed from videotaped recordings of the performances.

Prologue

Advance Preparation for the Project

With our critical and methodological baggage inspiring and leading us toward a new level of creativity for our foreign-language performance project with our students, I'd like to take the reader through a step-by-step process to get the show first on the drawing board and then on the road. Whether the dramatic and performance experience of the reader is that of a high school instructor or a university academic looking to do her first foreign-language play with students, or that of a seasoned director of either campus or community theatre projects, or any variation between, the ideas in this chapter and those that follow should provide food for thought and new and effective instructional, analytical, and performance techniques and strategies that will enhance the experience for student and instructor, director and actor alike.

SELECTING THE PLAY

Play selection can be both the most and the least difficult decision to make. In the re-creative project you will choose a work that a given culture considers to be a classic – meaning that contemporary critics continue to believe in the relevance and the influence of the work – and set out with the intention of contemporizing and vulgarizing, as well as de-familiarizing and re-familiarizing, the text's language and culture. So virtually any classic text will work for your project.[12] You will, of course, have your doubts as to whether you have a thorough enough understanding of Molière's *Dom Juan*, or Ionesco's *Macbett*, or Beckett's *Fin de partie*, whether you can bring your students to a motivational understanding of the text, or whether you can sufficiently abridge the artistic complexity of a text like Jarry's *Ubu Roi* while recovering its creative principle.

And let's face it, each of us has our own taste and artistic preference. Yet, surprisingly, once we commit ourselves to the task of reading any of these texts from a point of view that transcends the critical point of view of a teacher and adopts the artistic, receptive, and representational eye of the metteur-en-scène, things change. Given a certain level of resolve, the intention, good will, and innate performative talent of any focused group will come to successful terms with the text.

With this thought in mind, the teacher-director should choose a text that she trusts she can adequately render not merely comprehensible but exciting as well to the level of students in the class. On reading a given text do you get an intellectual and artistic buzz? Do particular scenes of the play seem to re-create themselves in your mind? Perhaps there are gaps in your analytical grasp of the text, but these gaps should represent more of a challenge than a fear.

Since designing and developing my re-creative approach to text performance, I have chosen the best of all possible texts that led to the best of all possible performances, including Voltaire's highly theatrical prose text, *Candide*. In 1994, at the University of Louisville, when I first decided to make a clear break with the conventional approach to mounting a foreign-language play, I had a group of eighteen students and I was determined to find substantial acting roles for each and every one of them. I was concerned as well about their knowledge of and experience with theatrical performance, so I thought a naturalist-symbolist-absurdist play like Alfred Jarry's *Ubu Roi* would provide much of the quantity and variety I sought, brimming as it is with interactive dialogue and action as well as a large number of characters to speak and act. From the beginning, I had planned to double and maybe even triple the number of actors playing the principal roles of Ma and Pa Ubu, but even with that, I still had to find other means to ensure all students a substantial moment in the spotlight. That's where the unusual but very theatrical prose text of Raymond Queneau's *Exercices de style* comes in. French directors have for many years produced this text on stage, selecting a small number of the work's ninety-nine different styles for representation, creating scenes from the styles, and adding transitions between the scenes. Each style I chose would accord one or more of my actors an independent and more or less central function in this second dramatic work. As it turned out, however, the (re-created) text of *Exercices* did not simply alternate with the action of the main story of Ubu; it wound up merging and assimilating into that action.

The next year, 1995, when I moved to my current home at the University of Tennessee, I had a group of ten students in my first practicum class. The outcome of the previous year's re-creative project was so successful that I determined to continue my exploratory journey into the art of combining texts, a topic I develop in chapter 7 ("Regeneration through Combination"). I also decided to try a text from an earlier historical period. So I chose Molière's *Dom Juan*, again with some consideration for its comprehensibility, its dialogue, the dramatic action and movement from one space to another, as well as the dynamic duo at the heart of the story, Dom Juan and his valet, Sganarelle. To complement this text, we developed and played it in tandem with Rostand's *Cyrano de Bergerac*, the neo-romantic jewel from the late nineteenth century. One problem I hadn't considered sufficiently was the sheer length of *Cyrano*. Ideally, before the play proceeds to the stage of production, the students will have had the time to examine its dramaturgical system and subsystems and its production potential. The length of *Cyrano*, in addition to the Molière text, makes it difficult for intermediate students of French to keep up with the reading. Consequently, I'm sure some of the less experienced students did not read (at least not closely) the entire text. If ever again I have the opportunity to combine these two plays, I probably would reduce the reading assignment for *Cyrano* by summarizing some of the scenes.

The Dom Juan-Cyrano project had piqued the curiosity of a couple of colleagues in the theatre department, one of whom, Bonnie Gould, had a good command of French and prior experience in foreign-language theatre and was truly interested in doing a project together the following year. I was in fact quite flattered by Bonnie's and the theatre department's exceptional gesture of outreach. So Bonnie and I would essentially team-teach the course. But since I had developed my own re-creative approach to the task, and because of the more or less advanced language and textual analysis components of the course requiring the experience and training of a foreign-language academic, we agreed that I would have the final word in determining the instructional and directorial structures of the project. In addition to her talent, experience, and insight, Bonnie brought to the project a key to the theatre department's costume and prop shops, and a team of advanced theatre students who worked primarily on lighting and set design.

In 1996 I decided to theatricalize Voltaire's short novel *Candide* for this project. While a student in Paris in the mid-eighties, I had had some hands-on experience with a theatrical version of the work, collaborating on a production and having an acting role in it, and two talented colleagues at the University of South Carolina, Jeff Persels and Olivier Debure, had mounted a very successful performance of the story with their students of French. Indeed, the story has lots of characters that move through a great variety of spaces. It has an abundance of action, dialogical situations, and the potential to produce fascinating imagery, and the character of Candide is so central that I had four of the twelve actors play the role.

The next year, 1997, I again chose to work on one text only: Jean Anouilh's *L'Alouette*, the story of Joan of Arc. Only seven students performed this play, five of whom got to play the central role of Joan – plus my nine-year-old daughter as a very young Joan for the brief but intense final tableau.

In 1998 I returned to the concept of combining two plays, but this time with a twist. My eight students and I first read a French translation of Shakespeare's *Macbeth* to understand the basic story structure and character-space dynamic. Then we turned to Ionesco's re-created version of this story, *Macbett*, with the instructional objective of gaining insight into Ionesco's process of writing an even more unrealistic-absurdist version of the original tragedy.

In the year 2000, I returned to the *Ubu* text, this time to produce it by itself and to see how much further I could take my students dramaturgically in a second production. After this project, I took a two-year break from my full-length performance projects in order to focus my attention on the completion of a book project.

In 2003, with twelve energetic students, including four graduate students, I decided to alter the structure of the practicum course by increasing the reading component so that it would conform to the requirements of a literature course in our program. The students would now have to read three full-length dramatic works (*Dom Juan*, *Ubu*, and Beckett's *Fin de partie*) and excerpts from others, including *Phèdre*, *Cyrano*, and *La Machine infernale* (Cocteau). I also experimented with an increased loosening of the directorial reins, allowing the students more latitude to produce the re-created written version of the text.

Most recently, in spring 2005, I originally had planned to return to the re-creation of one story and mount Giraudoux's *La Guerre de Troie n'aura pas lieu* (translated as *Tiger at the Gates*), a work with an abundance of central characters. I'm sure that my choice of this story had a lot to do with the current political climate. However, due primarily to a scheduling conflict in the French program for this semester, I wound up with only five students, all female. Though we still could have re-created Giraudoux's text to suit the five actors, I decided to change game plans. After reading a variety of dramatic texts to satisfy the reading component for the new course structure, we read four very short plays by the contemporary French playwright, Jean-Claude Grumberg, and more or less collapsed them into an integrated piece we called "Le Bombardement humain" ("Human Bombing").

SELECTING THE REHEARSAL AND PERFORMANCE SPACES

The location of the class, rehearsal, and performance space or spaces must be selected and reserved well in advance. If we agree with Augusto Boal that "one can do theatre anywhere, even in a theatre" (*Jeux* 20),[13] then any place is a good place to perform. So why concern ourselves with the choice of a venue for the class sessions, the rehearsals, and the performances? In an academic setting where most classes are conducted rather untheatrically and where rooms can vary enormously in size, layout, comfort, and acoustic quality, I do have my preferences when selecting the space for the course to be held. Much of each class session will be devoted to performance and rehearsal exercises, so my first choice would be one of the rooms used by the theatre department or by physical education to conduct their classes, rehearsals, or physical exercises. But these rooms are a distance from my office, which could pose a problem when I need to transport weighty and cumbersome materials to class. My next choice is a spacious, carpeted room, as sound-proof or isolated as possible from other classrooms to avoid disturbing others, and one with movable chairs and desks so we can make room for exercises and performance sketches. On occasion, I have had to settle for a relatively small, uncarpeted room. The time of the class will affect both the availability of classroom space and the availability of students to fill the space. The best time for this workshop is in the late afternoon, say 3:30 to 5:30. At this late hour fewer classes are being conducted, so it is usually easier to schedule a classroom that meets our needs and we have fewer neighbours we might disturb. In addition, though it is the end of a long day for instructor and students, students are generally more available at this transitional hour between class time and the part-time jobs that many of them keep. I teach the class twice a week. After doing three projects with a three-credit-hour class slot, I finally changed the course to four credit hours, and the two two-hour class sessions work fine. The rehearsals of the last two to three weeks before the performance will, of course, add many more hours to the schedule.

Despite Boal's upbeat news about the omnipresence of theatrical space, the selection of the space for the final performances elicits other concerns. Three key needs are a stage space large enough to contain the action of the play, an audience space large enough to contain the hordes of people who will attend the performances, and an overall layout that allows free movement between the stage and the audience space. With this in mind, my actors have played in the following "theatres": the campus's theatre-in-the-round, whose space we have been able to arrange or rearrange into a layout that suits our and the audience's needs; the ballroom of the university's student centre, where we used risers and platforms to create an elevated playing space divided into three distinct areas; the "chapel" of a student residence hall, where we placed a makeshift stage platform in front of the permanent stage (which also served as an altar); and the rather small but intimate and noble performance space of a converted church, where we performed our re-created Joan of Arc story. Finally, on several of our road trips to area high schools and community colleges, we settled for the schools' conventional "fourth-walled" auditorium spaces, where we again placed platforms in front of the stage to close the gap between actors and spectators, and to allow for interaction between the two groups.

It is, of course, extremely important to choose and do all you can to reserve your classroom and performance space as early as possible, usually before the semester begins. When you call the secretary or manager to negotiate the use of a preferred but usually unavailable space, I would advise emphasizing your desperate need to locate an adequate space, while conveying your pride and excitement for your project, which promises to be one of the premier end-of-semester campus events.

RECRUITING THE STUDENTS

There might or might not be two schools of thought on what species of foreign-language student would be sufficiently interested and motivated to commit him or herself to a project that requires a good deal more time and dedication than the average university course. Some of my colleagues seem to believe that only outgoing, active, or hyperactive students, especially those with some background in performance, are able and willing to sign on. To explain my position, I'll call on Augusto Boal's maxim that "anyone can do theatre, even actors" (*Jeux* 20) and expand this thought in the following way: Everyone can benefit from and succeed in theatre, even theatre professionals. In other words, there should be absolutely no auditions for this course. On the contrary, I attempt to persuade some of the most reticent, "nerdy," students in my other French classes to take the course. Notwithstanding my strong confidence in the therapeutic nature of theatre, I'm usually surprised at the metamorphosis of the most timid students entering the course.

On the other hand, don't be afraid to recruit seasoned actors from the theatre department for the project. If they have the foreign-language skill necessary, in all cases I have seen, including the three professional actors (members of the Actors Guild) who have enrolled in my projects, they will assimilate their performance skills to the collective will, spirit, and competence. They are happy for the opportunity to practice this alternative method of doing theatre and to do it in French.

One should, of course, be concerned to recruit a sufficient number of students to "fill" the class and achieve the goals of the project. So recruiting should begin long before the course is scheduled to occur, by regularly pitching the project to students in your other classes and by spreading the word to your colleagues, not only those in your own department but also in others such as English and theatre. In addition,

I have had native-speaking French students from majors outside the humanities and the spouse of a visiting theatre director join the class.

How many students are "right" for the course? Almost any number. In my latest project I squeaked by with only five student-actors, and my largest group was eighteen. The number of students might affect the choice of play for the project, but much can be done through the design of the re-created text to accommodate the numbers.

Be prepared for the difficulties of dealing with today's students whose college life has become increasingly complicated by extracurricular obligations such as part-time jobs and the growing number of clubs and activities that provide filler for the student's vita. These obligations seriously compromise the time the students are able to spend on academic responsibilities and on something so important as theatre practicum rehearsals. Some of our students claim to have more obligations than the faculty! (Sometimes it seems that all of them believe they do.)

The most productive stage of recruiting begins when I prepare and distribute the course description in the form of a flyer. Since the theatre practicum is a special kind of course, I ask my colleagues in French studies to advertise it to all undergraduate and graduate classes above the basic-language level. I also send an announcement to colleagues in the theatre and English departments. The flyer should include information on the requirements, nature, structure, and goals of the project. My requirements indicate the need for a certain competence in the French language, familiarity with literature and basic techniques of literary analysis, and overall high motivation, but I make clear that the students are absolutely not required to have any prior acting or theatrical experience. For the nature and objectives of the course, I note that the project is a particularly comprehensive and collective enterprise, focused on the analysis and performance of dramatic literature, with the overarching goal to produce a final performance piece. The grading guidelines reflect the prominence of performance and a performative approach to textual analysis. I also spell out the advantages and expectations for graduate students who take this course. See Appendix A, "Short Course Description for Promotional Purposes."[14]

I

Day One – You're On!

The important first day of class draws near. Because of the nature of this course, I try to make my first entrance into the classroom (before *my* audience of students-soon-to-be-actors) a memorable one – that is, a unique and theatrical one. One tactic I've employed is to enter the room as if on a stage, fully conscious of my body being mine/me, on display and integrally connected to space and the human environment (the student audience-cast). I then eyeball each and every one of the usually irregularly dispersed students, and, like a chef d'orchestre, with a prominent gesture I signal them to rise, to take up their seats and rearrange them in a half-circle in front of the class. While they are engaged in this activity, I do my best to choreograph their movement and instill in them the sense that they too are "on stage" and in a performance mode. While they perform this act, I rehearse the students in the refrain of a fairly well-known French song, such as "Chevaliers de la Table Ronde," and/or have them hum the song. Once this act is accomplished, I signal them to be seated.

The reader might perform this type of entrance, or not. You could simply enter the room and, accompanied by a stylized voice and gesture, say: "Bonjour, les acteurs." You might repeat this phrase + gesture until they imitate in concert your stylization in their response: "Bonjour, monsieur/madame [le professeur?]." Then you could tell them that this preparation of the space (*l'aménagement de l'espace*) will be their first responsibility of every session. As soon as two or three of them arrive for the class, they will open a playing space and position the chairs around it.

If you do begin in this "performance" mode, you do not have to worry about reverting to a more conventional instructional posture to do the administrative part of the first day of class, verifying attendance and discussing the course and the syllabus. With a well-established "performance pose" and the proper conditioning of the student-actors, the instructor can easily move in and out of the performance mode at will.

My next step is to have the students fill out a class roster (*feuille de noms*) that calls for the following information: name, phone, email, and "theatrical phrase" (*phrase théâtrale*), the latter of which could be as simple as one word ("*Merde!*") or as complex as a full sentence. With this simple instruction students write sentences like "*Ché pas,*" "*Tout est bien,*" "*L'Enfer, ce n'est pas les autres, c'est....*" The phrases are either connected conceptually to theatre/performance ("*Etre ou ne pas être*") or they are poetically or phonetically charged. They might be excerpts from classical poetry or philosophical writing, idiosyncratic concoctions, or pat phrases that resonate with the student's experience with French or theatre. An alternative to this exercise would be to show the class a picture in some way connected with the play they are going to study – Jarry's drawing of Pa Ubu, for example – and ask them: "What is this man thinking about?" ("*A quoi pense ce monsieur?*").

1.1 DISCUSSING THE SYLLABUS AND THE PROJECT
*Organizing the Class Sessions and Semester,
and Setting the Rehearsal Schedule*

While the class roster is circulating and students are creating their theatrical phrases, I distribute and discuss in some detail the syllabus. Besides the essential information relating to the instructor, office hours, textbooks, and reserve materials, the syllabus expands the short course description that was used to advertise the course and broaches the following topics for discussion (see Appendix A: "Sample Course Syllabus"). First, this is a unique course from which students can derive intellectual, artistic, and practical benefits; it serves the additional educational purpose of providing an authentic French-language cultural event for the local and campus communities. Second, the success of the project requires of the students not only prerequisite knowledge but also a high level of dedication and motivation: this is not academic "business as usual," but a creative *work project* with a clear mission and fixed deadlines. Many other people will be depending on us to provide an artistically sound event on a set date and time. Third, the student-actors are about to embark on a collective-collaborative journey that will depend on the development and nurturing of a communal work ethic. They will be expected to engage seriously in the evaluation of the performance work of others, offering their companions accurate judgment of their work; conversely, they should make an attempt at self-criticism and be open to the criticism of others. Fourth, they *all* will memorize roles and perform in front of an audience. Fifth, I give an introductory explanation and rationale for my performative approach to the text and my re-creative approach to its performance. Sixth, the syllabus outlines the classwork, homework, and grading criteria for graduates as well as undergraduates.

Finally, under "*Programme*," I give a broadly outlined timeline for the different components and stages of the course/project: 1) textual analysis and performance practice; 2) re-creating the text (indicating the dates on which the students must be available to meet in groups in order to do the work of re-creation); 3) first stage of the construction of the performance piece and rehearsals; 4) performances (on and off campus); 5) debriefing and preparation for final written work; 6) due dates for journals and papers. Given the experimental, *atelier* nature of the project, I prefer to supplement and update periodically this schematic program description, providing the students with small doses of more detailed information on class activities covering two to three weeks at a time.

To complete the discussion of the syllabus, we talk about the rationale and formula for grading, which includes the written component of the course in the form of a journal and final paper. I postpone the discussion about journal writing until the end of this first class session, but let me say a few words about grading. When I first began to conduct these practicum projects, I had some misgivings about according too much weight to the non-written portion of the course. Thus, for my first re-creative project at the University of Louisville, I included the study of a good deal of critical writing about theatre, and I even gave the students a written exam (with both in-class and take-home essay-type questions to develop) on the critical and dramatic texts we had read and discussed. However, I finally convinced myself that, unlike the conventional academic course, the non-written component in this course covers a whole lot more than simple oral discussion. Theatre courses in acting give students credit for creative expression and other non-written work, and for certain fields of study such as art, music, theatre, dance, and architecture, university administrators increasingly recognize that, for fulfillment of faculty responsibilities, creative activity is on a par with scholarship. Therefore, it is only appropriate that the theatre practicum be weighted heavily toward the area of creative participation and expression. Despite the grading formula, students still do an exceptional amount of somewhat informal but nonetheless effective and educational written work. Over the course of the semester, most undergraduate students will have written upwards of four to five thousand words for their regular journal entries and another two thousand words for their final analysis of the project.

In conjunction with the discussion of the syllabus, I distribute a schedule for the rehearsals and performances, to which the students must commit within the first week of class. I give them one or two class meetings to verify their availability for this schedule. If one student has a priority conflict (induction into the armed services? reception for Nobel laureates?; or perhaps an awards dinner, family wedding, or other significant commitment), the class renegotiates the schedule. One common problem is a conflict with another course. In this case, usually the student is able to have her absence(s) excused with a simple explanation to the instructor of the other course, but sometimes I need to write the instructor to assure him/her that our project is at least as important as all those extracurricular university sports activities and events that seem to provide an automatic excuse for the athletes on campus. Surprisingly, if you get to the students this early in the semester, before they have a chance to fill their agendas, they will have few conflicts, if any. Once the schedule is set by unanimous agreement, it is (almost) inviolable. It has to be, especially given the overly committed schedules of today's college student as well as the instructor. This said, I have had to deal with the case of an actor who had a legitimate and unavoidable conflict that arose about six weeks into the semester. Though it took some paperwork and some discussion with the other participants, we were able to accommodate it.

Where does one draw the line? In this type of project, students must understand from the beginning that you will do all you can to reduce time commitments to the bare minimum. But after that, they are required to dedicate themselves to the project and its scheduled meetings. This is the most important responsibility of the semester, their first priority!

An additional word on the rehearsal schedule. Over the years I have strived to reduce the number of hours I require students to be present for rehearsals. In chapter 2 I will enumerate strategies I have developed to this end. At this very early point in the game, however, I find it productive to have the students commit to a "worst case" schedule, which, I assure them, I will pare down as we approach that stage of the project. As an example of how much time I ask them to allow for rehearsals, let's use the example of my spring 2000 project. Our semester began on January 13 and ended on May 1. Accordingly, I indicated that rehearsals would begin in the third week of March, which is also the week before spring break. For this week of "official" rehearsals, I merely increased the two class sessions (Tuesday and Thursday, from 3:40–5:30) by one hour (to 6:30), and added a Wednesday rehearsal, from 3:30–6:30 (this is where the conflicts with other courses might begin). On the week following spring break, the last week in March, I increased the meeting times considerably: Monday, Wednesday, and Thursday, 3:40–8:00 p.m.; Saturday, 10:00 a.m.–3:00 p.m.; and Sunday, 4:00–8:00 p.m. The following week, the week before performance, I repeated this schedule. Then the week of the performance, we scheduled a final rehearsal for 3:40–8:00 p.m. on Tuesday, with campus performances scheduled for Wednesday at 4:30 p.m., Thursday at 8:00 p.m., and Friday at 4:30 p.m. We took the play on tour to three different venues during the next week. In reality, I eventually reduced this schedule by as much as one-third for all the students. For example, I only expected to have to rehearse three out of the four weekend days originally scheduled, and we wound up cancelling the first Sunday's rehearsal (see chapter 4 for the final schedule). But, at this point early in the course, the students had to block their time around the pre-scheduled rehearsals and performances, including one hour before and one-half hour after the approximately one-hour performance. One of our off-campus venues, a ninety-minute drive from campus, required a full-day commitment. (Going on tour is a serious drain on the students' time, but it does so much good, and they feel so professional!)

What about the rewards? If in this introductory discussion I seem to emphasize the demands of the course and the responsibilities of the participants, I do assure the students of the course's rewards. I am always happy and confident to tell my students that the work they do in this course will go a long way toward improving their communicative skills in the foreign language: oral, expressive, and written. They will have regular and rich opportunities to speak, express, and "play" with their French "in character," and in a format that is equally "true to life" and "bigger than life." Through this format they will develop a uniquely intimate working relationship with the group of peers and the teacher-director. Consequently, their attention will be diverted and will be so focused on the acting task at hand that psychological barriers to "foreign" communication will often fade into the background (see my introduction and the *parole* concept of language instruction). Phonetically speaking, they will have the opportunity to master foreign phonemes by playing with them. This ludic methodology and *parole* concept works for the writing assignments as well as the oral exercises. The overall atmosphere of the classroom/workplace will be very different from anything they have experienced up to this point in their academic careers. In addition to developing their abilities for theatrical and self expression, they will learn new analytical skills and learn to appreciate theatre and performance in any language. Last but not least, they will create unique characters, expressions, and imagery that will have a lasting effect on them, their fellow actors, and the audiences that come to see them perform.

"Any questions on the syllabus?"

1.2 SETTING A CREATIVE-CRITICAL-PERFORMATIVE TONE FOR THE PROJECT

Next, I begin at the beginning, at the most fundamental level of comprehension of the project. I tell the students that, rather than a class, this is an *atelier de théâtre*, a theatrical workshop, and I ask them to define this for me. After soliciting their responses, I relate these to Augusto Boal's definition for the *atelier* – the place where artists work together – emphasizing once again their status as "artists" as well as the collective nature of the project. Then I ask for a definition of theatre in terms of how we might distinguish dramatic art from other arts. What makes theatre different from prose fiction? From poetry? From other performing arts, such as dance and musical presentations? My ulterior motive is to guide the students to make the following observations: theatre is indeed an artistic act, but one that is especially comprehensive, uniquely "loaded" and multidimensional, because its nature and structure have the potential to assimilate and integrate all the other arts, from prose, to poetry, to dance, music, film, and even the plastic arts and architecture. Richard Wagner's observation in the nineteenth century about opera being the paramount art form is more true of all theatrical art today. Another point I make is that theatre also distinguishes itself as a uniquely social art, as the closest art to life and society, one that creates in and of itself a world within a world, a society within a society, one marked by concentrated speaking, listening, looking, and feeling. Finally, among the basic features of human communication in general and artistic communication in particular, theatre is an art in which of doing, showing, and telling, the doing and the showing are more determinant (than third-person telling) for meaning creation.

Then I remind the students of Augusto Boal's clever axioms (which provide the epigraph to this book's introduction) about how anyone can do theatre and they can do it anywhere (*Jeux* 20). I might also mention one of my favourite Antonin Artaud quotations: "The smell of shit is the smell of the living," or, more literally, "Wherever you smell shit, you smell life" (*Là où ça sent la merde / ça sent l'être*) ("La Recherche de la Fécalité," 81).[15] Among the many possible senses of this assertion, one is that true theatre (which, for Artaud, is more than simply the "double" of life) can represent a lot of things, but never business or communication as usual (as convention). In the name of civilization, reason, and propriety, we have rendered taboo the discussion, consideration, and even our awareness of some of the most fundamentally human traits and functions. Consequently, Artaud's poetry brings us back to the essence of life, which in turn is the essence of theatre. At all stages of theatrical production, actors would do well to banish their fears of embarrassment in order to get in touch with the primal "*merde*" of life, a prerequisite step to a truly organic and *genuine* presence and performance on and for the stage. Beyond this, as I pointed out in the introduction to this book, artists are always spectators as well as actors (spect-actors); they are receivers as well as producers of meaning. So a big part of their meaning production has to do with their ability to be attentive to (*à l'écoute de*) the "smell" – that is, the "being" – of their fellow actors.

1.3 THE INTRODUCTORY RE-CREATIVE EXERCISE

Perhaps more than our colleagues in theatre and English departments, we foreign-language teachers who do theatre need to de-emphasize the text and re-emphasize theatrical process. Perhaps more than any other method, my re-creative approach to the text forces the teacher-director and student-actors to de-emphasize the literary level of the text and re-emphasize its performance potential, the most profound potential for meaning production. Re-creative practitioners become producers in the full sense of the word because they remain conscious of the passage of the text into a composite, syncretic collaboration and fusion of a number of diverse signifying systems, such as complex human expression, movement, costuming, scenography, props, and sound. In a real sense, text "disappears" into the multidimensional dynamic synergy of performance.

To begin my re-creative initiation-induction to the synergy of performance, I use a form of shock therapy to expose and subvert the literary and authorial levels of the classical text and to empower the students' creativity and imbue in them a faith in the potential of performance. On the very first day of our theatre practicum course I take my student-actors through an introductory re-creative exercise. Many – if not most – of my students have never set foot in a (real) theatre, other than their high school auditorium. They all work in a foreign language, but the capacity to speak and understand French varies considerably among the students. So, compared to students learning to perform in their own native tongue, they probably derive more benefit from an exercise that de-emphasizes the conceptual component (along with a pre-established conceptual reception) of verbal language, employing it as a mere point of departure instead of an end in itself. As a process moving from familiarization to de-familiarization to re-familiarization, my re-creative exercise sensitizes students to deconstructing and reconstructing textual authority in the passage from the text to the stage. It is an important step toward understanding the potential of performance practices and an exercise that teacher-practitioners can use with any part of any text.

Let me use as an example Alfred Jarry's *King Ubu* (*Ubu Roi*), written in 1896 and considered a precursor to the post-war theatre of the absurd. It is, in fact, a preposterous, grotesque, excessive parody of Shakespeare's *Hamlet*. The first line, "Merdre!" (only off by one *r* from the French word for "shit" and rendered by one translator as "Pschitt") was absolutely scandalous for its time. The text's characters (including "The Entire Russian Army," "The Bear," and "The De-braining Machine"), its space (it takes place, as Jarry tells us, "in Poland, in other words, No Place"), language, and objects are all "deformed" in many ways. The principal character, Pa Ubu, referred to in the play as a "walking gullet," is a consuming, killing, and cowering machine. A creature of instinctual response, he is the epitome of the antihero. In other words, for arguably the first time on stage, Jarry displays a uniquely "authentic" model of human nature, and what Artaud might have recognized as the "*merdre*" of life. His wife, Ma Ubu, is just as engaging and "realistic."

The plot: The gluttonous Pa Ubu, currently a high-ranking officer in the army of King Wenceslas of Poland ("No Place"), is persuaded by his wife to enlist the army to slaughter the king and his royal family and ascend the throne. When the dirty deed is done, he despoils his subjects, nobles as well as peasants, torturing and massacring at whim, and sentencing many to the "De-braining Machine." Then Ma Ubu coaxes him to lead his army of Palotins (exploding soldiers) to war in Russia so that in his absence she can seize Poland's treasury. But the two scoundrels are easily reconciled and at the end of the play, both are seen fleeing Poland in a boat headed for a new place to call home, a place where aristocrats of their breeding can prosper. That would be Jarry's native land: France!

Now for the exercise itself. Since the group is working in a foreign language, I conduct all activities almost entirely in that language. However, an instructor-director can conduct this exercise effectively in any language.

Step 1: Read and discuss. In order to break with instructional convention and to avoid preconceptions, I neither discuss the text nor reveal the plot before my students begin to read the first scene. We do discuss the unusual list of characters, which precedes the dialogue of the first scene. This discussion might include comments on the characters' names, their identities and potential functions (the "De-braining Machine"?), and potential ways of grouping them. Then we do a collective reading of the very short first scene of the play, in which Ma Ubu rather precipitously throws herself to the task of turning Pa's mind – by insult as well as seduction – toward regicide. Students take turns randomly reading the lines of one or the other characters. I encourage them not only to try to understand the logic of the text, to ask questions if there's a word or concept they don't understand, but also to see, hear, and "feel" the (excesses of the) text's performance: the action accompanying the language, the rhythms of the bodies in space.

Step 2: Reductively and collectively re-invent the scene. I ask the actors to put aside their text and, based on the reading, to imagine the characters, the space, and the action of the scene. Attempting to strike a balance between preserving the "spirit" of the text and allowing each student's own personal interpretive competence and experience to intervene, the actors imagine one visual image that can stand for the scene. Based on this image, what do the two characters say to construct, complement, or round out the meaning of the image? Then:

A. I, the director, write on the board (or overhead projector – but, personally, I prefer the hands-on immediacy, and erasability of the blackboard) the framework for a very short dialogue between Ma and Pa Ubu: a total of no more than four lines, composed of one to two short lines each: Ma...Pa... Ma... (Pa...); or Pa...Ma...Pa... (Ma...)

B. Without consulting their texts, the actors suggest short lines for each character and the director writes key words only (further coaxing the actors to engage their creative memory) for each variation of the dialogue, all of which will contain varying amounts of and references to the original text.

C. The group reviews these lines, based on the key words.

D. The director erases the key words.

E. The director asks the actors to recall, to further reinvent, or to synthesize the most memorable, relevant, essential, and/or theatrical of the formerly proffered lines.

F. The group agrees on three to four lines, which they may refine at this point. These lines are written on the board and fixed for the re-created mise-en-scène. (Actors will become increasingly aware that the words alone do not make the show or create the message.) The four (re-created) lines for the first scene of Ubu that one of my classes came up with are as follows:

PU: Me? King?... Pshitt! [Moi? Roi?... Merdre!]
MU: What a coward! [Quel lâche!]
PU: Pshitt! I'm leaving. [Merdre! Je m'en vais.]
MU: All the same, I'll be queen of Poland! [Quand même, je serai reine de Pologne!]

It would, of course, be possible to omit this multi-tiered process of establishing a fixed text for the re-creative scenes that will follow. But this would diminish the collective-collaborative nature of the exercise (at least at the level of the plenary group). Furthermore, the exercise helps students to come to some sort of collective interpretation of the text, and it challenges each group to produce original performance solutions and structures for the text. Eventually, the actors will compare and contrast each group's performance of the fixed text, manifesting the unlimited potential of performance.

Step 3: The "textual" and physical warm-up. While any invigorating exercises will suffice, the following warm-up is a composite of exercises suggested in two different texts, one by Hahlo and Reynolds, the other by Boal, which I have adapted, especially to include references to the Ubu scene that the actors will perform.[16]

A. First instruct the actors to stretch (and bring to corporal consciousness) the joints and limbs of their bodies. The stretch is accomplished with a focus on the head, the parts of the face, and finally the mouth: Say "Oooh!" (lips in "O" shape)..., then "Aahh!" (the mouth opens wide). In an exaggerated fashion, say "Mer"..., then "Dre"..., then "Mer-dre!". (Since the group is working in a foreign language, the vocalization should include an array of sounds specific to that language.)
B. After the stretch and vocal warm-up, issue a series of commands that put the individual actors in touch with the group and the space.
1. Walk around the room, superconscious of the space: its shape and the forms contained within it; materials, textures, details. Moving through the air as a submarine moves through water, touch everything and keep focused on the

feel of your physical contact with the shape of your material surroundings, architecture and objects.
2. Move faster, slower, FREEZE!
3. Close your eyes. Think of an "Ubu sound and/or word" (one related to the Ubu characters or to the story itself), silently articulating it with your inner voice, the voice of your mind, and listening with your "mind's ear." Next, on the count of three, say it aloud. Repeat it. Repeat it again and again. Louder... louder...louder. Softer...softer...softer. (To ensure a smooth, collective response, I give the following command for each repetition: "*Un... deux... trois: Dites!,*" etc.)
4. Open your eyes and change the focus of your sight by turning your head only. Move off in that direction. Walk, negotiating your way through the clusters of other moving bodies.
5. As you walk, expand your body, becoming as big as you can. Take up as much space as you can. Bigger...bigger still. Stop! On the count of three, say your Ubu sound as "big" as possible. Repeat.
6. Change focus by turning your head only. Move off in that direction. Walk.
7. As you walk, shrink your body as small as you can, continue moving. Smaller...smaller still. Stop! On the count of three, produce your Ubu sound as "small" as possible. Repeat.
8. Change focus by turning your head only. Move off in that direction. Walk.
9. Look at another body that is not looking at you. Close in on it. Surprise the person/character/body with a touch and your sound, and keep moving, non-stop, on to your next surprise encounter.
10. Now, half the group faces the other half. Make eye-to-eye contact with someone, and:
    a. Produce successively the following expressions with your *face only*: smile, frown, anger, inferior, superior, dumbfounded, ecstatic (*Un... deux... trois: Souriez!*, etc.). Remember to retain eye contact with the object of your gaze.
    b. Now produce the same expressions with your *entire body* (*Un... deux... trois: Allez!*)
    c. Produce first an Ubu *face*, then an Ubu *body-face*; then, on the count of three, add either your original Ubu sound or a different Ubu sound that corresponds to your Ubu body.
    d. Hum a tune with your Ubu body. Louder...softer...louder...frenzied. Stop!

e. Say "mer-". Say "-dre". Say *"Merdre!"* Add the appropriate (big) gesture. Louder...louder...louder still. To the max! Stop! Relax.

Step 4. Plotting the re-creative performance.

A. The large, warmed-up group is divided into smaller groups, mostly groups of two, but also, depending on the number of participants, at least one or two groups of three, and one or two single individuals, a situation that will vary and challenge the creativity of those groups with one extra or one less character than the scene seems to require. (Actors will produce very interesting, thought-provoking solutions to this challenge.)

B. Give the actors the following instructions:
   1. Memorize and play each of the four lines as is. The only exceptions to this rule: a) the group may insert the word *"merdre"* anywhere in their text and with any frequency; and, at their discretion, b) the group may add one short line only.
   2. If there is a sufficient number of participants, one or two of the groups (one group of three, and one of two?), selected by the director, must find a way to involve the audience directly in the action.
   3. Clearly define and mark the beginning and conclusion of your sketch. The audience must readily recognize the conclusion.
   4. Each group *may* use one prop, one piece of costume, and one sound effect, but the prop and the costume piece must be readily available – that is, either on their person or in the room where they rehearse and/or perform.
   5. Rehearse in isolation from others.
   6. Ten-minute time limit to prepare.

C. At this point the groups of actors disperse to locate a place for their re-creative rehearsal.

Step 5. Rehearsing the audience of actors. Once the groups are ready to perform, I inform them that they now will have essentially two roles to perform: in addition to their performance role, they will serve as critics, as a critical audience. The director should "rehearse" their role as critical spectator, involving them in a discussion of the performative potential of the forthcoming presentations:

A. Ask the students to think about what they expect to happen, about possible variations of the presentations and how they might compare or contrast with their own.

B. Distribute a questionnaire for them to take brief notes analyzing the presentations with respect to the following:
   1. positioning of actors
   2. proximity of the actors to the audience
   3. rhythm of movement
   4. language: rate of delivery of text, rhythm, enunciation, volume, tone
   5. gestures
   6. prop?
   7. costume?
   8. sound effect?

C. Based on these specific and distinctive elements of each group's sketch, be prepared to provide a specific *title* for each sketch.

These analytical guidelines enumerate components or sign systems that the inexperienced theatregoer would not normally (or consciously) observe. Emphasizing the constructed nature of performance, they facilitate both the reception and production of the great variety of sign systems that contribute toward the construction, even as I limit the number of components to which the critics pay attention. They also provide a clear basis for the comparative analysis of the individual productions, the next step.

Step 6. The re-created/creative performances. Each group plays once, then repeats once. If the first and second performance of the sketch are flawed, if any of the actors do not seem content with their performance, they may repeat a third time. If anyone misses their line, they also may stop and restart at any time. In addition, the director might ask the audience to give the actors feedback on the general quality of their sketch, which might include, for example, advising the actors to speak more loudly, to articulate more clearly their language or their gestures, or to define more clearly the beginning or ending of the sketch. Then:

A. Comparison. After the first sketch, the audience comments on each of the categories listed above. These comments should have a comparative component, and, for the first sketch, the actor-critics can reflect comparatively on their expectations. Subsequent to the first sketch, remarkable aspects of each sketch are compared with those employed in the others.
B. Title. Audience members come up with a title for each sketch, and the titles are written on the board for future reference. In the 2000 Ubu project, for example, students offered titles such as *"La Rage de Père Ubu"*) ("Pa Ubu's Fury") and *"Mère Ubu à la drague"* ("Ma Ubu on the Make").[17]
C. Summary. The analytical session concludes with a summary of the divergences among the groups (each being referred to by the title), including those groups with one more or one less actor and those instructed to engage the audience. With respect to these divergences, what do the various performance practices employed tell us first, about the dramatic situation of the Ubu text being presented and second, about the potential of performance to essentially determine the written language of the text?

1.4 ASSESSMENT OF THE RE-CREATIVE EXERCISE

This exercise is in many ways a miniature model for my entire project. It sets the standard for the long-term task of re-creating an entire text. For this reason, I think it is appropriate for the instructor to consider the following questions at this point:

1. If you are an experienced director, how does this exercise differ from the usual steps you take to prepare the mounting of a play? If you have no personal experience directing a play, how does this differ from the steps you might imagine?
2. Is this practice of textual tampering a "legitimate" reading of the text? If so, why? If not, why not?
3. What are the relationships between the text and this type of performance?
4. Is the text really responsible for these *mises-en-scènes*, or is it more a question of the creative talent of the student-actors?

5. Is this truly a "collective" effort?
6. Do participants feel they were truly collaborating?
7. Can this practice lead to innovative productions?
8. Is this "art"?
10. Was this exercise instructive for the student-actors? For the audience (the spect-actors)? If so, in what ways? What do/can student-actors learn? Do they risk losing an artistic and critical appreciation or understanding of the original text? Is this method pedagogically sound?

Having explained my instructional position in the introduction of this essay, I think the reader can certainly predict many of my responses to these questions. While the range of conceivable responses are undoubtedly unlimited, a serious consideration of these questions should help affirm the extent to which my re-creative practice breaks with tradition, requiring and stimulating a variety of collectively creative reactions to text, performance, and the transitional spaces between the two. The exercise I have outlined includes a two-step re-creative demand, initially for the written text and then for the performance of the re-created text. First the actors collectively re-imagine, re-invent, and re-assemble the text they have read, determining a second-degree distillation of the original scene. Then they respond to the challenge to come up with a multidimensional performance context through which to render these verbal signs. In the ten minutes they take to collaboratively design the performance, they must consider at least three sometimes competing, sometimes complementary circumstances: the original text of the scene they read along with the original performance they imagined; the potential of theatrical art to convey feeling and meld meaning; and their own personal and communal relationship to the condensed story. Clearly, the re-creative approach to text and performance draws to the forefront of the final presentations the second of these circumstances, the extra-verbal world of theatrical art. Much more is going on at the level of production, in the full sense of the word, including the production of new cultural forms. Meaning is clearly rooted in the performance rather than the text, whether the original, classical text or the re-written version that the students collaboratively (re)produce before they begin to perform it. Consequently, theatre practitioners of all types, backgrounds, and capabilities, from academics in foreign language and English to experienced directors, can discover and convey new dimensions and degrees of artistic and intellectual creativity through instructional re-creativity.[18]

Put more simply in terms of immediate instructional benefits, the students certainly learn something about semiotics of performance, something about the way in which theatrical sign systems come together on stage. They also learn about the spectator's experience, the perceptual effects of performance. Perhaps the most cogent lesson, though, is the concrete demonstration of the open, contingent status of all verbal text, the precariousness of a disembodied utterance in isolation. In spatializing and performing the text, the students were completing an experience by creating form, so, in a sense, they began the course as creators. Finally, the language-instruction objective that falls within the "subject matter-*parole* concept" paradigm: perhaps for the first time in their experience with French, these students were focused more on their bodies and space than on the abstract language structure (grammar and vocabulary) itself.

1.5 HOMEWORK

The re-creative exercise takes us to the end of the class session, at which time I give the students the following instructions for homework:

Reading: The re-creative exercise has already (collectively and collaboratively) introduced the students to the task of performatively analyzing the *Ubu* text, which spares them the shock of discovering the text's eccentricities all by themselves, alone in a campus residence hall – though I don't feel that we should always try to avoid this type of discovery. I ask the students to read preliminary information in the text, including the "Préface," the "Chronologie du Père Ubu," the "Discours d'Alfred Jarry," the "Répertoire des costumes" (provided by Jarry) and the strange list of characters,[19] as well as the first act and the first two scenes of the second act. Since this class only meets twice a week, the reading assignments are usually fairly lengthy, especially on a Thursday when they have four days before the next class session.

Writing – the Journal: I ask the students to attempt a *critical* analysis of the first day of class, focusing on one or two aspects of the syllabus, the discussions, or the re-creative exercise that seemed particularly interesting, important, surprising, or puzzling to them. What aspect of the class, for example, was the most surprising to them? In addition, they should write a couple of paragraphs on one or two aspects of the text (space? action? character?) that they found particularly intriguing or absurd. At the next class on the following Tuesday I will collect their journals for review.

I wait until the next week to give the students more in-depth instructions on journal-writing assignments. At this point I simply instruct them to avoid simple descriptive comments and to try to be as critical and analytical as possible. This is, of course, easy for me to say. See the next chapter for more on journal writing.

Finally, I warn the students to be prepared to produce a verbal and gestural "recapitulation" of the first day's activities at the beginning of the next class.

2

The First Six Weeks of Performance Awareness and Textual Analysis

The second day of class (Tuesday, January 18, for my Ubu 2000 project) allows me to establish the basic structure and order of class activities for the first part of the course, which is largely devoted to performance apprenticeship and textual analysis. In the first six weeks, class activities are generally organized in the following order: 1) a recap of the previous session's activities and discussions, and questions about these; 2) warm-up exercises, including vocal exercises in French; 3) dramatic games, including game-like or "recreational" semiotic awareness activities; 4) analysis and discussion of the text; and 5) the re-creation of a scene from the play. All class activities are conducted in the target language, but given the inevitable range of the students' proficiency in the foreign language, some English may be employed sporadically for necessary clarification (and theatrical oomph!).

2.1 CREATING A PERFORMANCE SPACE, CHALLENGING HABIT, TRUSTING THE TEACHER-DIRECTOR

To begin, students should know that the first of them to arrive in the classroom will clear a "stage space" within the classroom, arranging the chairs or the desks in a layout that resembles a theatrical space – not just any theatrical space, but one that connects with the audience and facilitates audience participation. I find that a simple semicircle of chairs is best for my purposes, an arrangement that creates the *théâtre-sphère* associated with the popular theatrical traditions (medieval, Elizabethan) that preceded the infamous creation of the *théâtre à l'italienne* (or *théâtre-cube*) and its fourth-walled barrier and frontal separation from the audience.[20] In addition, I make a pitch to the students to get them to alternate on a regular basis their seating position with respect to the other students in the class. With the objectives of avoiding the familiarity of old friends (familiar faces, voices, and personalities) and of becoming familiar with new ones, they will begin each class session in a new seat. I also impress upon them that mutual trust is essential to our collaborative work. We all must trust one another, and for certain aspects of the project, they must, as a group, have confidence in me – in my experience and my judgment as teacher and director. Nevertheless, considering the co-operative nature of our work and the final production, this confidence does not preclude discussion of my decisions or critical challenges to them. In the end, to trust me is to allow me to take responsibility for a final decision.

2.2 QUESTIONS

Before we begin afresh and transition into the performance mode, I allow a little time for informal, reflective discussion, asking students if they have any questions whatsoever about the course or the syllabus.

2.3 CLASS ROSTER

I distribute copies of the class roster (*feuille de noms*) that the students prepared the first day, and we briefly discuss the theatrical phrase that appears alongside each student's contact information. This helps acquaint students with the different personalities and interests in the class, and it helps convince them of the potential for the theatrical, of the theatrical essence of life. As I do in almost all my classes, I direct students in a group recitation and dramatization of some of the more phonetically charged phrases, asking them to repeat the phrase with a specific tone and volume, accompanied by a certain gesture. (See chapter 1 for examples of these phrases.)

2.4 RECAP

This activity draws the students further into the performance mode. (If the instructor prefers, this exercise could follow the warm-up exercises.) I ask students to stand and give them the following instructions:

1) Relax, close your eyes and concentrate, trying to recall as clearly and as thoroughly as possible, in chronological order, what we did and said in the previous session.
2) Open your eyes and think of the Ubu sound you produced for the first day's warm-up exercise. First think about it, then allow your body to vocalize it. First in a whisper, slowly and precisely, then accelerating the rhythm of the word/sound. Feel its weight in your mouth and its effect on your body. Add the gesture to the sound. *Un-deux-trois: Dites!... Un-deux-trois: Dites!*
3) Close your eyes and concentrate on the re-creative exercise. Try to see the action and hear the words of all the players/characters who were presented, including your own.
4) With your eyes still closed, allow your body to re-create any pose, attitude, or gesture that you recall. Allow the words associated with this gesture to come to articulation in your mouth
5) Find a comfortable place in the room. Bring to mind the re-created Ubu text of the first day. Think of the entire scene and text, without dwelling on the individual role that you played in the sketch: Ma Ubu says... Pa Ubu replies... Ma Ubu retorts... Using the appropriate gesture, on the count of three, present the first line: *Un-deux-trois: Dites! Un-deux-trois: Dites!* And so on.

2.5 WARM-UP EXERCISES

Next, we all get in touch with our bodies through the warm-up exercises that we will do each session prior to proceeding to the first dramatic game or performance activity. The exercises loosen the tongue and the body, both physically and psychologically, and besides getting in touch with one's own body, they also serve to create an esprit de corps and to diminish individual self-consciousness. The physical exertion itself contributes to the "bondability" of the individual in that a warm, exercised body responds better and more readily to another body. I usually not only supervise these exercises, but also participate in most of them, especially after the third or fourth day when I pass the exercise leader's baton to the students.

The exercises should be simple, especially at first; as the semester progresses, I introduce some complexity into the exercises. They should exercise the muscles, especially the lungs, regulate the breathing, and reawaken corporal consciousness and connect it to the voice. They should put the individual in touch with her inner organs, her inner self, and the body in touch with the mind that is the body, and they should connect the individual body-mind to the group. Furthermore, while exercising our immediate corporal consciousness, we would do well to relate these exercises to the ultimate objective of the class project: the production of a particular text or story – in this case, the Ubu story. So even the warm-ups have a component motivated by performance.

My basic warm-up involves a progressively more comprehensive stretch: first we focus on the body, silent and at rest, and get in touch with its breathing, then we turn our attention to the body's primary joints and muscles, then body-breath, then body-breath-voice. The guidelines for this exercise are easy to present, proceeding linearly from the top of the head to the bottom of the feet. I call the exercise the *tourbillon* (whirlwind):

1. Stand up straight, but with your body relaxed. Listen closely to the instructions. Enjoy a moment of silence, listening to your body and concentrating on your breathing – air flows in and out, and the transition of the flow of air from in to out is almost imperceptible.

2. Eyes open. At the point of your scalp and hair, a whirlwind begins to affect the very top of your body *from within*, blowing from left to right, causing your body-voice to initiate a hum that coincides with the energy of the internal wind. It begins to make your hair turn round and round, in a circular motion toward the right (Feel it?). ("Hum.") Then, slowly descending, it reaches your forehead, while continuing to affect your hair: each individual part of your face swirls round and round, first the forehead, then the eyebrows, eyes, ears, nose, and chin all get caught in the whirlwind, which proceeds slowly and steadily from the head and face through the neck, the shoulders, chest, abdomen, hips, knees, ankles, and feet. Slowly but steadily. Once you've arrived at the feet, the

CHAPTER TWO: THE FIRST SIX WEEKS

entire body is consumed by the whirlwind, and all the major joints are engaged in the rhythm of the motion.

Then the wind gradually decelerates: slower, slower still, until the motion comes to a rest and the hum becomes silent, though your body remains energized. Then suddenly the hum starts up again and the internal wind changes direction, from right to left. The hum changes tone, and, beginning with the feet, the motion proceeds up the body toward the hair, the last area to surrender to the motion. ("Hum.") Once you've reached the top again, after about ten seconds of working the entire body, the motion slowly comes to a final rest. The whirlwind has passed, leaving the body fully charged and ready for action.

3. Now for the mouth, voice, and body-voice. Remain standing, at ease, but with a new warmth and energy in your body. Mouth closed tightly. With the lips remaining closed, slowly widen the space within the mouth to the maximum *without opening the lips*. Relax. Repeat. Then open the mouth as widely as possible and stretch your jaw through its entire range of motion, side to side and up and down, round and round. Relax. Without making a sound, mechanically initiate a major yawn, slowly opening your mouth and, on your tiptoes, stretching your body and limbs upward to the maximum. *Un-deux-trois*: Yawn! Repeat the great yawn, but this time with an appropriate but exaggerated sound effect. Now contract your entire face to the maximum. Close your eyes, compress and pinch your lips together, until your mouth is as small and compressed as possible. Hold for about ten seconds. From this contracted position, begin to open your face and your mouth to the maximum. Open to the max! Hold. Release.

4. Now you will do with your entire body and voice what you did with your mouth, with your mouth-voice as the focal point of your body. Slowly and progressively open your mouth and your body to their maximum extension, stretching all your joints, limbs, muscles, and body cells, and coordinating a sound with the action. Open to the max! Hold. Release. Now reverse the action. Contract your mouth and your body as tightly as possible, folding yourself into a cocoon, concentrating on all the components of your body, from your scalp/hair to your face, your trunk, and your toes. Employ an appropriate, exaggerated sound. Hold. Release.

5. Add the breath. Breathe slowly, deeply, and deliberately, filling and emptying what appears to be your abdomen. Inhale, filling your entire body with air until it stretches to the maximum. Exhale, trying to empty your entire body of air, contracting into your cocoon at the maximum point of release. Inhale and repeat the action. Exhale and repeat the action. Relax.

6. In a relaxed standing position, let's add a French voice. First the basic vowel sounds. Say Ah!... Oh!... Ah là là. Repeat all the vowel sounds individually. Then repeat the sounds in rapid succession, transitioning from one vowel to the next without a clear break or distinction. Do /a/→/i/→/u/. Now add the consonants: /da/.../da-da/, /dé/.../dé-dé/, and so on, using a wide range and variety of consonant-vowel combinations, including, of course, the nasal vowels, and then ending with amusing, resonant combinations of fabricated words, such as /din-don-fan/, /pas-ta-fa-zouille/, and so on. Say in clear, precise articulation: *"Ah là là!," "Hélas!," "Tiens!," "M'enfin!," "Chou-ette!," "Mer," "Dre," "Mer-dre!," "Merdre!"*

7. To complete the warm-up, I usually have the actors take a stroll through a delimited space weaving in and out of one another's path at varying tempos (faster, slower, stop!) while vocalizing sounds, words, and phrases related to our work and the text at hand. (See also the warm-up exercise that precedes the first-day re-creative activity in chapter 1.)

As I lead the group two or three times through these warm-up exercises, I make sure the students realize that the key objectives are the activation of the body; the bringing to mind of the entire body, including its least obvious and least visible parts; and the connection of the individual body to the group through kinetic rhythm and vocalization in French. With this in mind, on the third or fourth session, I turn these exercises over to the actors. On a rotating basis, one of the actors leads the group (including the instructor) in a three- to five-minute warm-up exercise. This sharing of leadership responsibility helps the students mature in their role as project participants and it allows them to be creative in their design of an exercise. It also gives them an added opportunity to construct and employ French commands of their own. Students introduce a variety of ideas for exercises. If I see that a given exercise lacks an important component, such as the engagement of a French voice or sound, or perhaps the bringing into play of a vital body joint, then I might discreetly step in with a supplemental command or two of my own. Since I ask the actors to volunteer to lead the exercises, they do not volunteer until they are ready, and they usually prepare something in advance.[21]

2.6 INTERACTIVE DRAMATIC GAMES

Once the group has completed these warm-ups, simultaneously focusing on their individual bodies and voices and working together and in unison, the actors are ready to become more interactive. The next step up the activity ladder is what I call "interactive dramatic games" (*jeux dramatiques et interactifs*), where "games" suggests the innocent yet rule-governed conventional activities of children and "dramatic" suggests action.[22] The following is an example of an interactive exercise that I have done on the second day of class.

"*Faire connaissance*" ("Getting to Know You"). The students begin to promenade slowly and casually around the space of the room. At a given signal (*C'est parti!*), they greet the first person they see with their surprised recognition of a face, but not a name. (Yes, this exercise requires them to do a rudimentary bit of role playing.) Taking the person's hand, they say: "*Tiens, c'est toi*" ("Heh, it's you!" or "What d'ya know!"). Then they remind the other person of their own name and ask him/her to remind them of his/her name: "*C'est moi, Charles. Tu t'appelles comment encore?*" ("It's me, Charles. What's your name again?"). Once they get their names straight, they can ask, "*Comment ça va?*" and begin to banter more or less formulaically with their partner. During their banal conversation, they also might employ something like the famous line from Eugène Ionesco's *La Cantatrice chauve* (*Bald Soprano*): "*Comme c'est curieux! Comme c'est bizarre! Et quelle coïncidence!*" ("How curious!" "How strange!" "And what a coincidence!") in any manner, combination, or improvisation they choose.

During their conversation, however, they follow this rule: Their hands must remain locked together in the handshake and they can only release the other's hand when they recognize someone else and have taken their hand, initiating a similar greeting and conversation. They must always have hold of someone's hand. This exercise continues until each individual has addressed all the other members of the class at least once. It can get awkward, but the students will improvise until they acknowledge as a group that the mission has been accomplished. If I see the activity wind down, I either instruct them to accelerate their pace or tell them to "Stop!"

I use a great variety of these interactive dramatic games, each one different with regard to the level of complexity, the use of spoken French, and the connection to the dramatic text we're studying at the time. Generally speaking, I try to use interactive activities of increasing difficulty as the project progresses and the actors acquire experience, though most of the games I use are fairly simple, not too time consuming, and supple enough to allow me to tailor them to the subject matter of the project's text(s). See appendix B for descriptions of these exercises.

2.7 LA PETITE MISE-EN-SCÈNE (THE SHORT SKETCH)

In this second day of class, instead of doing a sketch based on the text we're reading, I like to do an exercise that further conveys to the students the potency of performance, diverting their attention from ready-made meanings of verbal text and toward the importance of the physical, material, and the social context of the verbal. As an extension of the first day's re-creative exercise, before we take up the analysis of the Ubu text, I do an exercise that I call *"Dis donc"* ("Say there"). Its structure is as follows: I ask the students to propose a number of pat phrases in French. They usually come up with something like *"Dis donc,"* *"M'enfin"* ("Well"), *"C'est con"* ("How stupid"), *"C'est chiant"* ("How shitty" or "What a pain"), *"Pas vrai"* ("No way"), *"Chouette!"* ("Cool!"), *"Pourquoi pas"* ("Why not"), *"Ah là là"* ("Oh no!"), *"Bon bem"* ("Well then"), *"Voilà"* ("There you go," "There it is," "That's right"). I write these on the board as they suggest them, and I divide the students into groups of two to four, depending on the size of the class and the need for variety in the structure of the sketch. Then, as I did with the first day's re-creative exercise, I give them ten minutes to produce a situation-sketch in which they will use at least four of these phrases and only these phrases. Thus the emphasis is on the spatial, physical, and expressive contexts of the language and not the language itself. I impose only one other rule: Each phrase must be accompanied by a well-defined gesture. The open-endedness of this

CHAPTER TWO: THE FIRST SIX WEEKS 65

exercise produces a great variety of scenes and actions. At the conclusion of this exercise, we have a brief discussion on the creativity of each of the presentations, paying particular attention to the situation selected: What was the situation? Who were the players? What gesture accompanied each of the phrases employed in the sketch? How effective was it? In today's class, this sketch has substituted for a sketch based on the Ubu text.

2.8 TEXTUAL ANALYSIS

Following the first part of this second class, the part dealing with performance awareness – awareness of the individual body and its potential for performance through its alliance with the communal body of the group – we move to the textual analysis component of the class, in which we study the text from a performative point of view, which I will discuss in more detail later in this chapter.

We base the analysis on the reading assigned for homework. First we discuss the paratext, paying particular attention to Jarry's prologue ("*Discours*"), the suggested costumes, and the list of characters. For the "*Discours*," we discuss what Jarry wrote about the fundamental nature of Pa Ubu's character, developing the discussion by reference to the key words, phrases, and ideas located in the text, such as Ubu's "*ventre*" (belly)[23] and his "*forme sphérique*" (spherical form); the idea of "*grotesque*"; Jarry's intention to portray his characters as/through marionettes; and especially the fact that the action of the play takes place in "*Pologne, c'est-à-dire Nulle Part*" ("Poland, in other words No Place"). The "*Répertoire des costumes*" ("*List of Costumes*") and the list of characters add equally to the students' insight into the structural and thematic underpinnings of the work that lies ahead and to their wonder at the text's strangeness. I ask the students to consider the list of characters and to conjecture as to how the story will play out. They attempt to categorize the characters individually and in groups. Some names are more conventional and realistic than others; some are more suggestively ironic than others ("Capitaine Bordure," for example, where "*ordure*" means "garbage"); some are less referential and comprehensible (the "Palotins," for example, which turn out to be exploding soldiers); some are a bit extravagant (The

Entire Russian Army!); and some "characters" are downright "unreal" (The De-braining Machine?), though perhaps no more unreal than a play (like Howard Ashman's *Little Shop of Horrors*) that has a huge flower on stage demanding to be fed human bodies ("Feed me!"). The list of characters and settings, located at the beginning of a dramatic work, is a trusty peephole to the larger text, and this is true for drama of all types and from a variety of historical periods. Consider the commander's statue of Molière's *Dom Juan*, suggesting the metaphysical nature of the play, and the enormous inventory of characters in Rostand's *Cyrano*, reflecting all walks of seventeenth-century French society. Cyrano's cast of characters includes "the crowd," "the poets," "the bakers," and numerous references to the society of theatre, references that reveal for this neo-romantic world a special link between theatre and society at large.

We then discuss the text proper: act 1 and the first two scenes of act 2. At this point I encourage students to volunteer their initial reactions to the Ubu story, comparing it to other plays they have read. I especially emphasize not only its "absurd" or fantastic nature, but also the fact that the unrealistic elements of the story (characters that explode, strange foodstuffs in the form of human waste, invented language, etc.) are contained within and framed by a more or less comprehensible and believable storyline. It is not an entirely unrealistic or absurd text. So what "label" might we give it: Realistic? Hyper-realistic? Semi-naturalistic? Symbolist? Fantastic? Surrealist? Existentialist? Or, absurd? I coax students into a closer, more attentive reading by asking them to suggest titles for the acts and subtitles for the scenes and to explain their choices. The first act might be titled "*Le Complot*" ("The Conspiracy") and the first scene, which we used for the first-day re-created sketch, might be titled "*La Mère sait mieux*" ("Mother Knows Best"). We discuss the action, the spaces, and the progression and transitions from one space, one situation, and one action to another. I choose one or two short scenes and pose a few more exacting questions about the language, action, and characters. Finally, I ask the entire class, a group of students, or an individual student to do an improvised reading of selected dialogue or an improvised performance of a specific mini-scene, such as the scene where Ma Ubu gets unusually excited about the veal: "*Ah! le veau! le veau! veau! Il a mangé le veau! Au secours!*" ("Oh! The veal! The veal! Veal! He's eaten the veal! Help!") (1.2).

2.9 A PERFORMATIVE APPROACH TO THE TEXT

At least since the early 1980s, teachers and scholars have tended to de-emphasize traditional, literary approaches to reading and interpreting dramatic texts and to seek new strategies to read these texts *as* theatre: that is, as blueprints for performance.[24] Today many of us who work closely with the genre of theatre realize that reading theatre for its literary value is somewhat (though not exactly) like reading poetry for the narrative story. Dramatists write plays primarily to *enact* language, action, and images (visual and sonoral, including human bodies acting and uttering language within a material, social world) that might or might not tell a story in any conventional sense; they write for "readers" who, like directors and actors, have a strong sense of performance. Consequently, many of us who teach theatre practice what we call a "performative approach" to reading the dramatic text with our students. This involves much more than keeping an eye toward the vocal production of the lines and the visual display of the body. I'm not sure, however, that we all agree on what this approach should entail. Neither am I sure that we have really taken this term as seriously as we should by developing clearly defined techniques to draw out the supra-literary, performative dimension(s) of the text. After all, if reading performatively simply means to read or to project the text *into* a/the *mise-en-scène* (and the *mise-en-scène* into a text), we have only to turn to the traditional practices of theatre directors, who, for the purposes of transposing them to the stage, have always had to read these texts performatively. This might be a good start, but I think it is also possible to take this performative approach to theatre in new directions that could enhance the instructional value of the reading as well as the performative response to the text.

My particular performative point of view relies on the art and science of theatre and performance semiotics, an approach that classifies and defines the specifics of *"systèmes signifiants"* ("signifying systems") such as space, time, rhythm, props, language, and action, examining the ways in which these systems signify individually, in conjunction with one another, and in a local and global context. The performative reading should pay close attention to at least four specific properties of the theatre text: 1) the stage directions, and not only the (explicit) stage directions proper, but also the (implicit) directions that are embedded in the dialogue; 2) the "holes" in the text (the un-said), which according to Anne Ubersfeld constitute one of the defining characteristics of the theatre text; 3) the need for a community of reader-practitioners belonging to a specific contemporary culture and subculture to collaboratively negotiate and renegotiate possible and alternative stagings and meanings for the text in *contemporary* performance; and 4) the need to evaluate each aspect (each sign system) of the text conjunctively as well as individually. Thus, a performative approach to reading the dramatic text initiates insight into theatrical process, especially sign production and sign system management (semiotics), and it provides students with terminology to discuss it – and not necessarily the sophisticated vocabulary of the semiotic specialist.

As is evident by now, my re-creative approach to the text-stage transposition includes specific "hypertheatrical" techniques to underscore the performative-performable subtext and to intensify performance practice, techniques that place a good deal more emphasis on the medium of theatrical art than on any social, philosophical, or psychological message. Like Artaud, I believe the artistic medium and life are one and the same (theatre is a form of plague), and, to a large extent, the art is the message and not at all a gratuitous one. Accordingly, when I do textual analysis with my students, my objective at the level of the text is not only to anticipate the production but also to encourage the re-creative innovation that I believe is legitimized by the nature of the text: "art re-creates the creative principle" of the text that is already created (see my introduction to this book).

For many of the dramatic texts we plan to re-create, I develop a "performative" guide, consisting of staging-related questions to which students respond in one or more of three ways: they can respond orally during class discussion or rehearsal, in writing in their journals, and/or in the performance of their daily sketches. Some questions address the theatricality ("theatrical" identity) of characters; some address the theatricality of the space; others address relations between characters and space. Some questions ask students to offer ideas for filling in some of the "holes" and the transitions between scenes, and others require students to play a very brief scene, originally written for as many as six characters, with only three, then two, and finally with one actor (How will they "cover" the presence and the action of the missing characters?);

contrariwise, I ask them to play a scene, originally written for only one or two characters, with as many as four or five characters (What new character-functions will they create and how do these relate to the original characters and their situation?).

2.10 GUIDELINES FOR PERFORMATIVE-TEXTUAL ANALYSIS

On the second day of class, once the discussion of the first textual assignment is complete, I distribute a couple of handouts, one consisting of key citations from scholarly criticism related to the Ubu text and the other, a two-page list of guidelines for the class work for the next two weeks. (For the French-language version of these guidelines, see appendix C, "Sample Study and Performance Guide for a Literary and Critical-Creative-Performative Approach to *Ubu Roi*.") Let me elaborate on each section of the guidelines here and explain their rationale. The numbers below correspond to those that appear under the subtitle "*Le Texte (et sa mise-en-scène)*" in the study and performance guide.

1. *Criticism on the play.* This section refers to the handout with short excerpts from three French-language critical works on the play by Linda Kleiger-Stilman, Henri Béhar, and Robert Abirached. I place the complete texts on reserve and encourage students, especially the graduate students, to consult them either during the textual analysis part of the course or near the end of the project in preparation for their critical analysis of our performance. Though a bit dated, I find these texts to be very accessible and particularly enlightening for this type of course. For example, Kleiger-Stilman speaks about how, in *Ubu*, "the character is dehumanized" and "conversely stage properties become animate" (5). Pa Ubu is "[t]he perfect anti-hero ... the apotheosis of anarchic destruction, the repressed side of man" whose "ignominious force of annihilation ... creates a reversible world (that of the non-sign)" (26–27). Language in the play becomes "a concrete object, opaque, in any case hardly open to a 'clear' translation" (21). Robert Abirached argues that "returning to the very origins of mimesis, Jarry assigns to theatre the objective of creating life through abstraction and synthesis and with impersonal images.... [Jarry] treats the character like an autonomous mask, rid of any imme-

diately figurative identity, while he demands that the stage preserve its radical strangeness" (187–88). For his part, Henri Béhar identifies and classifies the various structures of the play: narrative, internal, external, gestural. Though today's university students appear to be less critically oriented than we would like (than we believe we and our generation were), and many of my students probably will not be capable of grasping the full critical context or value of these critical writings, the ideas and language provide insight into the complexity of this "absurd" text and a bit of vocabulary to discuss it.

2. *Structure/Action*. Like the other functional categories of the text (space, character, language, time, sound), the isolating and naming of these systems helps instill in the students the essential principle of our (semiotic) comprehension of reality and art: the principle of difference, which I discuss below. Students learn to break the text down into its constitutive elements. They are encouraged to pay close attention to the external structure (acts, scenes) and the internal structure, the sequence of "moments" that move the action forward. Furthermore, they should try to characterize these moments according to such criteria as how "realistic" or immediately comprehensible and logical they are and how they contribute to the representation and development (progression? digression? suspension? transmutation?) of the action of the story. Students will become increasingly aware of the mixing of the realistic with the fantastic and the absurd. The functional category of time in the form of the rhythm or pace of the movement is relevant here. (This is, of course, different from the historical time or period in which the action takes place.)

3. *Space*. On the one hand, I ask the students to hypothesize a spatial context for the performance of this play, beginning with the type of theatre in which the play could be most effectively mounted. On the other, I ask them to consider the most global of the spatial contexts of the text itself: "Poland ... nowhere"? They should pay attention to the specific characteristics of each of the multiple spaces or settings of the text, the differences among them, and the sequencing from one setting to the next. Consistent with the re-creative bent of the course, I also ask students to hypothesize another possible space, perhaps a space belonging to our contemporary world, that would be re-creatively suitable for the action and characters of this story.

CHAPTER TWO: THE FIRST SIX WEEKS 71

4. *Characters*. The first rule of semiotics is that in fiction we are dealing not with any actual historical space or characters but with artistic-fictional entities that were created and/or adapted to perform a certain *function*. So characters are functions (hence, I use the term character-functions), and as such they do not have personalities or psychological motivation in the same way that we readers or spectators do (see Pavis, Pruner, and Ubersfeld). So how do these characters function with respect to their spatial situation that represents an immediate "theatro-social" context, the *functional* individuals within the *functional* society of the story? How might we classify them as individuals and as members of groups of characters who share a similar function? Can you imagine another possible or hypothetical character that would be re-creatively suitable for the space, action, and other characters (the character scheme) of this story?

The essence of theatre is the character-in-space, and, by extension, the character-space relationship.[25] So in considering the category of character, students should examine it in terms of how it relates to and interacts with the space it inhabits. Also, how do the characters relate to the comprehensive material world (the set and the objects) within a given space? Several quotations from Kleiger-Stilman and Henri Béhar are relevant here, such as the one about how in Ubu, the character becomes dehumanized while the object becomes animate, or the one about how the characters are every bit as schematic as the plot and this is the way they generate a certain theatrical force.

5. *Language*. Explain the form and the content of the language in relation to the other functional categories mentioned above. Be aware that not all of the text's language is created equally, and make the distinction between the two basic kinds of language in theatre text: all the words that are attributed to characters in the form of *dialogue*, on the one hand, and the author's direct address to the reader, or the *didascalia*, on the other, which is all the language that is not dialogue, including the stage directions, paratext, title, character list, and so on. Pay particular attention to the *implicit* stage directions – the words in the dialogue that relate to the action, attitude, or expression of the character ("Come back here!," "Don't give me that look"), to setting ("Pull up a chair," "Are you able to read in this light?"), to objects ("Why are you holding that gun?"), and

so on — as opposed to *explicit* directions, which are usually italicized or otherwise distinctively marked in the text.

6. How do the sound and sound effects specified by the text relate to all the other sign systems? *Ubu Roi*'s stage directions indicate all sorts of loud and abrupt noises, from the "clamour" and cries of a mob, to the sound of fanfares in battle, to doors being knocked down, to isolated explosions and exploding characters.

7. As a final step toward anchoring the Ubu story and its performance potential in the students' memories, and to provide a critical point of reference or "key" to the structure of the text, I ask students to determine for themselves one, two, or three of the most "theatrical" images, actions, or utterances of the play; they also should choose the most powerful theatrical moment of the play and explain their choice.[26]

2.11 THE JOURNAL

As indicated in the guidelines, I usually collect the students' journals on Tuesday for review and return them to the students with my comments on Thursday. If the class is rather large and/or the instructor prefers a more manageable alternative, the journals can be collected every other Tuesday. (One could argue that a two-week interval would allow the students to develop more completely some of their ideas.) Whatever the interval, however, the instructor should expect students to make entries for each and every class session and as soon as possible following the session.

The journal is an excellent sounding board for every aspect of the project. Students can dialogue with the instructor-director – and with the rest of the group through the instructor – and raise questions about the text or any other component of the course, including their rapport with other members of the class. Besides the evident value of the journal for focusing the students' attention on the critical and artistic work at hand and guiding them toward objectives, it is also an excellent way for them to develop their writing skills. It allows students to practice their French written expression in a more relaxed, informal mode, since the content is emphasized over the form and the performative and collaborative nature of the course removes at least some of the psychological barriers to expression. Nevertheless, I bring to the attention of students any serious or chronic deficiencies in French expression, while allowing for differences between undergraduate and graduate students in the quality (of form and content) and quantity of work.

In the journal writing for the first part of the project – in the second half, guidelines for journal entries will change, as noted in chapter 3 – I expect students to write analytical and critical (not descriptive) comments about the three different components of the class sessions: the dramatic exercises and games, including the semiotic awareness exercises that I describe below; the daily sketches, including their own participation in these sketches as well as their perceptions of others; and their performative "reading"/analysis of the text. In addition, I often ask them to write responses to specific (re-creative) exercises or questions about the text and its performance. I sometimes provide these exercises/questions well in advance, allowing them time to reflect and write their responses. To give an example of this type of assignment, I might ask students to reduce a certain long tirade of Ma or Pa Ubu successively to three sentences, to one sentence, and then to only one word. Or just before they hand in their journals on a Tuesday, I might give them five minutes to complete a spontaneous written exercise. An example of this type of activity would be to select a certain specific point of the work (say act 1, scene 3, line 4) and ask the students to quickly invent a line (or a stage direction) that could easily assimilate to the language and spirit of the work.

Given conventional learning processes, the university's institutional mentality that affects these processes, and variations in student personalities, lifestyles, interests, and abilities, many students will not get an immediate grip on the "critico-analytical" demands of the journal writing. Consequently, I give students feedback in my comments and I reinforce and elaborate the guidelines and analytical objectives for the journal writing throughout the semester. I expect them to focus on one or two aspects of a dramatic exercise, sketch, and text. For the dramatic exercise, they will recount their experience – their personal development, attitude, and inhibitions – attempting to explain what the exercise has or has not done for them or for others. In retrospect, what might they have done differently? Breaking down the exercise into parts or steps, how did they feel at any given moment of the activity? Were they hoping, for example, that someone else would volunteer to initiate it? Were they worried about what the instructor or others would think if they did or did not participate? Were they surprised at any other actor's contribution to the exercise? For the sketch, they will expand on the post-performance discussion that comes after each sketch, usually discussing the sketch's relation to the text, its creativity, and how it compares to others. For the text, they will deal with its performative dimension as outlined above: space, character, space-character relationships, language, stage directions, and so on.

Each time I return the journals to the students after having evaluated them, I reiterate my caution against being too abstract and general with their remarks and analyses. For example, I might tell them that it is not sufficient to say they felt frustrated while doing a certain exercise or reading a certain part of the text. They should try to explain this frustration and give an example of a specific aspect of the exercise or text that frustrated or perplexed them. Or if they feel that they haven't really grasped a certain idea or exercise, they should explain as concretely as possible what it is that they *have* understood and why they believe this is not accurate or adequate. To clarify and reinforce this point, I usually give examples of articulate, appropriate, detailed comments made by students.

2.12 SCHEDULE OF RE-CREATIVE SKETCHES (PETITES MISES-EN-SCÈNES) FOR EACH CLASS

For each class session, students perform a re-creative sketch, what we call "*petites mises-en-scènes*." As our reading progresses, students regularly re-create some part of the text, some particular moment in the Ubu story that we have read and discussed. I emphasize the guidelines for all sketches: a) abridge and concentrate, performing only the essential action or image of the scene (they can, for example, reduce a ten- or twenty-page scene to a thirty-second sketch); b) contemporize and personalize; and c) vulgarize the language, with the purpose of making the dialogue more comprehensible to an audience with a wide range of competence in French. Students are assigned to groups of two, three, four, or even five, depending on the number of students in the class and the nature of the

CHAPTER TWO: THE FIRST SIX WEEKS

sketches, and I rotate the members of each group to ensure that actors get to work with different actors each time they perform. Unless otherwise specified in the guidelines, all sketches are prepared and rehearsed outside of class. I give the groups an additional five minutes preparation time in class before they perform.

To stress performance over text, enhance performance learning, and ease student-actors into their roles, I often ask the actors to run through their one- to two-minute sketches in ways that isolate the various components or sign systems of performance while progressing toward an integrated performance. First they simply recite the verbal text of the sketch in a fixed stance and without expression. Then, still without the accompanying context of the action of the scene, they recite the text with the appropriate expression. Then they act out the scene silently, without the spoken text. Finally they do the integrated performance with the full complement of components (spoken text, expression, movement).

To advance further the re-creative and performative mission of the project, I provide assignments and/or specific instructions that will challenge the "face value" or "surface value" of the text and the immediate, conventional response to it, such as exercises similar to the ones mentioned above and noted in the "Guidelines" (appendix C). The assignment for Thursday, January 30, for example, required the groups of three actors each to play the battle scene, originally written for four characters/actors, in two different ways: first with three characters, then with one character and two narrators. How do they compensate for the lack of bodies, or to put it semiotically, the lack of character-functions called for by the text? For Tuesday, February 4, groups had to re-create the conclusion of the play in a way that would incorporate the audience. Finally, on Thursday, February 6, each actor did an individual sketch, with a re-created text of three or four sentences that would capture the essence of *one* of the Ubu characters. In spring 2003, for the final re-creative sketch of Beckett's *Endgame*, I asked students to create a scene that would come *after* the concluding scene of the text.

The re-creative sketch also functions as a covert audition for the roles the actors will assume in the subsequent rehearsal stage of the project. Frequently, the actors self-determine these roles by the roles they choose in these sketches.

2.13 INDUCING A SEMIOTIC UNDERSTANDING OF THE PERFORMANCE WORK: VIVE LA DIFFÉRENCE!

By the third day of class, I will have introduced students to the most fundamental types of class activities that will dominate the schedule of the first part of the semester. Let me complete this orientation to my approach by explaining and describing the activities I use *not* to teach or present performance semiotics as a critical practice but rather to initiate or *induce* a semiotic understanding of our re-creative work by drawing students into the constructive and reconstructive processes related to individual sign systems.

From the very first day of class, in the premier re-created sketch of the first scene of the play, students learn to take a (re-creative) semiotic approach to the project and the play through their evaluations and comparisons of one another's work – the different positions, rhythms, and gestures. Their critiques emphasize the differences in each of the sketches, and, giving each sketch a different title, they include the act of naming, or classifying as a critical manoeuvre. As we saw in chapter 1, this initial exercise functions as an introduction to the potential of performance by actively involving the students in the regenerative construction process while distancing them from what they usually perceive as the authority of the fixed, canonical text. The students are not so much interpreting the text as reacting to it, giving an impression of it, producing the traces that are relevant to their world. They are also learning to collaborate and to work collectively. Most important, however, by comparing and contrasting the usually very different ways in which each of the groups has presented the same text, this exercise draws their attention to the concept of *difference*, on which all artistic as well as linguistic meaning is founded: not so much the Derridean sense of the deferral of meaning, or meaningful deferral, but the original structuralist sense introduced by Ferdinand de Saussure, which asserts that the basic premise of language and all human understanding is referential non-similarity. The colour blue, for example, is "blue," not because it fills a slot on some predetermined semantic scheme but because it is not white, red, or green. Thus, the "meaning" of blue derives from what it is not: all the other (different) arbitrarily assigned effects we have come to call colours. In one of the first-day sketches, for example, the student-spectators deemed the rhythm of the action to be "lively" and the positioning of the characters to be "intimate." They based their assessments on how this rhythm and these particular characters compared either to the prior notions of "liveliness" and "intimacy" they had derived from their own personal, social, and cultural experience, or to the degrees of "liveliness" (or non-liveliness) and "intimacy" (or non-intimacy) enacted in the sketches of the other groups. The more one pays attention to semiotics or sign systems, the more one understands that meaning is not a substance but a *system* of differentially derived values and forms.

Both the art and analysis of meaning production are all about distinguishing, acknowledging, and classifying difference. The dual and multidimensional role of the actor as spectator or spect-actor – and the multidimensional potential for spectating that the actor might achieve – which I wrote about in the introduction of this book, suggests that the properly trained actor becomes critically conscious of her capacity to produce and control her meaning production, and with a higher degree of experience, she becomes better able to forecast both her fellow actor's and the spectator's reception of the meaning she wishes to produce. An acutely and actively acquired sense of performance semiotics can only enhance the spect-actorial sensitivity and potential of our actors.

"Semiotics" remains a scary term for most students because it evokes a rather mystifying, arduous lexicon of its own. Over the years, I have realized how difficult it is to teach theatre semiotics normatively, by explaining principles such as kinesics or proxemics to students and then describing and even demonstrating conceptually how different spatial positions among actors on stage create different meanings for the same verbal text. I now prefer to draw them into a performance practice that involves meaning production, such as the first-day sketch detailed above, and then ask them to evaluate themselves and others only after they have intuitively or half-consciously worked out their solutions and their critique. They are more likely to perceive art as a process and truth as relative, and they become aware of their own personal and collective spect-actorial stake in the creative interpretation of a text.

2.14 THE DISCOVERY OF SEMIOTICS THROUGH RECREATION AND RE-CREATION

We know performance presents a veritable cauldron of interdependent, overlapping sign systems. Roland Barthes refers to the "thickness of signs and sensations that builds up on the stage."[27] As Anne Ubersfeld reminds us, signs can only take on meaning with respect to other signs (to the "differences" among them), and it is impossible to isolate the sign in theatre (*L'Ecole* 21–22). The context and what the French call *parcours* (development, evolution, or trajectory) of any sign are the real determinants for its ultimate meaning. For example, once the colour white is relationally established (it is not blue or black), it can suggest emptiness or fullness, whore or saint, depending on the cultural and aesthetic context within which it is placed and within which it functions. The cultural context can be one of national culture or one of a local, temporary subculture produced by the performance work itself. But to prepare students to deal integratively (syntagmatically) with sign systems – with the way *different* systems work together – they first should learn to recognize and categorize the (paradigmatic) differences among specific elements of costume, objects, and so on.

As an analytical guide and critical backdrop for the course, I have adapted Patrice Pavis's performance questionnaire to analyze performance from a semiotic point of view. Though this guide helps me to orient discussions of our practices throughout the project, to enhance the students' sense of freedom and creativity, and to divert their attention from the straightforwardly analytical, they do not see it until I have introduced them to the method inductively in the first few weeks of class. The questionnaire is organized into signifying systems (*systèmes signifiants*) such as stage design, actors' performance, costumes, lighting, sound, props, rhythm, and pace, which are treated as categories of spectator reception (see appendix D). As the course progresses, students participate in exercises that focus on one specific signifying system at a time. Since there is not sufficient time to introduce specifically and individually all the different systems and subsystems, I find the following to be the most instructive and those that will contribute most effectively toward the actor's understanding of the global system: 1) the overarching aesthetic principle of the presentation (its *mise-en-scène*), or its style, such as comic, tragic, lyrical, prosaic, or fantastic, to name a few; 2) costumes; 3) props; and 4) music.

During the first phase of the project, I present these signifying systems in three basic steps to stimulate students' semiotic awareness. First, I present the principle or system *recreationally* in a dramatic game or exercise, such as the style exercise and hat game described below. These exercises provide a level of diversion and amusement as students "play" intuitively with the sign systems. Second, we move to exploring the system's *re-creational* value when I ask the students to incorporate a rudimentary application of it in a re-creative sketch. The re-creative sketch provides an opportunity for more controlled and intellectualized semiotic behaviour, and it serves as the template for practicing a semiotic approach throughout the first six weeks of the class.

After the recreation and the re-creation comes the third step, group discussion. We discuss the importance of the signifying practice, its revelatory and instructional aspects. What differences were there among the sketches with respect to the actors' choices and uses of style, or costume piece, or prop? Which choices and uses seemed to produce a more or less coherent, insightful, or perhaps challenging, controversial, or subversive response to the text? Which of these choices and/or uses seemed to carry over from the introductory recreational exercises of the day?

2.15 INTRODUCING THE "SYSTEMS" OF STYLE, COSTUME, PROP, AND MUSIC, AND THE STYLES OF JEANNE D'ARC

Styles. What Patrice Pavis calls the aesthetic principle behind the *mise-en-scène*, I like to think of in terms of style. As an organizing principle, the styles provide the basic structure, substructures, and rhythm for the performance projects. The artist speaks of "style" as an aesthetic approach to the production of a play (or a scene of a play) or another work of art; the critic speaks of it as a judgment that classifies the play or one of its parts. Depending on our experience, we may produce or label a performance piece very generally as "comic," or more specifically as "cartoon-like" or as "slapstick." Raymond Queneau's famous fictional work *Exercices de style*, in which one very absurd and banal anecdote is recounted in ninety-nine different "styles" (from "botanical" and "zoological" to "geometrical" and "precious"), foregrounds both the unlimited varieties and the force of style, and it demonstrates humoristically that form or style can *make* the message. In theatre, of course, style has much to do with theatricality, that "thickness of signs and sensations" (Barthes) occurring on the stage.

From the initial dramatic exercise, to the rehearsals, and finally to the finished performance, my "re-"constructivist-collaborative approach to theatre benefits from what Augusto Boal calls "stylistic eclecticism." In the chapter titled "Poetics of the Oppressed," Boal advocates for "techniques ... to create chaos," one of which is "stylistic eclecticism": "Within the same performance we ranged from the simplest and most 'soap opera'-type melodrama to the style of circus and vaudeville" (*Theatre of the Oppressed* 170). Boal writes:

> With the "Joker" we propose a permanent system of theatre (structure of text and cast) which will contain all the instruments of all styles or genres. *Each scene must be conceived, aesthetically, according to the problems it presents....* Thus realism, surrealism, the pastoral, the tragicomedy, and any other genre or style are available to the director or author, without his being obliged for this reason to utilize them during the whole of the work or performance. (176; my emphasis)

I acquaint the students with the concept of style in the following dramatic game: In a circle, each student thinks of a word or a short utterance related to the Ubu story, usually an improvised version of Jarry's text. They then find a highly exaggerated, stylized form of delivery, which includes tone, facial expression, gesture, and rhythm to express this utterance. After all of the actors have "performed" their utterance, I ask each of them to recall and mimic as thoroughly as possible another actor's utterance, until all styles are fairly vivid to us all. I then ask students to label each of the styles. For the Ubu story they proposed styles that were labelled "indifferent," "grotesque," "melo," and "un-tragic." One actor performed *"Ah! le veau! le veau! veau! Il a mangé le veau! Au secours!"* ("Oh! The veal! The veal! Veal! He's eaten the veal! Help!") in what others described as an "indifferent" manner; another performed *"Tais-toi, ma douce enfant"* ("Shut-up, dear child") in a "grotesque" style; and another performed *"Cornegidouille!"* ("Horngibolets!") in a "melodramatic" style.

In another project, based on Jean Anouilh's version of the Joan of Arc story (*L'Alouette*), students proposed the following: sacred, tragic, comic, bizarre, zero, and clown. One actor, for example, performed "*J'obéis*" ("I obey") in what the actors felt was a "sacred" style, while another performed "*Je ne suis ni homme ni femme*" ("I am neither man nor woman") in a rather "styleless" or "zero" manner.

To establish a progressively more discrete awareness of style, the students apply what they have sensed about styles in the daily re-created sketch, the consummating activity of each session. I ask the groups to perform their re-created sketch in three different "styles" – say, first in an "ironic" style, followed by the same text in perhaps a "cabaret" style, and then a "metaphysical" style. At a certain point of each one of the renditions where the group seems to have reached an image that is representative of the sketch and its style, I give the command "*Figé!*" ("Freeze!"). Then I ask the audience of actor-spectators to critique it and especially to point out those elements, traits, and key words that might be representative of the style in question. Students might respond by explaining the manipulation of an object, the display of a costume piece, a remarkable gesture, or the tone of a voice as indicative of the style. (For a variation of this exercise, and in the hope that two groups will choose a similar style and allow a comparison in the discussion to follow, I might simply instruct the groups to perform the piece in only one of three styles: indifferent, grotesque, and un-tragic, for instance.) This focus on style production, together with the obligation of the audience to explain its reception, increases and fleshes out style awareness.

The purpose is to refine their sensibility and develop their acumen for style, a concept that even in the most simplified of performance exercises involves the full physicality of vocal expression, gesture, and movement. What's more, our late twentieth-century and early twenty-first-century American and Canadian students have to think about reconciling the stylistic repertory of their native culture with whatever knowledge they have – much of it stereotypical – of a foreign culture and a distant historical period. Since I believe it is unrealistic to expect anglophone students of French at any level to perform an "authentic" and unaccented French play (including French voices and styles), I encourage the actors to produce a "localized," hybridized performance out of the juncture of

Fig. 1. "Jeanne d'Arc." The narrative introduction. Tim Nagy, Florence Barat, Stephanie Wyatt, Patricia McCoy, Bijou O'Keefe, Elisabeth Pitts, Lourdes Betanzos. Laurel Theatre, Knoxville, TN. Photo by Les Essif.

the different cultures, languages, individual experiences, and attributes of each member of the group.

The Styles of Jeanne d'Arc. At this point I'd like to jump ahead to a later phase of the re-creative practicum and expand on this essential system of style. The example of a play project in which style came to the forefront of the re-created text will illustrate in greater detail the validity and usefulness of these semiotic exercises and how they carry through to the final performance. In spring 1997, I instructed the students to rewrite Jean Anouilh's story of Joan of Arc – a phase of the project that I will discuss in detail in the next chapter – by dividing their re-created text into a number of tableaux based on different phases of Joan's life and to designate a certain "style" for each tableau. Thus the aesthetic principle or "signifying system" of style, especially style variation, became the primary organizing engine for the finished performance. Consequently, our re-written text was organized into seven separate phases (tableaux) of Joan's life, each of which was labelled and eventually performed in a different style. These styles were more specific and complex than the more generic ones (tragic, comic, etc.) that the students had applied in the initial exercise on style that we had done early in the semester.

The first "style" of the play was used for the introduction. We called it "Narrative Neutrality." *Joan* played on three different stages to over 600 people. In addition to the three campus performances in a converted church chapel, attended by members of the community as well as students and faculty, we played on the stage of a high school auditorium and on a makeshift stage in the student union building of a community college. Many of our spectators had a very rudimentary knowledge of French and little experience in theatregoing. In the five-minute introduction to the performance, the actors took turns summarizing and explaining much of the action in English while rehearsing many of the key phrases of the

CHAPTER TWO: THE FIRST SIX WEEKS 83

Fig. 2. *"Jeanne d'Arc." Joan as a child.*
Elisabeth Pitts, Tim Nagy,
Stephanie Wyatt, Bijou O'Keefe.
Laurel Theatre, Knoxville, TN.
Photo by Les Essif.

play in French with the audience. They attempted semiotic neutrality through the use of the costumeless bodies in black and the neutral space – the bare stage – that formed the backdrop for the collective narration of the story (fig. 1). In this sequence of the performance, the actors attempted to be as "styleless" and "natural" (naturally themselves) as possible. This attempt at semiotic neutrality prepared first the actors, then the audience for the application of subsequent semiotic markers. The opening section of the performance foregrounded the act of constructing semiotic meaning.

In the remaining seven tableaux of the play, we used seven different styles corresponding to the seven stages of Joan's life: 1) Joan as a child, a "rustic-innocent" style (fig. 2); 2) Joan's precocious confrontation with Capitaine Beaudricourt to get an escort to see the king, a "smart-pragmatic" style (fig. 3); 3) Joan's visit to Charles's corrupt political court, a "carnivalesque-Fellini" style (fig. 4); 4) Joan's infatuation with the divinely ordained battle at Orléans, a "lyrical" style (fig. 5); 5) Charles's coronation, a "sacred-ceremonial" style (fig. 6); 6) the trial and condemnation of Joan, a "sombre-sinister-fascist" style (fig. 7); and 7) Joan's execution at the stake, an "apocalyptic" style (fig. 8). This process of successive styles was an offshoot of our metatheatrical approach to performance: our desire to expose and explore the theatrical construction of the story. It also accommodated role-sharing, which enhances simultaneously the semiotic framing of our project and the "spect-actorial" awareness of the participants. Five of the actors performed the role of Joan in at least one of these styles/tableaux. Though all but one of

Fig. 3. *"Jeanne d'Arc."* Joan with Captain Beaudricourt. Elisabeth Pitts, Florence Barat, Tim Nagy, Stephanie Wyatt. Powell High School, Knoxville, TN. Photo by Les Essif.

Fig. 4. *"Jeanne d'Arc."* Joan with King Charles. Elisabeth Pitts, Bijou O'Keefe, Florence Barat, Lourdes Betanzos, Stephanie Wyatt. Powell High School, Knoxville, TN. Photo by Les Essif.

Fig. 5. *"Jeanne d'Arc."* Joan at the Battle of Orléans. Patricia McCoy, Lourdes Betanzos, Stephanie Wyatt, Tim Nagy, Bijou O'Keefe, Florence Barat. Powell High School, Knoxville, TN. Photo by Les Essif.

Fig. 6. *"Jeanne d'Arc."* King Charles's coronation. Elisabeth Pitts, Lourdes Betanzos, Patricia McCoy, Bijou O'Keefe, Stephanie Wyatt, Tim Nagy. Laurel Theatre, Knoxville, TN. Photo by Les Essif.

Fig. 7. *"Jeanne d'Arc."* Joan's Trial. Elisabeth Pitts, Bijou O'Keefe, Stephanie Wyatt, Patricia McCoy. Powell High School, Knoxville, TN. Photo by Les Essif.

CHAPTER TWO: THE FIRST SIX WEEKS   85

Fig. 8. "Jeanne d'Arc." Joan at the stake. Stephanie Wyatt, Tim Nagy, Lourdes Betanzos, Davenne Essif, Patricia McCoy, Elisabeth Pitts. Powell High School, Knoxville, TN. Photo by Les Essif.

the Joans were limited to playing a different "style" of Joan's turbulent heroic life, they claimed to benefit from their opportunity to observe (as a second-degree spect-actor) the similar character-function played by other actors. In our final version of the story, for the politico-theological cataclysm of the conclusion, we decided to reintroduce the innocence and puerility of a youthful Joan, so my daughter (age 9 at the time) was burnt at the stake. She didn't mind one bit.

By collectively experimenting with the designing, conscious naming, and active construction of these highly differentiated and theatrically magnified styles, the students came to understand *difference* from a broader and more comprehensive and complex angle. The other semiotic systems consequently were more determined and determinable since they were constructed in relation to the particular style of a given tableau – "rustic-innocent," "sacred-ceremonial," or "carnivalesque-Fellini" – either to fit the style, to enter into a dialectical relationship with it, or to subvert the standard logic of its message. We set out to elaborate on the styles through costumes, set, music, and props. Our minimalist setting, for example, consisted primarily of a cloth-covered table and a varying number of cloth-covered chairs. To reflect the changes in styles, actions, and stages of Joan's life, each tableau featured a tablecloth and chair covers of different materials, colours, and patterns. The table and chairs, in various positions and handled in a variety of ways, signified successively a kitchen table, an altar, a podium, a tribunal, a prison cell, and a stake for execution.

Costumes. To introduce the semiotic causes and effects of costuming, we play the "hat-character" game, which I revised and expanded considerably from the Jango Edwards workshop I attended in 1996 in Périgueux, France. I ask the actors to bring an interesting hat or headdress to class. The day of the exercise, I spread the hats on a table, adding several of my own uncommon specimens, and I give the actors the following instructions:

1) Choose a hat different from your own contribution.
2) Examine your hat, considering a) its history (Who could have owned or worn this hat? What was its wearer like? Where and when did he/she wear the hat?) b) its materiality, shape, and functionality (What is it made of? Why? Its shape? Why? Its function? What do the materials and the shape have to do with the function? Its "look"?) c) other information it provides, or feelings or ideas it suggests.
3) Close your eyes, and, holding the hat in your hand, assume the attitude of its original owner/wearer.
4) Open your eyes and walk with your hat, in your hat-character.
5) Stop. Note your pose and your attitude. Observe the other actors, their attitude. Is anyone looking at you? If so, do you note any reaction that you believe is a response to your hat-character?
6) Place the hat on your head. Feel its presence and think of the character the hat imposes on your body.
7) Observe the others. Do you (your hat-character) belong in this group? How should you behave to reinforce or challenge your association with this group?
8) Now, begin to move around, to stroll as your hat-character, greeting other hat-characters along the way.
9) Stop. Say something. Repeat the utterance with an exaggerated gesture.
10) Now say something in French. Repeat the utterance with an exaggerated gesture.
[In this foreign-language project, verbal improvisation is a tricky practice. When we ask anglophone actors to speak French, we jeopardize their spontaneity. Even the most advanced non-native students often must make a special effort to find a French utterance. My approach to this exercise is characteristic of my overall approach to the project that I asserted in the introduction to this book. Unlike many of my professional peers, I don't pretend to transform my student-actors into authentic native speakers. Thus, I first solicit a spontaneous utterance (step 9), which often will appear in the actor's native language, before specifying the French, a response that will require a more intellectual, learned, academic effort. *Tant pis!* Also, if the actors show signs of inspiration

CHAPTER TWO: THE FIRST SIX WEEKS   87

at this point in the exercise, I might encourage them to strike up a conversation among themselves, hopefully in French; if not, in "franglais."]
11) Start to stroll once again, continuing to speak in French when so inclined and in response to the perceived environment.
12) Take your hat in your hand again and use it for something. Touch someone with it.
13) Remaining in your hat-character, replace the hat on the table, at its "proper" place.

After the first run-through, actors change hats and repeat the exercise. Then I solicit observations on how they felt and what they saw in others, and their opinions about the role of the hat in meaning production and the differences between the two hat-characters they have assumed.

This exercise increases the students' (spect-actorial) awareness of the material properties that produce the image and "feel" of a hat, its meaningfulness and suggestibility beyond its function, and the sensorial effects this costume piece has on their own body-mind. Subsequently, after the students have performed their sketch of the day without the use of any costuming, I ask them to perform it again with a hat. Hats can be worn, held, or used in some other way. Needless to say, I encourage them to look beyond the immediate naturalistic/mimetic authenticity of their selection and to consider its theatricality and the way it might fit into an original theatrical context. We then discuss the differences between the two performances – one with the hat and one without – with special attention to the selection, contribution, and effect of the hat. Then, for the next day's sketch, students choose a hat that they think will add to the effectiveness of their performance. The hat serves as an introduction to other forms of costuming as well. Once they have accomplished this semiotic rite of passage, the actors have an inventory of articles of headdress at their disposal to perform all subsequent sketches.

Props. The exercise I use for props was inspired by a dramatic game that I learned at the Monod-Ryngaert workshop at the Université de Paris in 1985–86 and that we called *"À quoi ça sert?"* meaning "What's that?," or more literally, "What do you do with that?" I prefer to call this exercise *"Le sens détourné,"* or in English, "The Object Reimagined." I give the actors an object such as a ballpoint pen, a belt, or an empty milk carton, and I ask them to propose and perform first a conventional use for it in a clearly articulated or perhaps stylized manner, then an "unconventional, suggestive" use for it, and finally a reimagined, radically transfigured, or deviant use for it (*sens détourné*). Conventionally, with the pen, for example, an actor might perform (theatrically, gracefully) the gestures of a writer writing, trying to get an idea, or simply posing. Unconventionally, she might perform a policewoman using the pen to connote power, menacing a motorist with a ticket: "Ya gonna move yer cah, right now?" In its *sens détourné*, however, the actor might use the pen as a weapon: "On guard!" Thus, the pen can be "used," practically and artistically, literally and figuratively, not only to write – the original, normal, straightforward function of the object – but also (practically but imaginatively) to point. When imagination (or theatricality?) gets the upper hand, however, it can be reimagined as a sword, to fight or to kill. To give another example, a ball can be used to juggle, to hit someone or break something, or to "climb" or "drive," as if it were a mountain or a vehicle. Of course, the distinctions between these functions or "meanings" of the objects are never exact.

Next, as they have done with the hats, toward the end of the day's session and after they have performed their sketch once (in a certain style and with a selected hat, but without a prop), they must use an object in their second performance of the sketch. But this time, in order to advance further into the re-creative dimension of the project, instead of allowing them to select the object themselves, I randomly select an object and ask them to find a use for it when they repeat their sketch. Following the sketches, actors (spect-actors) and spectators (student-actors observing the sketch of another group) make observations. Similar to the strategy for costuming, for all subsequent sketches of the first half of the project, they must choose one and only one principal object to help design their re-created enactment of a character in space. Once again, I try to coax the actors toward the re-creative theatrical dimension of the object, which is more forthcoming when they reimagine the object and reconceptualize its use.

Music. Erika Fischer-Lichte points out that music poses a particular semiotic challenge in that, unlike costumes and props, it is usually considered an "autonomous art." To facilitate semiotic inquiry, she prefers to bracket off the artistic function of music and focus on its "practical" functions as well as its relations to social situations. As a semiotician necessarily dedicated to the study of *difference*, Fischer-Lichte strives to classify different types of musical meanings (which, like all meanings, do not evolve naturally but conventionally "on the basis of cultural codes"), meanings such as those "related to space and movement," or "to objects and actions," or "to character, mood," or "to an idea" (122–23). Another important characteristic of music in theatre is its "indeterminacy." While sounds can refer to concrete things such as a streetcar, the sea, or a knock on the door, "music tends to create meanings that are related to abstract elements" (126). Nevertheless, Fischer-Lichte infers that the indeterminate and abstract nature of music is counterbalanced by its context within other semiotic systems: "music is never employed in theatre as 'absolute' music, but rather always in particular functions which are related to the context of the other signs produced" (123).

Given the indeterminate nature of music and the increased role of context, the recreational step of our introduction to music consists solely of listening to recorded segments of five to seven musical pieces, which I select, that represent a wide range of styles: the group Enigma's "pop" version of a Gregorian chant; "Pie Jesus" (from *Jesus*); background music from the French films *The Return of Martin Guerre* and *The Visitors*, the Franco-British film *King of Hearts*, and Philip Glass's *Koyaanisqatsi*; and a variety of tunes and excerpts from Cirque de Soleil musical scores. Within contemporary Western culture, all these contemporary pieces have some connection to the Middle Ages, but they have very different rhythms, modulations, and tones, thereby evoking or suggesting different events, spaces, moods, ideas, and imagery. Furthermore, the fundamental indeterminacy of music will facilitate the eventual recoding into an immediate re-created theatrical context of any piece that has attained even a well-established cultural or historical coding.

For this initial exercise, I do not ask the actors to distinguish among the various classifications for the possible meanings of the music, such as whether they are related to space, a particular character, a mood, or an idea. Rather, while listening to the different pieces, I advise the students very simply to ponder the manifold categories of difference (the associative differences of rhythms, difference of context, application, etc.) among the pieces. They then try to relate these differences to the different aspects of the story in anticipation of the contextual choices they make for their sketch of the day. These differences become progressively more discrete as the actors move from the preliminary brainstorming for the sketches, when they make a conscious effort to integrate music into the context of other systems, to the actual performances of the sketches, and finally to the subsequent discussions when they compare their uses of the musical pieces with those of others.

After we listen to the pieces, I divide the students into groups and provide each group with an audiocassette on which I have recorded all the musical segments. Actors select one or two musical pieces for use in their sketch of the day. They can use the piece in whatever way they think it will work: intermittently and selectively, or as background music, or as a before (prelude) and/or after (finale) musical frame. Again, first from the points of view of the spectators and then from those of the spect-actor/performers, we discuss the music's contribution to their scenes. Perhaps more than the rhythm, tone, and immediate associative elements of the musical piece, its placement within the comprehensive scheme of signifying systems determines its specific, local meaning. As Fischer-Lichte puts it, "In Western theatre, music also functions as an integrating component of the theatrical code" (128).

In subsequent re-creative sketches, I encourage actors to bring to class recordings of their own choices of music. As do styles, costumes, and props, many of their choices survive into our finished performance (musical excerpts from the *Star Wars* movies, the *Riverdance* concerts, and the rock song "Bad to the Bone," for example). Invariably, we wind up with anywhere from fourteen to forty cues for musical pieces representing an exceptionally large variety of traditions and styles. In our performance of the Candide story, for example, we ended up with over thirty different musical pieces.

2.16 DAY THREE AND BEYOND

With this explanation of the semiotic recreational activities, the reader should have a good sense of how to organize the daily "game plan" for class activities that I listed at the beginning of this chapter. By the end of day three, the students have experienced the different modes of activities that will provide the basic structure for the first part of the course. In appendix B I list the dramatic games and exercises that represent my standard repertoire. Through a mixture of these exercises and the inevitable personal creativity you will bring to them, you will have a good template for this part of the course.

This is not to say that the first part of the semester will adhere to a strict pattern and soon become routine. Considering the different types of class activities and the possible variations within each type, each class, though progressively more familiar, should seem sufficiently and re-creatively fresh to stimulate the instructional and artistic interests of the project. In addition, given the project's serious bent toward performative creativity, many other performance-related activities practically insinuate themselves into the program. One particular highly instructive and routine-breaking activity that I do with the class is to have the students attend a local performance of a play, usually one of the campus theatre department performances, and render an analysis of it based on our semiotic questionnaire. We spend part of a class session discussing the performance, and students write in their journals an analysis focused on some aspect or semiotic system of its *mise-en-scène*. Despite their interest in performance, many of our students rarely attend live theatre. This assignment not only gets them to attend but to do so with a newfound ability to do a "close" if rudimentary semiotic analysis of the stage work. Most college campuses and high schools offer good, or even excellent, sophisticated productions of plays. Whatever the overall quality of the performance, students will be able to critique the various aspects or sign systems at work within it, or the lack thereof. Even in the case of a not-so-accomplished production, students might point out problematic areas of sign system management, apparent incompatible or incoherent staging decisions. Consequently, they can suggest possible solutions to perceived problems, or they can offer new ideas of their own for staging the text.[28]

3

The Collaborative Re-Creation
of the Original Text

Working solely on *Ubu Roi*, by the end of the third full week of the course, the seventh class session, we have achieved a deep and multidimensional analysis of the text, at least in a preliminary text-to-stage, performative phase. But the analysis continues, of course, throughout the re-creative writing, the rehearsals, the production, and the final written paper.

As I've already pointed out, there are alternatives to limiting the project to the study of one dramatic text. Several of my projects have involved the combining of two texts, which were thoroughly treated in class, and in a 2003 project my students studied three complete works and a number of excerpts from other texts. Despite these alternatives, I would argue for the instructional legitimacy of focusing on one text only, which the students will study in greater textual depth and in greater performative scope. In fact, I would recommend that instructors with little or no experience in mounting plays focus first on one text only. To simplify matters, this chapter will outline the comprehensive rewriting exercise for the Ubu 2000 project. At this point in the semester, the course changes course.

3.1 THE "HOW TO" GUIDELINES FOR THE COMPREHENSIVE RE-CREATIONAL ASSIGNMENT

At the beginning of the seventh day of class, we spend at least thirty minutes discussing the process of collaboratively rewriting the Ubu story. I provide a handout that contains some rather comprehensive guidelines and objectives for this task, many of which the students have been practicing since the very beginning of the project. The task at hand is merely more comprehensive with respect to the text, which it covers in its entirety.

In the past, when working with larger groups of students, I actually had all the groups rewrite the entire play. Time and experience have persuaded me, however, that students can benefit as much from a more limited assignment, rewriting no more than about one-third of the complete text, including the two parts of the text that are most determinant for the whole: the introduction and the conclusion. The assignment has two principal objectives, one instructional and one artistic. On one hand, working co-operatively with their re-creative focus, the students' creative understanding of the text and its performance potential will reach a new holistic level. On the other, their work will provide me – the secretary-scriptwriter, in a fashion – with a model that represents the ideas of the various constituencies of the class as well as those of the ensemble.

This is a tremendous learning opportunity for all students. The most aggressive and motivated get to put their organizational and creative skills to work, and the less dramaturgically inclined still contribute something, though they might be more inclined to follow the advice of their peers and contribute fewer original ideas. Most important, all students involve themselves to a lesser or greater extent in a rich and highly concentrated experience of peer learning, collaboratively negotiating and renegotiating the meanings of the text.

The "Textual Re-creation Guidelines" (*Recréation de textes théâtraux*) handout (see appendix E, "Textual Re-creation: Guidelines for Ubu 2000") is the key to understanding the task, so let me explain it section by section:

Section I of the handout enumerates the key words and phrases that describe our goals.

Section II provides a list of themes related closely or remotely, directly or indirectly, to the Ubu story. Most of these themes correspond either to the written text, to our preliminary textual and performative work with the text including students' comments about it, or to my personal-professional views on the re-creative potential of the text. I include some of them simply to push the critical envelope of the exercise, providing food for thought and illustrating subtle differences that exist from one theme to another. While avoiding any rigorous form of classification, I try to group the themes into a casual logical order. I expect the rewriting teams to link their ideas for their characters-in-space and the actions of these characters to one or more of these themes. One action, for instance, might suggest the (theme of the) nobility of a character, a space, or an action, while another might illustrate sensuality or a supernatural aspect of the story.

Section III shows the groups within which the students will collaborate to rewrite the text. Yes, I do take into account the particular traits, abilities, and personalities that each of the students have displayed up to this point in the program, assuming that they will bring this baggage to their respective groups. But given the four-week re-creative apprenticeship and the re-creative dynamic itself, I'm still not convinced that a random mix of students would be much less productive for the exercise.

Section IV proposes a working structure for the full performance text. I have always used a narrator for my projects, and not only because the narrator's character-function reinforces the Brechtian principles of distance and mediation by occupying an intermediate position between stage and audience. In our particular play, the narrator can also guide the audience's comprehension of the foreign-language text. I also prefer to frame the play with an introduction, one which – as I tell the actors – should serve as a useful instructional tool for the audience. While the actors involve themselves in writing this introduction, and later when they perform it, they will learn more than a little about the structure and the possible meanings of the text. Then I remind the actors of the basic stages of the story, and I encourage them to include songs, recitations, and other activities in which the audience can participate. If the students feel especially re-creative and enterprising, they are, of course, free to overstep this suggested structure as well as any of these guidelines.

In our performative approach to analyzing the text, we have paid close attention to the didascalia/stage directions. Now, shifting roles from receiver-interpreters of *the* text, with its sign systems and code management, to producers of *a* text, I instruct the actors to include detailed instructions for the staging, including both explicit and implicit stage directions, as well as a list detailing costumes of the characters for each scene and a list of the objects that the characters will handle.

Each group will prepare a rough sketch of the introduction and the conclusion, plus a preliminary draft of any two or three scenes or phases of the action that come between the beginning and the end. With larger classes that I can divide into a larger number of groups, I usually assign two groups the same portions of text. This guarantees two versions of the same scenes and makes for a good point of comparison. I require titles and subtitles for each separate scene because the technique of devising and providing titles helps the actors and eventually the audience to understand and follow the essential movement of each scene. And recalling the importance of style and Boal's practice of incorporating a variety of style changes within the same performance, I also require an indication of the style in which the scene is to be played. I provide a list of possible styles for the students to think about. The novelty and strangeness of some of these suggested styles might rouse the students' sense of invention.

In section V of the guidelines, I list the principal, secondary, and what I call "collective" characters of the play. I also allow the group to invent a new character, "*Un autre?*" ("Someone else?") that will fit their creative rewriting of the script. In addition, I usually give special instructions for each of the projects, based on my vision of the potential for the particular stories. For the Ubu story (and the Macbett story), I asked them to consider including the use of a life-sized marionette in their text, and I provided them with one to use in the demo sketch they would perform upon completion of the rewritten text (see below).

Section VI offers self-explanatory pieces of advice, some of which reiterate guidelines enumerated above but most of which are reminders of previous class discussions and dramaturgical practices already employed in the first part of the class.

I conclude the guidelines handout with the due date for the re-created drafts and a reminder that in addition to the writing, each group will perform before the class a re-created piece from their already re-created text.

As I hope the reader will attest, I have tried to give these guidelines a certain provisional, non-normative, experimental tone. They should be "guidelines" in the suggestive sense of the word (not rules) and should not represent an authoritative and calculated blueprint for the task at hand. With this in mind, at the end of the guidelines I also remind the actors that, like all other aspects of this project, this collective and comprehensive writing assignment is merely a new beginning of the rewriting process toward a "finished" text, a process that will continue throughout the rehearsal stage of the project. Therefore, the emphasis is on process.

The students have anticipated this rather weighty, demanding task, a key rite of passage that I've scheduled and emphasized on the syllabus, since it will require them to be available to meet in groups. On Tuesday I provide them with their group assignments so they can arrange meeting times. On Thursday I distribute the guidelines, and require the completion of the assignment on the following Tuesday. This is, of course, a rapid turnaround time, but given the collective and creative nature of the assignment, I find that a concentrated timeframe helps the students achieve their goals. It further encourages them to consider the task to be outside the framework of their other academic responsibilities and instills in them a special sense of exigency and commitment.

This is a memorable weekend for most of the students. On Tuesday, they come to class with copies of their rewritten text for distribution to each individual of the other groups. They also prepare themselves to discuss and explain the rationale behind their re-creative decisions, to defend the logic, coherency, and creativity of their choices and their text. Thus, this exercise provides yet another opportunity for the students to get a good hands-on lesson in textual construction: that is, the idea, method, and art of the dramatic text, the problems that arise, and the choice of solutions that lie ahead in a never-ending series of dialectical construction.

3.2 D-DAY: PIECES COME TOGETHER AND THE FULL STORY TAKES SHAPE

The following Tuesday, the groups arrive with the requisite number of copies of their re-created text. (Some students arrive late with an armful of papers in need of stapling.) We have a brief, informal discussion of their impressions of the process, a discussion that I urge them to continue in their journal writing. Did they feel creative? Re-creative? (Can they explain the difference between these two terms and/or feelings?) Did they feel that the exercise was truly one of collaboration and that the end product represents a collective work? Did they make new discoveries about textual process? How much of their prior re-creative apprenticeship in the class showed up in the process and the results? Did some of their ideas move in a different direction from those they developed through earlier interpretations of the text and their experiences with it? Did they see brand new possibilities for the introduction or the conclusion? Can they comment on the basic style or styles they've emphasized?

After a warm-up and a couple of recreational exercises, including perhaps the "imaginary sword" (with music) and a "tableau vivant" (see appendix B), the students prepare to perform the scene they have chosen from their rewritten text. Before they perform, each group writes on the board a title of the scene and one or two key phrases or words. If they desire, they may give a brief explanation of the context of the piece before they perform, but usually this is not necessary. Once again, in keeping with the spirit and the established standard of the project, these sketches are very brief, consisting of one to three lines per character.

When the performances are complete, the students discuss and compare them, commenting on the titles chosen by the other groups and guessing their respective styles. Besides the obvious lessons in textual construction and analysis, the students are improving their foreign language skills, as I have argued in the introduction to this book. It is true that all types of content discussion will improve the students' foreign-language skills, from the culture-oriented discussions of the language and composition-conversation courses to the interpretive discussions that take place in the literature courses. But in this type of exercise, where the students are presenting material in which they are so personally as well as collaboratively invested and which they have actively rehearsed, the potential for *parole*-situation language learning increases dramatically.

Homework for Thursday will include both individual and group assignments. Individually, the students will read and compare for discussion the several different versions of the rewritten drafts. The representative sketches they have seen will provide further insight into these different drafts. On the collaborative side, each re-creational group will reconvene to rehearse a two-step sketch for presentation on Thursday, consisting of a re-created and reduced version of the introduction and conclusion they've written (introduction-pause-conclusion).

CHAPTER THREE: THE COLLABORATIVE RE-CREATION 99

3.3 COLLABORATIVE EXAMINATION OF THE RE-CREATED TEXTS

While we still do warm-up and recreational exercises, the two principal activities for Thursday are the discussion of the re-created drafts and the performance of each group's introduction-pause-conclusion. In the discussion of the texts, we address questions about what they liked and disliked, understood and did not understand, in the other texts. We first focus on the big picture of each of the drafts: What is the overall style and structure that this draft suggests? Do we agree with the title and the style attributed by the group? Are the draft's content and form consonant with what we have seen in the course up to now, or are they radically different? What are the striking similarities and dissimilarities among the different versions? Then we address some of the remarkable detail and features of the texts: the use of the marionette, the strategies they used to involve the audience, a particular action or line by one of the characters, rhythm and movement, transitions from one scene to the next, an interesting theatrical device. Following this discussion based primarily on the written texts, each group performs its version of the introduction-pause-conclusion, after which we resume our discussion, this time taking into account the performance produced from the texts we have read. The performance of the written texts will provide additional insight into each of the texts as well as a valuable lesson on the principle of the art and practice of text-to-stage transposition.

For homework, I usually tell the students they can relax – for the first time since the beginning of the semester and for the last time before the intensive rehearsal work begins. Not so for the instructor: it's my turn to endure the weekend from hell.

3.4 MY WEEKEND FROM HELL!

I admit that I do dread this weekend, despite the creative gratification that invariably results from it. I spend the next four days exploring creative ways to produce a text that fits the following criteria: 1) it represents the spirit of the original text (that is, recalling Boal, it recreates the creative principle of the text); 2) it represents the spirit of this particular community's interpretation of the text, allowing the various individuals and student constituencies to see themselves and their work in the text; 3) it tells a story in a language that is sufficiently coherent and accessible to be easily understood by the mixed audience we expect, one with wide-ranging abilities in the foreign language of the play; 4) it does not have any major technical or material requirements that would jeopardize accommodating it to a variety of stages; and finally 5) it is sufficiently creative and original to represent a legitimate art form.

To this end, I read and reread the several versions of the students' drafts, taking notes on interesting ideas and text. Then, following the structure I prescribed for the story in the re-creational guidelines (see appendix E), I write a preliminary script from beginning to end, including abundant stage directions. I base the script partially on the original Ubu text and partially on the rewritten versions produced by the collaborative group work, the fusion of which I further refine in the interest of (what I believe to be "standards" of) coherence, congruity, and suitability. Throughout my writing, I remain mindful that the students must not see this text as a new source of authority or as an abuse of my authority, but rather as another step in the process, a giant step perhaps, but one that we can and will continue to mould and revise according to the demands of the direction in which our collaborative rehearsals take us. In the spirit of Victor Turner's theory, the performance will complete the text.

I cannot write the text with the expectation that it can stand as is. For the sake of (re-)creativity, I try to furnish the text with a good amount of adaptability and a fair number of "holes" by neglecting to write two of the most essential components, the introduction and the conclusion. I also expect that we will produce recreational interludes, transitions between scenes and acts in which the actors will step outside the action of the story and, in a kind of external narrational role, play with the audience while summarizing, explaining, critiquing, questioning, or demystifying the action and the progress of the story. Thus, I provide a note sheet with the text, pointing this out and bringing to the attention of the actors other needs of the integrated re-created text I have produced. For the Ubu story, we postponed the production of a narrative frame (*cadre narratif*) because, more than any other component of the text, this framing device would be contingent upon the course taken with (the development of) the rest of the text: it would clearly benefit from the point of view and ideas we would develop during our initial blocking, shaping, and reworking of the text's language and action (see appendix F, "Sample Narrative Interventions between the Tableaux of 'Père Ubu'"). The experimental, contingent character of this work-in-progress gives the actors a sense that there is always potential for improvement, and it makes them especially attentive to successive changes that are made. It helps us avoid routine and the concomitant onset of the tedium that develops with the task of persistent, repetitious work on refining the detail of the same old fixed, prewritten text. I strive to maintain a feeling of freshness and a mood of work-in-progress right through the final performance phase. When all is said and done, in the final performance, the acting of the actors evinces a somewhat rough, "rehearsal" quality that enriches the overall theatricality of the work.

In conjunction with the production of a comprehensive rewritten text, I also produce a very schematic list of costumes for the characters, as well as objects that they could manipulate (and that the spectator would associate with the character), costumes, and objects that might or might not vary from one act or scene to the next. As a supplementary journal exercise, I assign students the task of making further suggestions for possible costumes and objects.

The following Tuesday, at the very beginning of the class, I devise a ceremony for "*la remise du texte*" (the presentation of the text). Despite the relatively short time the students and I have worked together on this project, this is indeed a sacred moment. It consecrates the end of a rather eventful period of performance apprenticeship and creative production, and it leads simultaneously to the beginning of the most creative and intense part of the project, which will bring us progressively closer to the "finished product" that we will be proud to bring to our prospective audience. Each individual actor comes forward for the following exchange (parody, of course!):

— *Monsieur/Mademoiselle l'artiste, recevez-vous ce texte dans un esprit solennel, sérieux, artistique, et surtout dans un esprit ubuesque, fidèle à l'image du Père Ubu? (Mister/Madame Artist, do you accept this text with solemn, earnest, artistic, and above all, ubuesque mind, faithful to the spirit of Pa Ubu?)*
— *Oui, Monsieur. (Yes, Sir.)*

– *Dites: "Merdre!" (Say: "Pschitt!")*
– *Merdre! (Pschitt!)*
– *Allez, jouez bien, mon fils/ma fille. (Go and perform well, my child.)*

Once all the texts are distributed, I say to the group:

– *Au nom du Père, de la Mère et du fils Bougrelas, je vous dis "Merdre!" (In the name of the father, the mother, and the son Bougrelas, I say to you "Pshitt!"). (Note that, in French, to say "Merde!" to an actor before she performs is the equivalent of "Break a leg!") And, as a group, they respond in kind: "Merdre!"*[29]

I instruct the students to read the text very carefully, and to try to understand it as a culmination of the collective effort of the first part of the course. I encourage them to bring comments for discussion to the next class session. For additional homework, they should ponder the following: a title for the play, a name for our theatrical group, proposals for a poster design, and role selection. Bearing in mind the titles and subtitles indicated on the draft versions of their re-created texts, they can deliberate as they wish, either individually or in groups, on a title for our re-created work, one that reflects both its originality and its rapport with the original Ubu text. They must also think of a name for our new theatrical company, one that reflects our group personality and the experience and expectations we all share. The title of the play and the name designating us as a bona fide theatrical company are very important to our identity, focus, morale, and, most important, our re-creative esprit de corps: every group is different. In the next class session, we will discuss ideas for a poster design, and we will appoint two or three class members with artistic skills to draft a design. Finally, after having read the "complete" if preliminary text, all actors must submit to me a list of the four roles they would like to play, in order of preference. Once again, I encourage students to elaborate in their journals their ideas and questions about play title, company name, poster design, and their preferred roles.

The rest of the session includes recreational exercises, such as the "Perfect Impression" (film clips from French movies) and a *tableau vivant* (see appendix B).

3.5 DISCUSSING THE TEXT AND GIVING IT AND OURSELVES A NAME

We begin the next class on Thursday by discussing the rewritten story, first from a general, comprehensive point of view, and then in whatever detail the students care to discuss it. I'm particularly interested to know if they feel that the text represents a collective effort and shows evidence (though perhaps in an altered form) of their individual contributions. What surprises did the text contain? Puzzling or incomprehensible elements? Disappointments? Did this text influence and perhaps change the choice of roles they would like to play in the production? (See sample scenes from "Père Ubu" in appendix F.)

As a group, we decide on the title of the play and the name of the company in much the same way that we chose the dialogue for the first-day re-creative exercise, but with a bit more time and reflection. Students propose titles. I write them on the board, and we discuss and amend them. Students are expected to provide a rationale for their ideas. We do the same for the name of the company, considering it in tandem with the title since with our singular project the two are an ensemble and should coincide or complement one another: We have, after all, a one-play mission, unlike most companies. To avoid any rash decision, I tell the students to note the choices and reflect on them over the weekend. They also submit the list of the four roles they would like to play, in preferential order, and we complete the session with exercises and recreational dramatic games tailored toward refining performance technique (see appendix B).

On the following Tuesday, I distribute a sheet with the group's suggestions for titles and company names, and ask the students to reconsider them. After a short follow-up discussion, once I think we've arrived at a consensus and I personally feel that the title or titles proposed is/are acceptable (meaningful, clear, catchy, grammatically correct, inoffensive, not too controversial), we take a vote. I usually do not accept a simple majority rule but try to reach a greater, more collaborative consensus. At the end of this session, I reveal my casting decisions to the class. (See appendix F, "Proposed Names for Theatre Company and Play.")

3.6 CASTING: THE ANTI-(LONE)STAR SYSTEM, OR, EVERY STAR HAS A PROMINENT PLACE IN THE CONSTELLATION

My next major responsibility is to do the casting for the play. The obvious burden of the task is rendered less difficult for several reasons. In this performance, all actors will have the equivalent of a major role, whether they play one of the original text's title roles or not. Furthermore, the title roles are never played by one single actor but are always shared by two or more actors. Another casting aid derives from the structure of the project, which provides a considerably extended period of what I call "covert collaborative auditions." My casting decisions are largely based on the prior performance work of the students in their re-creative sketches. To a certain extent, the actors self-select their roles by the roles they choose, negotiate, or accept to play within the constantly changing groups that perform the daily sketches. I do take into account the preferred roles that the actors have submitted, but this usually is not a problem. In sum, thanks to my rotational scheme for role distribution, all students will have a significant and challenging stage presence. Those students who do not get a principal role will play a variety of other roles, which all-in-all are not so secondary.

To distribute the roles, I first create a chart showing all the scenes of the play and all the characters who appear in each of the scenes (see appendix F, "The Casting Chart for Ubu"). Then I begin by assigning the actors for the principal roles of Pa and Ma Ubu. To give you an idea of just how rotational and communal my casting becomes, for Ubu 2000 I assigned a certain male actor to play Pa and a certain female to play Ma for the first two acts (eight tableaux). At the beginning of the third act, the actors for these roles changed, with two new females playing Pa and Ma. The same female continued in the role of Ma for the next three acts, but a different female took over the role of Pa in the fifth and final act. (The reason for this decision had something to do with the prominence of the role in each act as well as with the type of actor.) However, in accord with the principle of identity propagation (and con-fusion) for the re-created play, in the final tableau, two females and one male played Pa, and two females and one male (who played Pa at the beginning of the

CHAPTER THREE: THE COLLABORATIVE RE-CREATION 105

play) played Ma. The play concludes with all six actors playing one of the two Ubu roles.

Another consideration for casting is to have an eye toward the rehearsal period. During the early rehearsals and also for some of the later ones, in order to save the actors some time and avoid requiring their presence during the rehearsal of scenes in which they might have either no role or a very minor, non-essential one, I am usually able to group the actors into teams and to work with group subsets of two, three, or four (depending on the size of the class) for several hours.

Other roles in the Ubu story, less principal but not quite secondary, include Captain Bordure (who first plots with Ubu to overthrow the Polish King Wenceslas and then turns coat and fights with the Russian Czar against Ubu) and the young prince Bougrelas, Wenceslas's son, who becomes Ubu's nemesis. Given the small number of actors for this project, both these roles were played by the same actor, even – with a good deal of dexterity and the help of a marionette – when the characters appeared together in the same scene (the king's assassination). In fact, this actor also assumed the marionette-assisted role of the Polish queen in this same scene, covering not two but three roles. The doubling and tripling of roles through the use of marionettes represented dramaturgical and interpretational challenges that added a beautiful bit of convoluted theatricality to the scene, which was not lost on the audience. Another "secondary-principal" role was the Bear-Narrator. In the original text, the Bear does not appear until the fourth act, and then its character-function seems rather gratuitous and merely incidental to the action of the play. In our play, we enlarged and significantly altered this role, combining it with that of the principal narrator of the first act. This role too was played by the same male actor throughout.

As an example of the provisional and transformative nature of our work, when I prepared the re-created draft and the accompanying casting chart, I plugged in the role of the Bear (*Ours*) throughout the play (see the casting chart in appendix F), though I had only written actual lines and actions for the role in the first act. The Bear/Maître d'hôtel/Narrator has the first lines in the play (see appendix F, "First Scene of 'Père Ubu'"). I encouraged the actor assigned to the role in the first act to experiment with continuing narrative intervention (as the Bear-Narrator, of course) throughout the rest of the play. However, subsequent rehearsals took us in a different direction, and in the end the Bear-Narrator did not expand as I originally had imagined it would: it wound up with a relatively limited presence after the first act, and the actor assigned to the role played a wide array of secondary roles in the rest of the play.

All six actors were able to have very substantial roles. When they were not performing one of these, they played one or more of the minor characters, like King Wenceslas, the Czar, the Messenger, the Magistrates, the Nobles, or the exploding Palotins, or the "collective" characters, like the Guards, the Whole Russian Army, the Peasants, the People. In addition to the equitable distribution of stage time and text, the casting assignments help push theatrical self-consciousness and Brechtian alienation to their limits, taking cross-dressing, cross-behaving, and cross-casting for granted.

I should note that this group was indeed the smallest I have ever worked with. As I noted in chapter 1, in my first Ubu play at the University of Louisville in 1994, there were eighteen student-actors to account for – the largest group with which I have worked thus far. So the casting was more complicated but nonetheless communal and distributional. In fact, this predicament of having to find "significant" roles for eighteen actors led me to explore the strategy of combining texts. We still had two actors sharing each of the Pa and Ma roles (though the two women who played Pa and Ma in the first two acts exchanged these roles in the final act of the play), one Captain Bordure, and one Bougrelas, so I had to find a way to get the other actors on stage in a "big" way: that is, with more than a collective or minor part in the action and dialogue. As I've already mentioned, my solution was to theatricalize and integrate Raymond Queneau's *Exercices de style* into the Ubu story. I deal with this topic of combining texts in chapter 7, but suffice it to say here that all students who did not get their share of the Ubu action were assigned a principal role in creating one or more of the "styles" in *Exercices*.

This shared re-creativity and complexity places performance as spectacular event at the forefront of the project and encourages further creative collaboration. What's more, it certainly takes the students' minds off French as a second language. The role sharing itself suppresses any kind of proprietary control over text and textual characters, and it increases the critical sensibility of both actors and spectators by allowing them to compare different renderings of the same role. It also encourages

CHAPTER THREE: THE COLLABORATIVE RE-CREATION 107

each actor to contribute something new and personal to the role. Given my experience with the Ubu story and the strategy of role sharing, I believe a director could mount this play effectively with as many as eight actors rotating through the roles of Ma and Pa Ubu.[30]

In addition to the actual performance roles of the actors, students also rotate through technical positions, including assistant director, stage manager, prompter, and lighting and sound technician, depending, of course, on the requirements of the particular project and the number of participants. For the smaller group of the Ubu 2000 project, I was more conservative with the tech assignments. For each scene, one of the six actors who did not have a demanding performance obligation was the designated stage manager. This meant she/he was responsible for the organizational, material, and technical duties of each scene (sound, light, set, props), which might also include some prompting, at least in the very beginning of the rehearsal period. This assignment was more important for setting the tone and the pace of the beginning rehearsals than it was for the work of the final production. As usual with my projects, the closer we got to the final product, the more organic and co-operative we became, and actors worked out the technical duties among themselves, in the thick of the action, so to speak. Almost invariably, actors are happy to be as active as they can in both the technical and the artistic sides of the production.

When I distribute the casting sheet to students, I warn them against reacting too hastily to it. They should take a good look at the entire assignment grid, especially since many of the roles do rotate, and they should think long and hard about what each role requires, comparing their roles not only to the rewritten text itself but also to its projected stage realization. Happily, I am able to assure them that whatever immediate doubts they might have about their role in the play, they will soon realize that each and every actor has a demanding and complex assignment on stage, to which they can bring to bear all their talent. More than the simple words on the page, they will have the (re-creative) opportunity to determine and re-determine the precise nature of the assigned role. They will not only be responsible for the physical image at the source of the text, but there will also be ample room to reconstruct the role and to alter, add, or subtract text and action during the rehearsal phase. They should also bear in mind that, given the nature of our project, at least some of these assignments are likely to be modified during the course of our rehearsals. To date, no student has ever asked to be reassigned. Despite these guarantees, I also assure them that if for some reason they remain unhappy with the assignment, they should let me know, and we can probably make some sort of adjustment.

Based on prior class discussions, student suggestions in the journals, their choices in the re-creative sketches, and my own ideas, I often produce a preliminary list of costumes and props, organized by scene, for each of the players. We need to begin to acquire and/or to otherwise produce the costumes and objects. We can easily and rather cheaply acquire some costume pieces and props at a party shop or novelty outlet. Other items might require manufacture by either the actors themselves or someone with sewing skills (like my wife), or, for props, someone with carpentry skills (neither my wife nor I). However, while it is a good idea to begin thinking about the material needs of the production, you don't want to be too precipitous. Unless you are definitely sure you will need an item that requires time to produce, it is better to wait until you see what the marvel of re-creative rehearsals produces in terms of material needs.

4

Co-operatively and Re-creatively Rehearsing, Revising, Refining, and Promoting the Performance

Enfin! On to the rehearsals. This point of the project roughly corresponds to the point at which most practicum courses, much like most theatrical productions, begin: that is, with a written text and a group of actors assigned to specific roles. But our project differs significantly from the others: although under conventional circumstances this would be a very late time to begin actual rehearsals for the final production, in many ways, our re-creative project is way ahead of the game, artistically as well as pedagogically. The troupe of mostly neophyte actors has learned much about performance from a practical and theoretical standpoint; the text has been very thoroughly and thoughtfully read, discussed, analyzed, and reconsidered; and, most important, in concentrated form, much of the Ubu story has already been performed: that is, performatively analyzed and "refitted." The actors have, moreover, an extraordinary investment in the project that will help them to learn, develop, and personalize their roles in the final production. And let's not forget, given the principle of shared, distributional casting, their roles will not have any exceptional demands in terms of quantity of lines. The focus, as always, is not on the text, but the performance.

The rehearsal phase officially began for Ubu 2000 on Tuesday, February 22, day eleven and week six of the project. By now, we have come to a satisfactory consensus on the title of the play, and the poster design will be finalized within the next week or two because we will need it for promotional purposes. The class has collectively, creatively, and precisely renamed our play "*Père Ubu, roi de nulle part*" ("Pa Ubu: King of No Place") and we have named our company "*Les Traveling Ubu.*" We will have our first (on-campus) performance on Wednesday, April

12, well before the end of the semester (May 1). This schedule allows less than four weeks before spring break (March 18–26) and thereafter, only a little more than two weeks before showtime. The actors are anxious about the approaching deadlines, but once they see how rapidly we are able to progress toward the finished product, they relax considerably – until of course the final rehearsal days when a bit of anxiety creeps in. I can say with confidence, however, that despite the relative inexperience of my student-actors, they are so thoroughly rehearsed *by and in* the collaborative re-creative process that they are less nervous and more prepared at curtain time than most actors would be.

4.1 EARLY REHEARSALS

I do my best to design a project and a rehearsal schedule that will not place too much of a burden on my students' time. The first phase of rehearsals, the three weeks preceding the week before spring break, all rehearsing is usually accomplished during regular class hours, four hours a week, though I do sometimes schedule extra time with subgroups of actors. I might simply ask the students to agree to extend a class session or two, three to four students remaining an extra hour or two one day and the others on another day. Extra time might also occur on a weekday other than the Tuesday or Thursday class sessions, perhaps even on a Saturday or Sunday. But the point is that at this early stage, outside of the regular class hours we concentrate on "key-character" rehearsals, in which only the actors playing essential roles are required to be present. For the Ubu play I required a few extra hours from four of the six students the first two weeks. Otherwise, we adhered to the prearranged rehearsal schedule, which only required extra hours in the week preceding spring break: one extra hour for two class sessions, which met 3:40 to 6:30 instead of the usual 3:40 to 5:30, and three hours on a Wednesday, 5:00 to 8:00.

The first phase of rehearsal is also remarkable because we do not immediately abandon the overtly instructional component of the course. In addition to the usual warm-ups that always precede a rehearsal session, I still take the students through increasingly more complex performance exercises and dramatic games (see appendix B) before getting

CHAPTER FOUR: REHEARSING

to the actual rehearsal activity. In fact, at the beginning of this phase, the rehearsal is largely a replacement for the textual analysis and the re-creative sketch portions of the regular sessions. This continuing work with general performance technique in conjunction with focused scene rehearsals expands the actors' perspective on the role(s) they are developing. The mimicking exercise (see appendix B, "The Perfect Impression") that I do with films like *Martin Guerre* and *Le Bal*, for example, broaden the actors' awareness of several significant features of their art that they can only learn through concentrated observation and practice. They learn something about the organic totality of a role, the need to be simultaneously subtle and demonstrative, and the range of actions and expressions at the actor's disposal. In fact, it's quite possible that some of the mimicked gestures learned during this exercise will find their way into the actors' portrayal of their Ubu characters.

4.2 BLOCKING THE TEXT

The primary duty of the director during rehearsals is to orchestrate a group of virtuoso performances into a comprehensive and comprehensible ensemble of dialogue contextualized within an environment of visual and aural imagery, an ensemble that meaningfully engages both actors and audience. In other words, the actors are sign-bearing systems that must be meaningfully moulded and situated within a sign-bearing space (and its signifying systems).[31] Blocking the text is the necessary first step in this "direction" (in both senses of the word).

In the first two weeks of early rehearsals, we begin at the beginning of the rewritten story, devoting much of the time to blocking the individual scenes – that is, determining and staging the actors' positions and movements – and to adjusting and refining the text. The rewritten text includes abundant stage directions that address questions of blocking, but they are never complete. In the interest of time, as the director, I prepare a preliminary scheme for the blocking of each scene. The actors move through it several times, trying to find their footing and the coordination of speech, movement, and expression. Aspiring directors can benefit from the many excellent texts on the general topic of directing plays, such as the ones I mentioned in the introduction to this book. However, we should also remember Augusto Boal's observation about the human being's natural, intuitive ability to act, an observation I would extend to the directing of actors in a play. In addition to some natural ability that we natural actors have to judge and direct our fellow actors, those of us who have studied theatre and have some theatregoing experience should have additional insight into the directorial task. Directors discover very quickly that ideas that look good or promising on paper do not always work in practice, so the blocking shouldn't be too precisely sketched out before the actual bodies-in-space are available to work through it. Once the blocking begins, the director must be ready to reshape her original ideas, taking into account suggestions from the actors themselves or from any non-performing actors who are present, as well as from her own perceptions. Nevertheless, the director should maintain a fair amount of confidence in her "educated" point of view and should at times resist making hasty changes, allowing time to consider and reconsider the workability of a blocking decision.

To prepare for a run-through of a scene, I use many of the usual pre-performance preparatory techniques that I used for the re-creative sketches during the apprenticeship part of the course, the ones isolating individual components of performance: actors repeat their lines first without acting them out; they execute the action without their lines; and I also might instruct them to decelerate or accelerate the overall rhythm of a scene. Another technique I use to make actors more aware of the intricate structure of their interpretive work is one I call "Stop-Rewind-Repeat." At a given point of a scene fragment being rehearsed, I tell the actors to stop the action, to "rewind" it, meaning to move through the action *in reverse* to a given point, and then to repeat the same action with dialogue.

The early rehearsals are quite rough, requiring lots of stops and restarts for (serious) corrections, problems, and questions. However, my initial approach is to allow the action to go as far as possible without stopping it, even when things might look a bit confused and off-track. It is better to allow the student-actors the opportunity to find their own way first. I do take written notes on any particular problems that I see during the rehearsal, and, subsequently, if I do not feel that the actors have remedied the flaw or at least that they are moving in the right

CHAPTER FOUR: REHEARSING

direction, I discuss possible corrections with them after the sequence is complete.

4.3 MEMORIZING TEXT AND INDIVIDUAL WORK WITH VOICE-ACCENT-INTONATION-EXPRESSION

As far as possible, I try to avoid allowing students to rehearse a scene with text in hand. To this end, we first do an "expressive reading" of the text, without the staging context. Then, before we rehearse each scene, I expect actors to have their text *more or less* committed to memory. During initial blocking, one actor is usually assigned the responsibility of providing prompting for the rehearsing actors. If the actor forgets a line, she simply says "*Texte!*" and the prompter provides a lead to the line. Or if the prompter notices that the actor has missed an important line, she will bring it to our attention.

As another time-saving technique (for the actors, if not for the director), I schedule meetings of thirty to sixty minutes with each of the actors to work with them individually on their roles, focusing primarily on vocal-gestural delivery and phonetic pronunciation. I schedule these sessions only after we have done the preliminary blocking for the entire play, which usually falls about two weeks before spring break, seven to eight weeks into the semester. They take place in a well-insulated office or another "safe" place where we will not disturb any neighbours. At the session, the student-actor performatively reads (including appropriate expression, gesture, and limited movement) all the lines she has in the play. Though the lines are taken out of the larger context, the actor has already rehearsed the lines with the rest of the cast, so she and I will not have a problem relating the lines to the precise performance situation. In this short session, we are usually able to rehearse critical lines several times and get the actor to "nail" a viable intonation of the lines and to at least approximate the correct pronunciation. The actors bring a tape and we record the session; I advise them to use the tape to practice their pronunciation and to memorize their lines. When they are available, I have also asked native-speaking French actors to produce an "authentically" pronounced version of the text or portions of it for some or all of the group.

4.4 THE JOURNAL

Students must also continue to keep and turn in their journals, but now, in addition to commenting on class activities, I instruct them to address issues regarding 1) their personal growth toward the final production and their role in the production, and 2) their perceptions of the growth of the production as a whole, including the continuing evolution and modifications of text, and the development of all the individual sign systems and the material context of the piece. Beyond the evident objective of keeping them focused and critically aware of our work and their contribution to it, the journal entries also prepare them for the final written assignment of the course: a semiotic analysis of our performance production.

4.5 THE WEEK BEFORE SPRING BREAK

The week before spring break, I require the actors to have their lines (nearly) committed to memory, and we hold about nine hours of rehearsal – three hours per day, Tuesday, Wednesday, and Thursday. For the Ubu play, the ideal achievement I had anticipated was the following: On Tuesday and Wednesday we would focus on getting through whole acts without a break, probably acts 1 and 2 on Tuesday, and acts 3, 4, and 5 on Wednesday; then, on the last day, we would do two run-throughs of the entire play. The first run-through of an act is done "express," meaning as quickly as is humanly possible. To maintain the momentum of the accelerated tempo, we don't use prompters. If an actor misses her line, we simply skip it and move on. Increasing the concentration on the text and avoiding all opportunity to relax their concentration prepares the actors for the next hurdle: the first non-stop, normal tempo but rough, run-through of the entire text.

As I said, this was my ideal. Now, back to reality: During the Tuesday rehearsal session I realized that the actors' rendering of the text was still too conditional and uncommitted to allow them to continue without correction, so I settled for something less. We spent Tuesday's session working on the first act and most of the second. On Wednesday, we completed acts 2, 3, and the beginning of 4. On Thursday, we finished act 5, briefly reviewed acts 1 and 2, which hadn't been rehearsed since Tuesday, and then did an express run-through of the entire play. Consequently, we did not do the complete normal tempo run-through as planned.

It is not absolutely necessary to adhere to the original plan for the rehearsal schedule and to require that the text be rehearsed comprehensively before spring break. Primarily, you want to ensure that the students will not leave for spring break with ambivalent expectations for the production in the making. Each and every actor should have a good idea of the overall configuration of the story, a strong sense of its performance potential and of her own contribution to the whole. In a project like this, the director must be flexible and prepared to reconsider her comprehensive plan in response to the actual progress being made. If I find that I'm falling behind my original schedule, I defer my original plans for adding the not-yet-written components of the text (the introduction, conclusion, and transitional interludes between scenes), and in the past, I have also resolved to cut certain large chunks of text that I deem problematic for one reason or another, especially if it looks like the running time of the play might exceed the one-hour limit I set.

The troupe had a pizza dinner together after the final rehearsal before the break. As always, I was sensitive to the comments they made about the project and what it meant to them. Though still rather rough and containing a number of "holes," and though we still had a narrative frame and some other features to add and to polish (such as songs and audience participation exercises), the students could depart for spring break with the confidence that we would be able to achieve our goal to produce a "real" full-length play. They were confident that something "big" was in the works and that they had a major role in it. Moreover, in eight weeks of working together re-creatively and theatrically, they had become – to the extent possible in our often cruel and egocentric society of "profit before people" – a solidary group of "professionals" who cared about their companions and were happy for one another's achievements. Every one of them had discovered and performed something beautiful in Thursday's culminating rehearsal. I also had the feeling they were happy to follow my mandate that they carry their re-created text with them wherever they went on spring break and return with the text fully committed to memory so that we could hit the ground running on their return.

4.6 AFTER THE BREAK
Discovering and Claiming Our Space

After the break, which for us amounted to an eleven-day gap in the rehearsal schedule, we had twenty hours of rehearsal time prescheduled for the first week, but I was able to designate at least some of the sessions for subgroups only. For the first time, we would be rehearsing on our actual performance space in the on-campus Wesley Centre, a residence hall sponsored by the Presbyterian Church. [32] The chapel area on the top floor of the building could be converted easily into a nice theatre space. I had asked the Centre's staff to build a 12- x 20- x 2-foot (3.6- x 6- x .6-metre) platform directly in front of the stage/altar area, allowing movement between this constructed space and the traditional stage space. Changing tables to hold costumes and props were located on either side of the platform, and the sound and light controls were located handily at the back of the platform on the threshold of the stage so that the actors could monitor them as needed. The theatre could hold about 120 spectators maximum.

Since this is the place where the students will become fully "professionalized" and perform for hundreds of spectators, it is important that they have the opportunity to both savour the transition and discover the new space by bonding with it sensorially and spiritually. So the first "chore" of the on-site rehearsal was the "discovery of space" exercise. Like the exercise in which they familiarized themselves with the first (classroom) performance space that we occupied, the actors went through their paces perambulating the space of our theatre, sensing themselves as a body-in-space on stage before a virtual audience and imagining themselves in the audience, getting an idea of what the spectator's point of view and gaze might be like: its cause and effect, so to speak. It is very interesting and rewarding to see the newfound sense of accomplishment in the attitude of the actors as they promenade around this space – a space that *belongs* to them!

The first post-break rehearsal, on Tuesday, March 28, lasted from 3:40 to 8:00 p.m., but I only required the plenary group to stay until 6:30. During the first part of the rehearsal, after the discovery of space and a quick warm-up exercise, we rehearsed acts 2 and 3. From 6:30 to 8:00, the essential cast of the first act (Pa, Ma, and the Narrator-

Bear) rehearsed three key scenes from that act. The second rehearsal, on Wednesday, March 29, lasted from 5:00 to 8:00 p.m. All actors were on call, and we rehearsed act 1 with the essential group noted above, and then act 4, in which different actors play Pa and Ma Ubu. On Thursday, March 30, we did the reverse of Tuesday's program. From 3:40 to 6:00, all were present to rehearse acts 1, 2, 3, and 4. Then, from 6:00 to 8:00, the core actors for specific scenes of acts 3, 4, and 5 remained. On Saturday, April 1, the session lasted from 10:00 a.m. to 3:00 p.m. The core actors for acts 1 and 2 rehearsed from 10 a.m. to noon. Then, after a quick pizza lunch, we reviewed the text with the plenary group to make definitive decisions on the supplementary stuff: the narrative frame, the transitions between acts that included audience contact and participation, and the conclusion. From about 1:30 to 3:00, the core actors for acts 3, 4, and 5 remained to rehearse their scenes. On Sunday, April 2, the entire group was present from 4:00 to 8:00 p.m. From 4:00 to 6:00 we rehearsed the integration of the added components; and from 6:00 to 8:00 we did a rough run-through of the entire play with the new stuff added.

As I mentioned earlier, this strategy of adding text and rounding out the action of the play at a point later rather than earlier in our program is beneficial to the overall health of the project from more than one point of view. It staves off the feeling of routine and gives the cast new challenges to confront, new ideas to build, and the revisions made are usually both more appropriate and more creative since they are part of a discovery process that could not have been anticipated at an earlier point of the writing process. The added text materializes more naturally and organically as a result of our performance practice, our performative putting to the test of the text, which has moved us in a more motivated direction in the process. The revisions and additions to the text are, in essence, part of a construction process that is largely guided and influenced by the performance practice itself.[33]

My class notes end on Thursday, March 30. On this day the rehearsal activity began to set its own agenda. I abandoned my classroom approach toward the project and went whole hog into a play production mode. The actors had a schedule indicating times at which certain scenes would be rehearsed. In addition, for the later rehearsal sessions, I often arrived with photocopied director's notes that I distributed to the actors. These were mostly concerned with fine-tuning, pointing out corrections that I thought should be made.

4.7 THE MATERIAL GENESIS OF THE PLAY
Set, Costumes, Props, Sound, and Light

As I've already pointed out and as anyone who does theatre comes to realize, the core of the theatrical enterprise is the body/character-in-space: a body, set in particular spatial context, that acts (or doesn't act) and speaks (or doesn't speak). This core can be exercised, rehearsed, and developed independently of the other material components of performance (set, costumes, props, lighting, sound effects, and music), the various signifying systems that are usually to some extent virtually present in the imagination of the actors and director. While it is entirely possible merely to imagine the non-living elements of the performance, this could not be done in the reverse, to state the obvious: that is, one could not productively rehearse a play with the set, costumes, props, and music, and imaginatively evoke and project the role of the speaking and acting bodies and their interaction with the material world of the stage. Rehearsals are made for human bodies and minds. What's more, the physical and psychological condition, conditioning, and predispositions of the human body require a good deal of work to elicit an effective verbal story and be properly moulded into the material world of that story. So the material support for the text necessarily follows the work of character interpretation. In my projects, it begins slowly but grows steadily, co-operatively, and, I would dare say, organically.

During much of the early rehearsal period in the classroom, the set is makeshift. The actors use chairs and other items to simulate elements of the set or delimit boundaries within a given space, but most of the set is imaginary. Remember that my actors have had some initial experience with props and costumes through the semiotic recreational exercises early in the semester. In addition, as mentioned above, I have produced a rough, preliminary list of costumes and props in conjunction with the rewritten text. This list is at least partially based on suggestions of the actors. As rehearsals progress, it happens that the actors or I introduce an item or two – such as a chair with wheels – with which the actors

CHAPTER FOUR: REHEARSING   119

become familiar and to which they develop a particular response. These props often find their way into the final production. With increasing frequency, I begin to introduce critical props and costume pieces into the rehearsals, ones that are not easily simulated or imagined and/or that might require substantial manipulation by the actor, or items that could be of sufficient size or weight to bear on the actor's ability to move and act. As far as sound and music goes, we often can effectively approximate a key sound effect by voice or action (such as the pop of a gun, the beating of a drum, or the chirp of a bird),[34] and background music will come much later in the process.

Given the collaborative educational goals of the production, I constantly remind the actors to think about solutions to our need for costumes, props, and set pieces as we continue to rehearse. Before we begin to rehearse each scene, I ask them what they think their material needs might be and whether they have an item they could use to fill the need. They also know that I have a considerable store of props and costume pieces and that if they do not respond to my casual requests to provide an idea or an actual item, I will either assign them to produce an item or step in myself to fill the need. They often bring to rehearsal props they think will work. They try them, and we discuss their use, their function, and their compatibility with the other signs and signifying systems of the production. Sometimes these items remain as is, sometimes they remain in altered form, sometimes we replace them with a signifying material that is more appropriate and coherent.[35]

The choice of costumes and props is never gratuitous; it is always motivated by the semiotic codes at work in the production. The actors have learned something about this through the semiotic exercises they performed early in the semester. To set the standard for the Ubu story, we discussed the extent to which costumes and props should comply with and reflect the "unreal" nature of the play. Some costume pieces can be naturalistic and have an historical connection, but most, especially those associated with Ma and Pa Ubu, will have something absurd, caricatural, or ridiculous about them. Thus, to recall the exercise on theatrical objects, we might look toward the "reimagined" sense of the object to fulfill this challenge to reality. Thus, in our project, we did not represent Ubu's sword by the rigidity, vigour, and force of steel (or a plastic prop that resembles steel) with all its historical baggage and stark realism. Instead,

Fig. 12. "Père Ubu," act 4, scene 2. The battle scene: Soldiers dance in the aisles, ballet-style, to Tchaikovsky's "Dance of the Sugar Plum Fairy." Emily Christianson, Diana Devy, Ashlee Sanders, Sara Boucher, et al. Wesley Foundation, University of Tennessee, Knoxville, TN. Photo by Les Essif.

we believed we could more meaningfully suggest the puerility and fantasy of the character by the ephemeral, mutable, and toyish qualities of a balloon. Likewise, costumes must reflect these meanings, and they must coincide and join with the objects to produce the strange yet meaningful story of Ubu. This does not mean that we are obliged to follow Jarry's surreal, cartoon-like (and perhaps tongue-in-cheek) design for Ubu, or his recommendations to have him wear a bowler hat. But we should take seriously these suggestions and their relation to the text: Is this the way we would have pictured Pa Ubu's or Ma Ubu's costume, based on the text and before seeing Jarry's list of costume suggestions? We also consider our company's re-creative reading of and approach to the text, our situation in the twenty-first century, East Tennessee's predicted response to the story, and quite simply, the need to be creatively and theatrically artistic and innovative in our attempt to produce a system of costuming for the play. The set, as well, must (cor)respond to these criteria.

As for the sound and music in the play, we remember that Fischer-Lichte pointed out the essential abstractness of music and how it easily assimilates to any context (see section 2.15, "Introducing the 'Systems' of Style, Costume, Prop, and Music"); so for the Ubu play, we chose an eclectic range of styles of music, most of which introduced an ironic allusion to historical reality within our realistic storyline replete with absurd action and drama. In short, the music frequently contrasted beautifully with the other sign systems of our work. Consider, for example, the use of the tango for the first scene of the play (see appendix F, "First Scene"). Also, in the battle scene the actors danced, ballet-style, to Tchaikovsky's "Sugar Plum Fairy" in the aisles throughout the audience space (see fig. 12).

CHAPTER FOUR: REHEARSING

Once the actors and I formulate a good idea of what our play is all about, I tell them to bring to rehearsal (in cassette format) selections of musical excerpts, usually lasting no more than one or two minutes. They indicate the source of the tune and the place in the text/production where they believe it would fit as background music. Then, with further input from the actors and usually by general agreement, I make the final decision on the music cues for the finished production.

For the Ubu play, the actors themselves took turns operating the "sound box," and as with the costume changing and props selection, they did so in full view of the audience, in an area that was designated as officially "offstage" but was in fact in full view of the audience.

Lighting is without doubt an important signifying system, but, in my projects, it is also the most expendable system and has a lower priority than others. Subject to technical difficulties, it is the least dependable and it often requires a lot of time and attention, not to mention liaison work with a technician. So I usually – though not always – limit the role of lighting in the project, which, I admit, equally limits the amount the students will learn about theatrical lighting, semiotically and practically. (This is, after all, an instructional project.) We usually incorporate lighting effects in the very broadest of brush strokes – light (day), dark (night), some variation between the two (twilight, shadow, fog, mystery, mood) – and I often use a projector to spotlight a particular character or event.[36]

I do not spend much time on the strategies and applications of makeup, especially since my actors will all be playing multiple roles, which, from a professional point of view, would require major alterations of makeup. In addition, a satisfactory application of makeup requires considerable knowledge of physiognomic effect. However, I do provide my actors with the basic red, white, and black stage makeup and allow them to experiment with discovering ways to produce a standard highlighting of their facial features, making them more visible on stage and more co-operative with the stage lighting. The objective is to render their facial features more perceptible and manipulable.[37] For a good French-language introduction to the art of stage makeup, see Maurice Chevaly's *Petit Précis*, "Le Maquillage," 159–62.

4.8 COLLABORATIVE, CO-OPERATIVE DUTIES
Stage Management and Promotion

As I pointed out above, role assignments include stage management and prompting duties for each of the actors. Beyond the evident practical benefits of such assignments, rotation through these non-acting, extra-performative functions also contributes to the feeling that we are indeed an egalitarian team of artists. Furthermore, it helps the actors derive a more holistic sense of the art of performance in general and the complexity of our production in particular, and it helps them to contextualize their role(s) in the production. The benefits do not end there. The grand and noble mission of our production is to present a collective artistic enterprise on the stage, one which makes the audience feel that they are both privy to and involved in the construction of this performance event and which helps them understand that all the world is indeed a stage. During rehearsals the actors become increasingly aware of the project's collaborative dimension, and they find their position within the greased machinery that feeds the performance. Not only do my actors change costume and props in full view of the audience – there are no wings or "backstage" in our productions – but they also move seamlessly between "onstage" acting roles and "offstage" management duties.[38] By the time the performance is presented to the "real" audience – the reader will remember that I do believe that throughout the rehearsal stage of the project my spect-acting performers perform for a virtual audience as well as for themselves – the audience witnesses the actors' collaborative and collective synergy, seeing it as part and parcel of the artistic event. This is certainly one of the more outstanding features of my re-creative productions and the one of which I am most proud.

The more the project evolves into a polished performance piece, the more the students are motivated to promote the play to as large an audience as possible. Of course, the teacher-director has confidently had the "big picture" in mind from the very beginning of the project. As early as the first week of class, once we have determined the exact dates for the final production, I send out an advance notice to an established mailing list of potential spectators, including French teachers in area schools and officers of the local Alliance Française, informing them that the play project is in the works. Since we do not have a definite title at the beginning of the semester, I simply tell the prospective audience that the work will be a "re-creation" of the Ubu story, or whatever text we might be working on.

What about the audience? I'm very concerned to have our projects seen by a large number and diversity of spectators. Our intense and complex work always leads to a high quality, original, and creative rendering of a dramatic story, and it deserves to be appreciated by as many people as possible. Too often, we foreign-language faculty are content to do only one performance before an audience consisting of the actors' friends, classmates, and fellow foreign-language students. Colleagues I meet at conferences are often surprised to learn that our productions play for as many as six to seven hundred spectators. While I would like to think that the design and reputation of our play projects accounts for much of this response, we should not underestimate the importance of promotion and marketing.

Where do we find the potential audience? Despite the usually large number of plays and other performance events on campus that might compete with our play for an audience, relatively few foreign-language plays, professional or otherwise, are offered here or in most parts of this country. Consequently, demand can be high for an opportunity to attend such a special interest event, especially among foreign-language educators in secondary and higher education who jump at the chance to offer their students an "authentic" French-language experience. I do believe, however, that an important strategy to increase the "market share" of the foreign-language play is to increase its comprehensibility and accessibility for a greater community of both francophiles and theatrophiles. Consequently, I do not believe, for example, that a play by the most prestigious troupe of French actors doing Molière has the "staying power" that a good re-created version of a classic text would have for a market consisting of mostly anglophone spectators. To be sure, any American or anglophone Canadian community with a good-sized university will have a rather strong demographic of francophones and francophiles, including an Alliance Française, and such a community will have a vested interest in the well-marketed professional French play. The frequent problem with such an enterprise, however, is that in order to attract an audience large enough to play at a decent-sized campus theatre and recoup expenses through ticket sales, the audience will need to include spectators with a very wide range of competence in the foreign language, including students with a limited capacity to comprehend a classical-professional rendering of a classic French text. If the reputation of the artists and the professional artistry of the performance will usually sustain the attention of the spectators for at least a short while, the less experienced non-native-speaker spectators will almost invariably lose interest. This is where the contemporized, re-created version of the story – one that abridges, vulgarizes, and simplifies some of the language, contemporizes some of the situations, and targets contemporary spectators by attempting to guide them through the action of the play while involving them in it – will have more appeal to a larger community of language learners and francophiles. If done at least semi-professionally, the production will not disaffect the native speakers in the audience. (I take up the topic of "rehearsing the audience" in chapter 5.)

I tend to think of our audiences in terms of a series of tiers, of zones of varying proximity to our project. The first zone of potential spectators for a French-language play by university students is, of course, the peer group of other students of French language and culture at the institution. For advertising purposes, it is also the most accessible group. Because of its on-site location, I have developed a successful strategy of "activist promotion," which I explain below. But even simple announcements of the play by your colleagues to their classes is fairly easy and effective. However, let me offer a word of caution about this. While I believe that all students of French, no matter how fundamental their training, should have the opportunity to see our play, I am opposed to a practice of applying pressure on the students to attend or to offering them enticements such as bonus points or extra credit, and I convey this to my colleagues in my promotional communications to them. Experience has taught me that the attendance of numbers of truly disinterested students might adversely affect the overall quality of the performance, especially one such as ours that attempts to develop and sustain an open and active rapport with the audience. Thus I prefer to limit the number of those students who arrive late, obtain a ticket solely for proof of attendance, and seat themselves with the intention to leave the theatre as soon as they can, often at an inappropriate time.

Yes, I do believe that there are a few student spectators who are (perhaps temporarily) beyond the reach of even the most effective theatrical

CHAPTER FOUR: REHEARSING								125

art, in a foreign language or not. Yes, it bothers me to see impassive or resistant spectators at our plays. But don't get me wrong – I do believe that colleagues and I would do well to coax seemingly unmotivated students to expose themselves to our theatrical event. Many of them can and have become sufficiently captivated by the creativity and energy of our show. However, given the relatively large audiences we play to, I'd rather err on the side of quality over quantity and attempt to secure the best possible experience for all.

Many students of theatre and literature on campus also attend our performances, especially at my institution, whose theatre department has strong linkages to France, Germany, and Eastern Europe. As noted in chapter 2, colleagues from the theatre department often contribute to my projects, and I have had the opportunity to team teach this course with a colleague from the department.

The next zone of potential audience consists of the foreign-language students from area high schools and junior colleges. If we develop a good rapport with faculty of these institutions, assuring them that we take our performance work seriously and are making an effort to reach out to the more fledgling language learner, many teachers will be happy to help organize the attendance of whole classes of their (usually advanced) students at our play. The director should carefully consider the time and scheduling of the play in order to facilitate the transporting of students to campus. For our area high schools, the best time is after the close of the school day. To give these students and faculty time to arrive on campus, I schedule two plays at 4:30. Another possibility is for the troupe and the play to travel to the local schools. This works especially well when high school and community college faculty are willing to collaborate with one another in order to consolidate their students, channelling them into the theatre of one of the high schools on the same day and at the same time. This consolidation results in an audience of from one to two hundred, instead of one-third or even one-fourth that number. I am very fortunate to know one particular high school faculty member who is always happy to coordinate a play performance at her school.

Arrangements for these events must, of course, be planned from the earliest stages of the project. For a performance at the end of the spring semester, I usually give my area contacts a heads-up as early as the preceding fall semester. Then, at the very beginning of the spring semester of the play, as soon as we set the performance dates, I contact my high school and community college coordinators and any other area French instructors who show an interest in hosting our troupe (time and schedule permitting) or in coming to campus for a performance. (One must realize that most high school teachers are unable to assume the organizational burden of hosting the play on a perennial basis.) Once I've made email or telephone contact with the facilitators, with the help of my actors I send out an early announcement explaining who we are and what our project is about (see appendix G, "Sample Promotional Letter to Potential Spectators").

One final word on playing to high school and community college students. Despite their usual lack of language skills, we have never had a behaviour problem with them. On the contrary, they are usually so attentive and pleasantly surprised by some of our "outrageous" techniques that we hold post-performance discussion sessions with them, in which they ask the actors questions about the text, the performance process, and more generally, about taking French at the big university.

Beyond the act of inviting students and faculty from other institutions to see the play on campus and the more enterprising exploit of transporting the play to their home institutions, we have also integrated high school students and faculty in the staging of one of our plays. Saralee, the helpful and resourceful high school teacher mentioned above had organized a group of her students into a cancan dance ensemble that performed at high school and community events. In rewriting the Macbett story, I realized I might be able to work this cancan chorus line into the big battle scene. With the enthusiastic collaboration and personal participation of Saralee, we placed the cancan chorus smack dab in the middle of the raging battle. (The staging required no more than one very short rehearsal with the dancers two days before the first performance.) The integration was productive on the artistic, professional (inter-institutional), and socio-theatrical levels. It definitely enhanced the play's theme of war, adding an interesting layer of anachronistic absurdity. It also added to the play's theatricality and its diverse cast of characters while creating a closer rapport with the high school students and faculty, and giving the greater audience some idea of the "reach" and the openness of our theatrical endeavours. I really believe it enhanced the spectators' feeling of connection to the theatrical event: All the world's a stage! Needless to say, re-creative theatre has great potential as a wonderful and enjoyable outreach activity.

Further out in the field of potential spectators lie the francophone and francophile members of the local and not so local communities. Individual members of the Alliance Française are on my mailing list, as are colleagues at universities as far as one hundred miles away, some of whom have made the trek to Knoxville with their students to see our plays.

Included on my mailing-contact list are addresses for the local media. I send press releases to the following media entities: our city newspaper, Knoxville's one free alternative newspaper, the public radio station, the student radio station, and the campus TV channel (see appendix G, "Sample Press Release," for sample promotional letters and press releases). Though this advertising might not bring in more than a dozen or so additional spectators, our unique theatrical and cultural enterprise should be seen by all those with an interest in it. We're providing a unique event, and we are enlarging spheres of influence for our specific theatrical enterprise as well as for French culture in general. On one occasion, two French airline pilots told me after the show that they had seen the notice about our play in the alternative newspaper. Though they rarely had occasion to come to Knoxville, they felt fortunate for the opportunity to see our unique production with connections to their home culture.

4.9 POSTER AND PROGRAM DESIGN

During the week or two at the beginning of rehearsals when the actors are deciding on the poster design presented by the poster committee, we establish a program design committee, usually composed of a couple of students who are savvy with computer graphics. The poster design is usually duplicated on the program cover, along with other graphics, space permitting. I provide all the information that needs to be included in the program: the cast and other credits and usually a brief, scene-by-scene synopsis of our re-created story. The Ubu play had key re-created phrases in bold that would facilitate the spectators' participation in repeating those phrases and it would increase their comprehension of the action. When the program design committee completes a draft of the program, they photocopy it for distribution and class discussion, usually before a rehearsal session or during a break. Once again, all actors are invited to collaborate and offer suggestions for improvement. Once we agree on the design, we choose a paper colour, and then I take the original to the photocopy shop.

4.10 FINANCING THE PRODUCTION AND TICKET SALES

The director must decide whether or not she needs to finance the expenses of the production by requesting a modest fee from the spectators. Expenses will include costume and prop purchases, poster and program printing, and any payments for the rental of space and perhaps the services of a technician or two. In addition to the necessary funding, the sale of tickets – which, for the purposes of our non-professional academic enterprise, represents more of a spectator contribution to our show – is also a good way to encourage people to attend the performance. It gives the event an air of legitimacy, creates some hype around it, and anyone who buys a ticket feels obliged to attend the event. Selling tickets in advance also helps forecast the attendance at each performance and alerts you to the possibility that the demand for one of the performances might exceed the seating capacity of the theatre. However, the sale of tickets represents yet another responsibility, one that takes time to organize and manage. In the past, I've implemented a practice of ticket purchases, requesting from $2.00 to $3.00 per ticket. I arrange the campus sale of tickets through our department staff, we indicate on the posters that tickets are available for purchase in our main office, and I send memos to my colleagues to announce to their students the availability of tickets. For off-campus performances the high school or community college coordinators usually collect money from their students, sometimes preferring the receipt and souvenir value of a ticket, sometimes not. Either way, asking a modest donation for admission can easily generate enough money to finance the project with some left over to be used as seed money for future projects.

The design and printing of tickets is uncomplicated, especially since the modest fee will discourage any efforts to counterfeit. It suffices to place on the ticket an icon from the poster graphic and a date and time.

Since we usually present three campus performances, we colour-code the tickets according to the date.

One could, of course, avoid selling tickets to raise funds and simply request a $2.00 to $3.00 donation at the door. For my projects, however, we sometimes play at venues with limited seating, and as mentioned above, ticket sales allow us to anticipate attendance at each of the three on-campus performances and to avoid turning away potential spectators at the door. Either in lieu of or as a complement to requesting a spectator fee to fund the project, the producer-director could seek financial support from inside or outside the institution. My first re-creational project at the University of Louisville was supported by an internal department grant, and my first two projects at the University of Tennessee were partially funded by two successive Practitioner Research on Teaching Awards ($600 each). In addition to these grants, Cleveland State Community College, a ninety-minute drive from the university that required additional expenses for transportation of the troupe, paid my department a flat fee of $500 for each of the three performances we performed there in three different years.

4.11 ACTIVIST PROMOTION
"Storming" the Foreign-Language Classrooms

As I mentioned above, the on-campus students of the foreign language constitute the first tier of potential spectators. At all levels of French, our program has a combined student population of eight hundred to a thousand. In view of these numbers, a little aggressive marketing goes a long way, especially when I have developed a tactic that I believe provides an instructional benefit to our targeted French student patrons as well as to the actors themselves. In the last week before the scheduled performances, the production is fairly polished and the actors are increasingly anxious to go on with the show. My colleagues have repeatedly announced the play to their students, making them aware of the upcoming event. So this is the best time for my actors and their fellow French students to get a taste of what's in store for performance night.

I announce to all instructors of French that at some point in the week before the first performance, they should expect to have their classes *briefly* interrupted by a promotional "spot" for the play. I ask that any colleague who prefers to not have their class interrupted on a given day contact me. My students and I determine groups of two, three, or four actors, according to their involvement in especially active and striking key "moments" of the play. These "moments" or tiny sketches last no more than thirty seconds or so, and I provide the actors with step-by-step instructions on how to proceed with their "intervention," including suggestions for possible groupings of actors and scenes they might present (see appendix G, "Instructions and Suggestions for Activist Promotion"). We then take a few minutes at the end of a regular rehearsal to discuss and rehearse the intervention. A group of actors simulates an intervention and the other actors simulate the audience. This helps the actors get a grasp on the various dimensions of the activity. Our post-intervention discussions are beneficial in that they help the actors realize how their promotional performance activity might be received by a variety of surprised and unsuspecting spectators. Most important, however, this allows them to get progressively closer to the "spot" they will present, and through this activity, to the performance itself.

I then prepare a schedule of all the classes in French according to their locations and times and I distribute it to my actors, advising them that they each must visit at least eight to ten classes. At the end of one of the rehearsal sessions, they take ten to fifteen minutes to coordinate their schedules and agree on which group will visit which classes, attempting to visit as many classes as possible while avoiding the possibility of two groups visiting the same class.

When the actors feel ready, they are on their own to accomplish the objective. I find that once they have done one or two of these interventions, they are invariably motivated to do more. This exercise is as beneficial as the rehearsals themselves in reducing the inevitable stage fright they might face with the actual performance. In sum, it is a unique way to actively and realistically promote the play. What's more, it proactively "rehearses" the potential audience as well as the actors. Consequently, this exercise has had great success with student actors and student audiences alike (see appendix G, "Traffic Accident," for another type of intervention).[39]

CHAPTER FOUR: REHEARSING 131

4.12 THE FINAL REHEARSAL PHASE

About two to three weeks before the performance, we put out the word that we will need volunteers, preferably from the ranks of students of French, to help with ticket sales at the door and, depending on the number of actors involved in the project, possibly some of the stage management tasks. I usually find a number of volunteers from among the students in other courses that I am currently teaching, and I have used them to help as sound and lighting technicians – that is, to operate the music or lighting system on cue.

The long rehearsals on the weekend preceding the performance are the most critical for final preparations. For Ubu, we rehearsed five hours on Saturday and four hours on Sunday. With all actors present during the entire rehearsal sessions, we do final touch-ups to any particularly difficult scene, segment, transition, or function of the play before proceeding to complete run-throughs of the play from start to finish, including the interludes of audience participation (using some of the actors, their friends, the director, and/or other observers as a guinea pig audience) and all lighting and music cues. We usually use all necessary props, and the actors wear only those costume pieces that they need to get used to, especially headwear and special footwear, and some particularly weighty costume pieces that could influence or perhaps impede their movement on stage. I also have had the actors practice a pre-performance audience warm-up, for which in full or partial costume they promenade around the stage and audience areas, casually and informally mingling with one another as well as the audience. The final run-through on Sunday is a full-dress rehearsal. I make it a point to invite a few interested colleagues and students to these final rehearsals, and we ask them for their opinions.

If our first performance is scheduled for a Wednesday at 4:30, I try to schedule one final dress rehearsal for either Monday or Tuesday. It does not really hurt if there is a lapse of a day or even two before the final rehearsal and the first performance, as long as the actors have mastered their roles. In fact, it is preferable that there be some small portion of the performance – besides the audience reaction, of course – that remains adventitious, uncertain, and unexplored, such as a movement of an actor or group of actors that depends on a last-minute decision of one of the actors or on a certain audience reaction. This recourse to spontaneity only increases the collaborative (re-)creativity of the group, the psychological predisposition of the players, and consequently, the "natural," relaxed mood of the performance.

5

The Opening Show: *C'est fini!*
... *Ce n'est pas fini!*

The opening performance consummates a very complex process and brings together a great deal of work. It constitutes a demanding and sophisticated display of performance art. But who cares at this point? There is little time for this sort of disengaged reflection now, and we are all anxious to present our wares to a "real" live audience. Some ultimately unknowable force, with a concomitant adrenalin effect, will ensure that all the actors will be ready to perform the show.

To my surprise and relief, I have never had a problem with an actor not showing up for one of the shows, though at times one or two have arrived perilously late. But a director must be prepared for all possible contingencies, including a no-show or the incapacitation of an actor, and that's another advantage to the re-creative instructional method. In a pinch, if one of the actors were absent or unable to perform for a given show, I would simply alert the audience and ask one of the other actors (or a student helper, or an audience member) to "cover" the absentee's role by reading the text and allowing the other actors to guide her through the action. I am quite serious about this. Thanks to the exceptional degree of metatheatrical self-consciousness and self-representation in my projects and to the resultant rapport with the audience, it's quite possible that even the most serious alteration to the original plan would only increase the play's spontaneity and interest. In addition to the fundamental re-creativity that characterizes the entire project and extends through the performance, I have exposed the actors to other specific techniques to accustom them to change and spontaneity, to render them flexible and prepare them for improvisation. One exercise I use from the beginning of the semester and throughout the rehearsal sessions is the spontaneous interruption of one or two spect-actors into one of the daily re-creative sketches of another group.[40] In short, the actors are more or less trained to be spontaneous with their roles and their relationship to the performance. They and I have much less fear of the unexpected.

5.1 INEVITABLE DOUBTS AND PROBLEMS

Given the re-creative-recreational principle behind the instruction and the production and given the relative inexperience of my actors, opening night has a slightly different meaning for my actors than it might have in the case of a conventional play production, whether in a foreign language or not. Though it still represents a critical defining moment for the actors' individual and collective performance, I am happy to report that despite the considerable greenness of many of my actors, none has ever had a serious attack of stage fright or otherwise really screwed up on stage. Once again, this achievement is due largely to the nature of the re-creative developmental process and to the various components of its methodology and their effects: the creation of a community bond among the actors, the limited burden of the amount of text they are required to master, and their brief but influential experience with the art of improvisation. These facets of the process are all reflected in the instructions I am able to give my group of actors in the moment before they go on, which go something like this:

There is no way you can really mess up in this play. The only difference between this performance and your last rehearsal is that here you will have a larger live audience to work with. The spectators will not only acknowledge you; they will to some extent reciprocate what you do on stage by guiding *you* with their eyes, voices, and gestures, especially when you reach out to them.

If you miss a word or two of your line, don't worry about it. You can simply skip it, or if you prefer, openly acknowledge and confess the omission to the audience and then repeat your line. At worst, you might miss more than a small piece of text or do something that might mislead the audience, distort the story, or disorient your fellow actors, or simply something you're not happy with. In that case, you have my permission – and the authorization of our re-creative mission – to step out of your role, tell the audience you messed up, and call on your fellow actors to redo the scene, just as you've done in all your sketch and rehearsal work to date.

Think about this in the context of the overall spirit of our work. Think about who we are and what we do: the audience will have no way of knowing if you really and truly screwed up, or if both your "mistake" and its consequence were simply part of the alienation effect, the self-conscious distancing strategy of our production.

So the worst (or maybe the best?) you could do is simply re-create our re-created story.

5.2 REHEARSING THE AUDIENCE[41]

Audience participation has come into its own in many types of contemporary theatrical productions. Proof of the artists' interest in extending the boundaries of the stage is the recent book *Audience Participation: Essays on Inclusion in Performance*. In her introduction, the editor of this volume, Susan Kattwinkel, speaks of the audience as "co-creators" of the production: "Whatever technique they use, chances are the artists [who seek audience participation] have the intent of engaging spectators in message-making.... They want the audience to speak the message as well as hear it" (x). As I pointed out in the introduction to this book, I do not view the actors simply as performers performing for an audience, but, much more complexly, as "spect-actors." The actors perform first for themselves, then for their fellow actors on stage, and finally for the audience. To put it another way, what the spectator perceives and processes is not always, or not entirely, an actor communicating directly to them but a much more intricately rendered (human) sign-bearing system in the form of a spect-actor whose communication with herself and with her fellow actors contributes to the message being produced and conveyed. In the same vein, I also believe in a more intricately co-operative and synergetic role for the audience. Though the role of spectator is not exactly commensurate with the role of the spect-actor, it is far from one-dimensional. The spectator is first and foremost conscious of herself sitting in the theatre. Most likely, she is at least semi-conscious of two sorts of human company (co-spectators) in her immediate environment in the theatre: the more intimate company of a friend or a relative and the larger group of people whose attention is primarily focused on the stage. This focus on the stage usually varies according to the spectator's comprehension of and interest in the action, imagery, and language presented. When actors directly address the audience, or when they draw the audience directly into the action and/or language of the story – that is, when they get the spectator to "speak the message [of the story] as well as hear it" – the interest and attention of the audience increases, thereby increasing the potential for comprehension of the play, especially the foreign-language play.

In rewriting the (language) content of our play, we already have contemporized, vulgarized, and abbreviated some of the more difficult and perhaps culturally and historically specific language; we have also designed and added a prominent and visible narrative structure to guide the audience members – who have varying abilities to comprehend the French language – through the story and involve them to the extent possible in the action of the play. To meet this objective, my projects have over the years employed a great variety of metatheatrical narrative strategies, one of which is to summarize or comment on the action with a certain amount of English text. Most strategies have had a good deal of success, but I guess I will always feel I'm still in the experimental stage.

In the Ubu play, we created an elaborate plan to ease the spectators into the reality-challenged language and culture of the nineteenth-century French text and, to a lesser extent, into the language and culture of the text's historical source culture, its medieval "intertext," in narratological terms. First, the performance begins when the Narrator-Bear places a cassette in the stereo and listens to an ornate piece of baroque music – operatic pomp and fanfare. Then all the other actors, who are visible to the audience in the perimeter of the "offstage" area, say "*Merdre!*" The Bear, decidedly uncomfortable with the choice of music, shakes his head and addresses the audience, explaining in English with a heavy French accent that this music is not appropriate for Ma and Pa Ubu, and the reasons he gives serve as exposition, summarizing the situation in the first scene of the play. He says that Pa Ubu "*iz 'appy to manger 'iz andouille*" ("he's happy to eat his sausage"), which cues the offstage actor playing Pa Ubu to assume his role and gluttonously repeat the phrase "*De l'andouille!*" ("Sausage!"). The Bear then coaxes the audience into repeating the phrase "*De l'andouille!*" But Ma Ubu is not happy

CHAPTER FIVE: THE OPENING SHOW　　　　　　　　　　137

Fig. 13. *"Père Ubu." The Grande Finale.
John Gonsoulin, Ashlee Sanders,
Sarah Boucher, Diana Devy,
Emily Christianson, Josh Hopkins.
Wesley Foundation, University of
Tennessee, Knoxville, TN. Photo by
Les Essif.*

with this situation, says the Bear, because she "wants 'im to put his cul (with a gesture towards his buttocks) sur le trône," in response to which the actress playing Ma Ubu assumes her role and repeats the phrase: *"Je voudrais installer ce cul sur un trône!"* ("I'd like to place that butt of his on a throne!"). The Bear shows the audience a placard with the French phrase and asks the spectators to repeat it, as he gestures toward his buttocks. Once the audience has satisfactorily complied with his request, he asks them to repeat the key word *"Merdre!,"* and saying "Now I play la bonne musique," he puts on a tango. Ma Ubu once again "comes alive" and begins to dance to the beat of the tango. She approaches Pa and seduces him into dancing with her.

From this point on, most of the tableaux (scenes) of the play are preceded by a short narrative interlude, which is presented each time by a different actor. In either heavily accented English or a mix of French and English, with a length of about three to four sentences, the narrator comments on the preceding scene and introduces the action of the following one. As part of her introduction to the following scene, she pronounces a key phrase, which is repeated "in character" by the actor who has the line in the scene. The narrator shows the audience a placard with the phrase – something like *"Il a mangé le veau! Au secours!"* ("He's eaten the veal! Help!") or *"Ce n'est pas moi! C'est la Mère Ubu et Bordure!"* ("It wasn't me! It was Ma Ubu and Bordure!") – and asks the spectators to repeat it. Besides appearing on the placard, the key phrases are also listed on the program as the titles of many of the twenty tableaux from the play. Also appearing on the program is the *"Chanson de décervelage"* ("The Debraining Song"). After the eleventh tableau, where Ubu condemns all the nobles and magistrates to the debraining room, the whole troupe will direct the audience to sing this song and guide them through it (see fig. 13). On the back of the program, there is a one-paragraph synopsis of the play in English. See appendix F, "Sample Narrative Interventions," for the text of these and other narrative interludes.

While this might strike some readers of this book – and perhaps, initially, some spectators of the show – as too much like French 101, the overall theatricality and sophistication of the play ensures a more engaged and enlightened overall reception. There are many benefits from this narrative operation of "rehearsing the audience." In addition to rehearsing the French language and providing the less initiated and less confident audience members with key markers to follow the story, it involves all the spectators in the action of the play and keeps them more attentive, as mentioned above. It also provides the actors with the opportunity to improvise, connecting them circumstantially to the spectators and the spectators to the actors, helping both sides of the absent curtain to relax in their respective roles. Judging by the reaction of the various types of spectators and by the comments we received on the audience survey (see below and appendix H), I am confident that even some of the most sophisticated francophone members of the audience were able to connect with the art and energy of the play. We might not win all of them over, but we can certainly shoot for the max.

The play should not last more than one hour: short and sweet. Why? Most of the audience members for this type of play are neither seasoned theatregoers nor seasoned speakers and listeners of foreign language, so they might not have the discipline and the attention span to sit through a longer performance. While director and actors will have attained a certain pride and confidence in the power of their performance, the actors will be short of a certain professional expertise. Under the circumstances, the director should assume, rightly or wrongly, that the troupe as a whole will not have achieved the necessary sophistication and finesse to keep the spectators on the edge of their seats – and that's where we'd like them to be – for an extended period of time. Whether I care to admit it or not, the same goes for the director, who, in most cases, is primarily a teacher (or teacher-scholar) of foreign language, literature, and culture, and only occasionally dons the hat of a theatre practitioner.[42] This means that, overall, the director should remain mindful of the unascertainable risk that the performance that she has designed will necessarily will lack something of a professional stamp. A shorter play will reduce this risk.[43]

Despite the preceding caveat, this is the evening that your student-actors begin to feel and act like professionals. They will come together like never before, and inevitably, most of them will begin to consider acting as a career.

5.3 AUDIENCE FEEDBACK
The Survey

At the end of the performance, following a thundering round of applause, I make a brief announcement acknowledging individuals and entities who have helped support our project and thanking the audience for their patronage. I also ask the audience to consider completing the spectator survey we provided to them when they entered the theatre. Requesting the spectators to offer their opinion about the play is to some degree a continuation and confirmation of the bond we feel we have created between them and us, spectators and artists, resulting in identities or positions that, in the spirit of Augusto Boal, we might redefine as "spect-artists": spect-actors all! But the primary purpose of this survey is to obtain a more or less objective, considered, and critical evaluation of our work and to seek ideas for possible improvement.

No doubt, most of the audience will not have the time or the inclination to complete the form, no matter how strongly they feel about what they have just experienced. Yet even a brief, limited response provides some very useful information, so I urge the audience to take the time to provide whatever comments they can. I also inform the students in the audience that they may submit the survey through their respective instructors, if they prefer. Some instructors actually require their students to complete the survey as a class exercise. If they do so, I discourage them from attaching any system of reward or penalty to the exercise, a practice that would without doubt jeopardize the objectivity of the survey. Off-campus instructors often have their students complete the survey in their classes and they mail them to me. Consequently, of the five to seven hundred people who have seen the play, I usually wind up with around one to two hundred completed survey sheets, some of which are quite detailed. This response is sufficient for our purposes.

The questions should be short, easily comprehensible, and to some extent specific to the performance: that is, they should refer to one or two of the specific narrative, theatrical, or metatheatrical strategies that were used in the particular performance. See appendix H for the survey form used for "Père Ubu."

I usually read some of the more thoughtful comments I've received to my students, who are very happy to hear them, especially the flattering ones. I take seriously all the positive and negative comments that are sufficiently detailed and seem to represent a consensus. By and large, the survey comments are quite positive, and I understand that many spectators would be reluctant to be too critical, whether because they feel unqualified to be so or because they are simply trying to be polite and supportive. I realize as well that the absence or scarcity of negative comments about certain features of the performance does not necessarily mean that there were no problems and no room for improvement. Similar to the validity of the confidential written student evaluations of teachers (a standard practice of the American university), this form of assessment requires a close and honest analysis to be effective and useful.

5.4 PHOTOGRAPHING AND VIDEOTAPING THE PROCESS AND THE PERFORMANCE

With the intense work of the rehearsals, the director will not have much time to think about making a photographic record of key images, moments, or "tableaux" of the progress toward the finished product. Post-performance, however, if you haven't kept such a record, you likely will regret it. The easiest solution is to designate one of the actors, a friend of an actor, or another available individual to be the company photographer for a couple of rehearsals. You can provide the camera, and you should provide the film, of course. Barring this solution, it is up to you to remember to bring a camera to rehearsal to take shots of the work-in-progress. This will provide a rough material record of the evolution of the project. On the other hand, since you have few other duties during the performances themselves and you better than anyone can follow the action and anticipate the best shots, you can do the photography throughout the performance phase of the project. Pictures I have taken have found their way into my journal articles.

The most complete and comprehensive record of the performance is the videotaping of one of the performances – or even two of them since they all do vary slightly in content, form, and audience reaction and participation. Many professional theatre practitioners prefer to respect and safeguard the ephemeral nature of performance art by refusing to produce any film document of it. In the case of my projects, however, which have a determined instructional mission in addition to their artistic design, the video record is a valuable teaching and learning tool for me, my colleagues, and my students. You will remember that my students will use the video to evaluate the performance.

I have videotaped rehearsals or certain portions of them,[44] but we create the primary videotape record during one of the performances, a task for which I usually provide double coverage, one film created by an independent camera and one by my own. The university's Photography and Video Centre is generous enough to send a video team (students or staff) to tape our performance, and I also set up my own camera from another angle of the theatre. Since the Video Centre personnel are not familiar with either the action of the play or the foreign language, I cannot expect them to do any kind of sophisticated camerawork, with suitable close-ups and long shots, and shots that precisely follow the action. Hence they usually position their camera at a point and distance where they can shoot one large frame that covers the apparent boundaries of the stage, boundaries that the actors will repeatedly cross when they interact with the audience. With my camera, I do the close-ups and cover all the action outside the stage frame, including the audience interaction. Almost invariably, however, the visiting camera operators are not content to provide an entirely fixed point of view of the production. They adroitly pick up the pattern of the movements of the actors and they wind up achieving a rather articulate film document of the performance. Consequently, I usually can rely on their tape as the primary record of the play, to which I add at the end of the tape a number of noteworthy close-ups of key scenes that I have filmed. I also have recourse to my video document when I need a specific close-up or two to show at professional conferences or workshops.

The results of the double videotaping are quite sufficient. My purpose is not so much to create a filmed version of the play that could be seen and appreciated in lieu of attendance but to provide a record of the various creative strategies that have come to fruition in the production. I have used this record in my instruction of other courses and at conferences where I do presentations of my students' work, though I usually find myself warning my audience of the "semi-professional" quality of the camerawork and the lack of editing. With the multiple video recordings I have of each of the plays, I'm fairly confident that if at some time in the future I need a high quality record of one of my plays, I will have the raw materials to achieve it, as long as I get the funding to pay for it. The fact is, the director's judgment of a given play production is more critically accurate and reliable in retrospect than during the heat of rehearsals or even in the midst of the "roar of the greasepaint the smell of the crowd."[45]

I generally schedule three on-campus performances, two at 4:00 or 4:30 p.m. and one at 7:30 or 8:00 p.m. The three performances allow the actors to consummate their training, fine tune their roles, and relax; they also offer the potential audience alternative show times. As I mentioned above, the late afternoon shows usually accommodate off-campus students coming from other institutions, and they also seem to work for a great many of our campus students who prefer to see the show during the day, while they are still "on-duty" and on campus. The evening performance is usually the best attended, and it has the added aura of being a bona fide extra-academic event like any other play, music concert, or dance performance for the campus community. This is also the performance attended by most of the off-campus community, especially the francophones who work during the day. I find Thursday to be the best day for the evening performance because it's toward the end of the week but doesn't interfere with the community's weekend agenda.

When the last on-campus performance concludes, we pack up our costumes and props and prepare them for the off-campus performances. After we do what is necessary to leave our borrowed space in the best of conditions, we bid adieu to the theatre, but not to our play.

5.5 ON THE ROAD
Another Space, Another Audience

I always do the road trips after the campus performances. The play achieves a definite, polished form in the on-campus theatre with which the actors are most familiar, before the company is experienced, comfortable, and confident enough to tackle the challenge of moulding it to another playing space.

The director should have considerable control over the configuration and design of the off-campus space. If the theatre is nearby, as in the case of an area high school, I visit the space with the resident staff person in charge of its management, and together we work out the logistics. My two chief concerns are that the playing area be at least as large as the on-campus space and to some extent approximate its shape, and that it allow the actors to comfortably and safely move between the stage and the audience. At high schools that have only conventional, concert-type auditoriums available for plays, I negotiate modifications with the on-site staff. In one case, I had the staff erect a simple playing area (a slightly elevated platform) in front of the elevated stage – making sure that the space is still fully visible to the audience. At another venue, we created a bridge to the spectators by adding steps leading from the stage to the audience seating area. On occasion, I have discovered a suitable playing area in unlikely locations of the school or its campus, locations such as the cafeteria or the library.

Other concerns are the visibility of the stage, the proximity of the audience, and the sound and lighting systems. As is probably evident, the less "formal" quality of our performance allows us a great deal of flexibility with the material and spatial conditions of the production. (I like to muse that if ever the need arose, we could produce the play in a vacant lot in the rain, and probably with great effect.) The off-campus venues and their staff can usually provide more than we need. At high schools and community colleges, I'm frequently greeted by a resident theatre director who is proudly prepared to provide state of the art technology for our production. Not surprisingly, these people often seem at least initially disappointed to see how uncomplicated our needs are and how technically and technologically independent we can be. For me, that's the proof of "real" theatre. Remember what Boal says about being able to do theatre anywhere, *even* in a theatre? I'm sure one could even do theatre on a high-tech stage, but the technology also could be a handicap to the original, anthropological sense of performance as a social ritual, the consummation of a life experience (Victor Turner), the ritual (re-)framing of sociocultural processes and the eventual regeneration of inter-human awareness and understanding. All the glitter could, in fact, camouflage or even inhibit the very soul of theatre: those communicating and communing bodies-in-space on the stage.

Since we only do one performance at each off-campus venue, the performance is scheduled either in the morning or the afternoon to accommodate the targeted audience, not only the students and faculty in foreign language but also those in theatre, and maybe even those in literature. For Ubu, we did two high school performances and one community college performance. Each high school performance was attended by French and theatre students from at least three other schools, and the community college performance was the feature event of a local foreign-language fair, attended by students and instructors of various foreign-language programs (French, Spanish, German) at area high schools as well as by other interested individuals from the community. The high school audiences numbered about 150 and 100, and the community college, about 150 to 200. All the more reason to have created a play that is accessible to a wider community thanks to its narrative strategies, its tactical use of English, and its emphasis on theatricality, performance, imagery, and audience participation.

I rent a large university van, and my students and I show up about one and a half hours before the scheduled performance. This allows us enough time to make all necessary adjustments, check the sound and lights, and do an express run-through of the play (text is glossed over while the primary action is executed at an accelerated pace) to check for any unforeseen glitches or unaccommodated needs.

The high school and community college audiences we play for are usually more surprised than our home audiences at our breach of theatrical convention. Their ability to comprehend the play is generally weaker, and they are usually a more conservative and less mature audience. Some of the language in some of the plays might be a bit objectionable (when it's understood by some students and the teachers). With the Ubu play, even the infamous "*Merdre*" seemed to raise a hair or two, not to mention the huge breasts we designed for Ma Ubu and Pa Ubu's impassive fon-

CHAPTER FIVE: THE OPENING SHOW

dling. But theatre's artistic license, the uniqueness of the event, the foreign-language filter, and (I'd like to think) the artistic and instructional merit of our play seem to coalesce to dispel any sustained discomfort in even the most reverent and proper audience members. After the performance, we usually hold a short discussion session with the audience to help the students and faculty better understand the nature, structure, and objectives of our project. The actors are happy to field these questions about their work.

One of our destinations is more than an hour's drive from Knoxville, so the drive gives us time to talk informally and openly with one another. (Also, on one occasion when lunch was not provided by our hosts, the actors and I went to a restaurant at the destination city, which made the trip more of an adventure.) To my knowledge, my actors have never had considerable difficulty in meeting the demands of the road trips. They enjoy the notoriety of doing them, the challenge of a new space and a new audience; if they had more time available, I'm sure most of them would be willing to do an extended tour. The demand on the students' time is the primary reason we don't accept more invitations to perform at off-campus venues.

The last off-campus show is the end of the performance part of our project, but there remains another activity that gives the students the opportunity to relive the entire process from a critical point of view.

6
Post-Performance Student Evaluation of the Performance and the Project

Our schedule usually calls for all performances, on and off campus, to be completed at least a few days before the end of the regular semester. This gives the students time to relax a bit and work (or catch up) on their other courses, and it allows us to meet once more to take stock of our work, indulge in a bit of self praise, and discuss the final analytical assignment for the course. Despite the absence of any physical work in our final meeting, I can't help having the class begin with one final collaborative gesture that will call to mind our humble beginnings: a final warm-up exercise together. When this is completed, we're ready to discuss the concluding written assignment of the project.

I divide the final analytical work into two parts. First, the students must reread their journals and their class notes, reflecting on the process of the course from the first day to the final performance. As a first step, I tell them to think about specific surprises, doubts, or revelations they have experienced with respect to the meaning and impact of their personal role in the project as well as the outcome of the project itself. This leads to the second step of this part of the assignment: from a critical-analytical point of view, students write a four- to five-page critique of the course, focusing on one or two of the course components, strategies, or objectives, such as:

- the importance of a specific set of activities or exercises for increasing their corporal awareness in class and on stage
- the importance of the course in creating a group community that might or might not have manifested itself on the stage
- the value of the semiotic awareness activities in developing a sense of the constructed quality of theatre

- the use of the sketches to orient, prepare, and even build the re-creative performance

We discuss possibilities and suggestions for this short essay, emphasizing the need to present precise, concrete examples of exercises and their effects, and students field some ideas about it. I encourage them to be open about any criticism they might have of any particular part of the course: format, exercises, discussions, and so on. It seems that most students are fairly candid in this exercise – one student, for example, felt that I over-emphasized the "imaginary sword" exercise throughout the first part of the course. In addition to the evident learning benefit for the students, these assessments of the project from the actors' points of view complement the feedback from the audience survey – two sources of input that influence my own point of view of the project's process and outcome.

The second part of the writing assignment involves a focused semiotic analysis of one of the signifying systems of the performance. I provide the students with their own personal videotape copy of the performance. Working from the semiotic questionnaire (which they used earlier in the semester to evaluate the theatre department's play performance: see appendix D) and based on their personal experience in conjunction with the video document, they do a semiotic analysis of *one* of the following: 1) the semiotic function of a group or specific category of objects, a particular type of costume, an acting technique or gesture, voice work, rhythms, or other staging strategies or 2) the elaboration of a certain theme of the play through our production's use of several different signifying systems, from text through *mise-en-scène*. I remind them that the re-creative premise of our project means that it is always a work-in-progress susceptible to modification or improvement, and I encourage them to pay particular attention to these three questions: What makes sense? What doesn't seem to make sense? What could make better sense, and how? Thus, I honestly attempt to encourage them to address what they feel was a bad choice in our construction of the performance by offering a critical, semiotic explanation for the problem and advice on how we might have corrected or avoided it.

We discuss these questions and instructions, and I ask them in class to give me some examples of what they might write about. Then, in order to make the exercise more comprehensible and interesting for them, I show a couple of clips from the play and we discuss the signifying systems and

CHAPTER SIX: POST-PERFORMANCE 149

possible connections among them. The undergraduate students compose these one to two thousand-word essays in their journal. Needless to say, I invite the students to contact me with any further questions, either via email or a visit to my office. See appendix I for instructions for this assignment.

The Graduate Student Research Paper. Graduate students also write the project assessment part of the written assignment in their journal, but for the second part, the course critique, they write a properly formatted research paper. I have a separate meeting with these students, usually one month before the end of the course, to allow them time to do the extra reading and begin the writing. Early in the semester, I provide them with a short bibliography, indicating both required and recommended reading, and I encourage them to use this bibliography as a stepping stone to other research that will suit the needs of their specific interest. Required reading includes Michel Pruner's *L'Analyse du théâtre*, Anne Ubersfeld's *L'Ecole du spectateur*, and Patrice Pavis's *Dictionnaire du théâtre*, in which they must read the entries on *"Dramaturgie"* ("Dramaturgy"), *"Espace"* ("Space"), *"Temps"* ("Time"), *"Théâtralité"* ("Theatricality"), *"Personnage"* ("Character"), *"Sémiologie"* ("Semiology"), *"Questionnaire"* ("Questionnaire/Survey"), *"Métathéâtre"* ("Metatheatre"), and browse the rest. Recommended reading includes Antonin Artaud's *Le Théâtre et son double*, Martin Esslin's *The Theatre of the Absurd*, Ubersfeld's *Lire le théâtre*, and Bert O. States's *Great Reckonings in Little Rooms: On the Phenomenology of Theatre.*

In light of the critical texts they will have read, I ask graduate students to reread the primary texts for the course – the principal work (*Ubu Roi*) and any other texts I have introduced into the course (usually excerpts from other plays) – reading these texts from our usual performative point of view, that of a spect-acting director. I usually suggest that they pay particular attention to one aspect of the text. In the case of *Ubu Roi*, for example, I asked them to consider the relations between Ma and Pa Ubu, and the relation of these characters to the different spaces or objects as these are indicated in the text and eventually played out in our performance. If their reading and reflection do not take them in a different direction, they may follow the instructions I gave for the undergraduate semiotic analysis of the play, with the added research dimension, of course. In their journal writing throughout the semester, the graduate students try out some of their ideas for a final paper, and in the final month of the course, these ideas begin to gel. The week before the end of classes, they submit an outline of their paper and discuss it with me for approval and to flesh out their ideas.

I have problems getting the students, graduate and undergraduate, to meet the deadline for turning in the final assignment. It is very difficult for them to accomplish yet another *corvée* when they have already given so much and already feel a great sense of achievement. Yet I insist that they take this one extra step. Once they begin to put pen to paper, the task is relatively easy for them. Because the writing component in this course carries less weight and has a less formal aura to it, they are more easily drawn into it. In the absence of conventional, "formal" pressures, they can learn and retain more. This is the capstone assignment of the course that will help them engrave the semester-long experience in their memory. Not all the final essays are particularly strong, but they all contribute to the student's and my knowledge of theatrical art in general and our re-creative approach to it in particular.

On the whole, I have a reputation among students and colleagues for being a very tough grader. When all is said and done, however, as the reader might expect, my students in this course usually receive grades that are stronger on the average than those I give in other courses I teach. This is due in part to the fact that students can (im)prove themselves through their performative and collaborative investments in the project in terms of quality as well as quantity (see appendix A, "Sample Course Description and Syllabi," for grading criteria). On the other hand, my student evaluations for this project are always in the highest range, from 4.6 to 5.0, on a 5-point scale. In the past, a few students have taken exception to some of what they can't help seeing as my "draconian" demands on their time and my refusal to compromise with some of the scheduling to meet their personal needs. But almost all the written (qualitative) evaluations are exceptionally positive, and they demonstrate how meaningful the course has been to all types of students, the most passive and the most aggressive, the more and the less academically inclined, the leftist radicals and the more traditional, conservative individuals. Many students have come to me in person at the end of the semester to tell me how important it has been for their overall education and their life, and an exceptional number of my former student-actors stay in touch with me long after they've graduated.

7

The Analytical-Subjunctive Art of Combining Texts and Confusing Character Identities

In this chapter, I pick up where the theoretical background in the introduction left off. In the introduction, I showed how the basis of the theoretical framework for my re-creative approach to doing foreign-language theatre with students is a shift from one artistic/cultural (and instructional) mode to another. Victor Turner refers to this shift in terms of moving from the traditional indicative mode of interpretation – the understanding of world, of human relationships, of life "as is" or as we think they are – to a subjunctive "what if" mode or condition: What if things were different? While all my dramaturgical strategies to regenerate collaboratively and subjunctively classic texts have a performative bent – that is, they consciously work toward the material enactment of a story and its images – the strategy of re-writing the original play is largely a textual approach toward a performative act, at least at one stage of its development. I say "one" stage and not the first stage because, as we have seen, the "reductive" rewriting of the play takes place only after my students have already re-created large portions of the story in a number of regular sketches. Furthermore, the re-created text in its first comprehensive form is only a preliminary version of the final re-created product since, subsequent to the text's creation, it undergoes substantial performative revisions during the rehearsal process. No text is fixed or sacred in this project, not even our own (re-)creation. Further still, during the rehearsal and performance phase of the project, the strategy of sharing the principal roles of the story also contributes to the subjunctive mood of our project by destabilizing any fixed interpretive subject position for the characters in the story. I have already discussed these two strategies for textual regeneration (re-creating the text and the sharing of roles) in the body of previous chapters. In this chapter, I discuss other creative strategies for textual regeneration: 1) the com-posing (original sense of the Latin *cum-ponere*, 'to put together') of two very different, previously written texts into a new, integrated performance text and 2) the con-fusing of character identities within a given story.

7.1 REGENERATION THROUGH COMBINATION

At least four of my projects have involved the combining of texts in various forms and to varying degrees. After the combination of *Ubu* and *Exercices de style* in fall 1993, and then the full-blown combination of *Dom Juan* and *Cyrano* in spring 1995, we achieved a different nature and degree of combination between Shakespeare's *Macbeth* and Ionesco's *Macbett* in 1998. Most recently, in 2003, I considerably altered the structure of my practicum project to include the reading and analysis of more dramatic texts, providing my students with a more comprehensive overview of French theatre. As a result of this increased exposure to texts, I challenged my students to venture into the most overt and aggressive of the combinatory projects, one that brought together *Dom Juan*, *Ubu*, and Beckett's *Fin de partie* (*Endgame*). In all of these projects, the decision to combine texts was made up front; it was part of the overall organization and structure of the project. On the other hand, the con-fusing of character identities is a strategy that more or less (re-creatively) insinuated itself into the process of regeneration. Consequently, I devote most of this chapter to the first strategy, and I discuss the effect of the second on two specific projects, the 1998 Macbett story and the 2003 Dom Juan – Ubu – Hamm project.

My initiative in 1993 to intersperse the Ubu story with theatricalized versions of Queneau's *Exercices de style* increased the complexity of the project and the spectacular quality of the performance. The strategy had two principal objectives: to increase the acting contribution of those students who had less than major roles (usually group appearances as soldiers, peasants, or nobles) and to increase the demand for collaboration, since transitions would have to be developed to ensure the flow of action. In addition, the strategy would contribute to other objectives of the project: to encourage the students to think critically of the play as a comprehensive spectacle or event rather than as a representation of a text, to challenge the students to investigate the theatre's ability to create form, and to decrease the students' consciousness of and preoccupation with the strangeness of speaking French text.

The creative and re-creative nature of the practice of combining texts is evident. The subjunctive (What if?) mood or condition becomes operative when one text, with its story, actions, and bodies-in-space, intrudes on another text and its signifying systems. Therefore, I will move beyond this assumption in order to address the following primary questions: How do students and director carry out the integration? What do they discover about literary-dramatic textuality that they could not discover through the conventional practice of reading and performing one single canonic text? Does the integrated production educate and stimulate the audience as well as the actors? Should it?

Despite the late twentieth century's revolutionary incursions on the imperialism of the written text, as I pointed out in the introduction, to my knowledge very few directors have given serious thought to the practice of combining texts, other than the medley-like presentation of excerpts from a variety of thematically related plays.[46] The most likely explanation for this is the myth of textual integrity leading to a fear of tampering with the autonomy of a written document. The act of combining one text with another to create a new performative, contextual whole clearly violates this principle of integrity, this *author-ity*. Notwithstanding the evident risks involved with copyright laws, the lack of experimentation in the combining of texts surprises me, considering the revolution of the *mise-en-scène* in this century. If dramatic texts constitute an intensely rich form of culture-in-process, if they are inherently more open than narrative texts to creative and personal reception, and if they cry out for transformation in the form of a *mise-en-scène*, then why not explore the opportunity to engage and energize constructively the creative process of one classic text by confronting it with another? What better way to divert the attention of the student simultaneously from the literary dimension of the dramatic text to its performative potential and from the interpretation of one individual text to the creative, dialectical processes of textuality and intertextuality?

To be sure, any *mise-en-scène* of a prewritten text has some creative and subjunctive (What if?) quality, especially owing to the inevitably individualized characterization carried out by an actor guided by a director (What if Dom Juan wore a lily-white cowboy hat, which he handled with a stylized gesture?). In my projects, however, in our collective search to reassert creative principle rather than message or interpretation, I have added another parameter of creativity, the rewriting of the original text. The practice of structurally altering one previously independent story to accommodate another further increases the students' awareness of and control over textual structure, and it toys with Aristotle's belief that the arrangement of the actions (plot) constitutes the soul of the tragedy. Following Turner's argument outlined in the introduction, if left untouched, the once subjunctive mood of the original written text belonging to a former generation of Western culture – be it *Ubu* (What if an outrageously gluttonous cartoon character came to lead a nation?), *Dom Juan* (What if a man devoted his entire existence to female conquest?), or *Cyrano* (What if there were a soldier whose military prowess, poetic genius, and passion for one singularly "precious" woman were equalled only by his physical ugliness?) – will necessarily fall back into an indicative mood. But the complex architectural reinvestment required by the practice of combination deliberately and radically breaks with the indicative rigidity of the canonic text and embeds the project in the subjunctive: What if Queneau's absurd "exercises" interrupted and eventually infiltrated the story of Père Ubu? What if Dom Juan, victimizer of all women, and Cyrano, victim of one unrequited love, were forced to cross paths on the theatrical stage?

Let's take a look at the ways in which textual integration took place in my first two very distinct re-creative theatrical projects. In the first project, "Ubu Roi déformé," the (rewritten) *Ubu* text was integrated with theatrical adaptations of a small selection of the ninety-nine different styles of Raymond Queneau's *Exercices de style*. Why combine these two particular works? How arbitrary was the choice of plays? While there are few common threads to link these two plays, the "looms" from which they are woven have a fundamental similarity: the stories of *Ubu* and *Exercices* are both examples of what critics have called "absurdist" texts. There is, of course, a difference in the historical time frames. *Ubu* was written at the end of the nineteenth century, while *Exercices* was written over half a century later. There is also a difference in the theatrical time frames, the times in which the action of their stories occurs. Though not clear in this regard, the action of *Ubu* definitely takes place centuries before the action of *Exercices*. Despite these divergences and many others,[47] both works are constructed around denaturalized characters and action. So having characters from both plays alternately occupy the same stage during the one-hour duration of the performance was initially probably more curious than shocking for actors and spectators alike.

A total of nine exercises were presented: two at the end of each of the first four acts of *Ubu* and one, titled "Comédie" ("Play"), at the play's conclusion. During the first four acts, our theatrical version did not substantially integrate the two plays. Throughout the play, the transition from *Ubu* to *Exercices* was cued by placards displayed by the actors, so most of the combining of *Exercices* with *Ubu* was a matter of alternation and juxtaposition instead of real integration. While the need to weave the exercises into the Ubu story forced the students to take a closer look at the content of both works, the weaving did not automatically transcend the indicative mood of performance. Only at the beginning of the fifth and final act does the integration become more evident and poietic, more regenerative.

At the beginning of act 5, the narrator interrupts the action.[48] He admonishes Pa Ubu for jumping too far ahead in the story, and he blames this deviation on the confusion caused by the interruptions of the exercises. This was, in fact, the only written dialogue in our revised text contributing toward integration. It is nevertheless noteworthy that the rehearsals (the early active phase of performance) created a conclusion to the play that fully absorbed *Exercices* into the Ubu story. At the end of act 5, the four actors who have alternated in the roles of Pa and Ma Ubu are all reassembled aboard a ship in search of a new country to plunder. After they recite the final line of the "*Ubu roi* déformé" text, "*Quel délice de revoir bientôt la douce Louisville, nos vieux amis et notre château de Churchill Downs!*" ("What a delight it will soon be to get back to sweet Louisville, our old friends, and our Churchill Downs chateau!"), they dance out into the audience space still holding their cardboard model of a ship around them. Then the music stops, the action freezes, and the theatre goes dark. When the stage lights come on, the final "exercise" of the performance ("Comédie") is played out as a short dramatic sketch of the nonsensical *Exercices* situation. I assigned one of the students to direct this sequence, a move that permitted me to follow Claire Kramsch's

Fig. 15. "*Ubu Roi déformé.*" "*Exercices*" meets "*Ubu Roi.*" Tyler Thomas, Kenneth Cox, John Vickerstaff, Shannon Bennett, Rae Smith, Jennifer Barnes. *University of Louisville, Louisville, KY. Photo by Les Essif.*

advice and join with the students to "discover anew" the *Ubu* and the *Exercices* texts as we generated our own integrated text. Noteworthy were the parallels between the ubuesque behavioural patterns of the *Exercices* protagonists and those of Ma and Pa Ubu, not to mention the absurdist staging techniques. The *Exercices* characters acknowledge their *Ubu* stage companions by shouting the emblematic "*Merdre*" (see fig. 15). Either wittingly or unwittingly (probably both), the student director and his players were creating a poem that enhanced the metatheatrical dimension of the synthesizing process of the two plays: *Merdre* is the first and most memorable word in the original *Ubu* text, whereas *merde* has a theatrical application as the French equivalent of the expression "Break a leg!" meaning, of course, "Good luck in the performance!" (It was the first time I thought of Père Ubu's famous "*Merdre!*" from this metatheatrical angle.) Following the brief sketch, there is another blackout. When the lighting is restored, the reanimated *Ubu* characters dance their way back to the stage for the grand finale. The students were deeply involved in a process. Their ubuesque alteration of the *Exercices* sketch and the smoothness of the transition from one "text" to the other demonstrated that they were developing a unique hands-on, comparative-analytical approach to absurdist texts as they participated in a creative renewal of French, Franco-American, and foreign-language literary cultures.

This creative fusion of the two plays was, for me, profound from both theatrical and pedagogical points of view. The intervention of *Exercices* required the active participation of the student-actors in an intensification of the theatrical ("showing") process of Jarry's text, and consequently this intervention increased the students' textual, theatrical, and cultural consciousness. As teacher, I had avoided the normative authority

CHAPTER SEVEN: COMBINING TEXTS   157

that Kramsch says "discourages the reconstruction of the text necessary for its appropriation by the reader" ("Texts" 358). My simple proposal to bring these two works into confrontation with one another exploded the dialectical aspect of our encounter with their stories and characters. I began to see textual integration as a navigational process based on triangulation. In the same way that a ship at sea finds its bearings by reference to not one but two known geographical points, we construct a meaningful point of reception (the integrated text) with respect to the two original textual references.

Planning my next theatrical project, I decided to go further with the integration strategy. I chose two plays that, in one way or another, deal with the theme of passion: Molière's *Dom Juan* and Rostand's *Cyrano de Bergerac*, which in the integrated version became *"Dom Juan et Cyrano: la passion démasquée"* ("Dom Juan and Cyrano: Passion Unmasked"). At the very beginning of our re-created and integrated play, one of the narrators, Sganarelle, explains this common bond:

(*Pointing to stage right*) "Voilà Dom Juan. He loves women, lots of women, all kinds of women, all women. And (*pointing to stage left*) voilà Cyrano. He loves only one woman, but boy does he love this woman and boy is she beautiful, his cousin Roxane!... Dom Juan and Cyrano, two great stories of passion on the French stage. Unfortunately for these heroes – but fortunately for the stage – the expression of their passion is not without a problem. For Dom Juan, the problem is the Church and the notion of honour. For Cyrano, ...it's a certain appendage."[49]

The narrator thus registers the theme of passionate love, which at once connects the two plays and separates them. I realized by this point that our performance text would not produce answers to the operational "what if?" questions. Instead, the juxtaposition of the stories and characters would provoke and sustain an elaborate interrogatory process, within which my students would read and respond actively as second-degree authors. I also hoped that the confrontation of the *Dom Juan* structure of passion with the *Cyrano* structure would tease out for my students an interrogatory attentiveness to the creative decisions made by authors actively involved in textual production – by all authors, including the original ones. For instance, why did Molière decide to create the "street-smart" Sganarelle to accompany the aristocratic Dom Juan, and why does Cyrano seem such a loner? These questions became more relevant for my students when Sganarelle literally switched stories and imposed himself on Cyrano in the conclusion of the integrated text, a text they helped to produce.

In our integrated story, based more on the intensity of passion-as-process than on the object of passion (thus, the "passion unmasked" of the title), the major chain of events of the original plays remain largely intact; there is some revision, however, much of which stems from the confrontation of the two texts. Already at the point of the project where the students were engaged in the rewriting of the original texts, a substantial linkage between the works materialized in the dialogue, the action, and the characters. As with the *Ubu* project, I divided the students into four groups: two worked on acts 1, 2, and 3 of both plays, and two on acts 3, 4, and 5. In this way we would have two separate versions of acts 1 and 2 to compare, two versions of acts 4 and 5, and four versions of the transitional act 3. For the re-creative exercise, I instructed the groups to 1) juxtapose the two stories, alternating chronologically between each of the acts of *Dom Juan* and each of the acts of *Cyrano*; 2) create a narrator's role for each of the stories; and 3) seek new ways to tie the two stories together, especially by having the two narrators (Juan's valet, Sganarelle, and Roxane's governess, la Duègne) and the two protagonists (Dom Juan and Cyrano) exchange dialogue and gestures. As before, once the students had completed their rewriting, copies of the rewritten versions were distributed to all, read, and discussed in class, before I prepared a first written version of the integrated text.

If still a long way from total integration, the students' versions included ideas that I wrote into the re-created text as a series of remarks made by the narrators of each of the stories about the protagonists of the other story. There was also some dialogue exchanged between the characters of the different stories, an example of which is the exchange between Dom Juan and Cyrano at the point of transition between the end of act 2 of *Dom Juan* and the beginning of act 2 of *Cyrano*. After Dom Juan declares his eternal love first for one countrywoman (Charlotte), then for another (Mathurine) – a situation our *mise-en-scène* transformed into a stylized *Dating Game* sketch moderated by Sganarelle – Cyrano crosses the stage composing his love letter to Roxane. Dom Juan calls to him,

CHAPTER SEVEN: COMBINING TEXTS   159

"Would you like to play, Cyro?" Cyrano replies, "No thanks. I've made my choice," and returns to writing his letter, a move that launches act 2 of *Cyrano*. There are also a number of exchanges between the two narrators as well as between the narrators and the protagonists belonging to different stories. The narrators also address the audience. Most of these exchanges and comments are judgments about the amorous protagonists' behaviour, judgments that contribute to the comparative and analytical bent of our integrated version.[50]

The rewritten text also enhances the integration through the use of props and character cross-overs. The introduction of the telephone, a modern tool that many young people associate with amorous relationships, dehistoricizes and contemporizes the imagery and the action of our play. What's more, the telephone conversation becomes probably the most prominent action linking the two separate stories. But how do we integrate such an anachronism while attempting to safeguard some of the semblance of honour and solemnity constructed within the original texts? We decided to tone down the assault on history by employing an "archaic" telephonic device: a tin can. This way, the device still provided support for the notions of distance, mediation, and deferral that undermine the passion of both Dom Juan and Cyrano, though in different ways and for different reasons.[51] So the famous expression-of-love scene with Cyrano, Christian, and Roxane is carried out by telephone. The climactic first kiss between Christian and Roxane, too, is "telephonic." Alternately, on the Dom Juan side, the portentous visits from Done Elvire, the Father, and the Commander with their warnings of divine retribution are likewise communicated by phone.

Character transplants help interweave the structures of the stories and generate new text. Sganarelle functions not only as Juan's valet, as he does in the Molière story, but also as a double narrator, narrating on one level the Dom Juan story and on another, the integrated Dom Juan-Cyrano story. In the transition between the last act of *Dom Juan* and the last act of *Cyrano*, Cyrano is mortally wounded when he tries to intervene against the Commander, who is sending Dom Juan to his death. After Sganarelle's "*Mes gages*" ("My wages") tirade, which for over three centuries has provided the literal-textual conclusion to the Molière *Dom Juan*, in our play Sganarelle endures, though briefly, as Cyrano's valet. The subjunctive fusion of his textual, then visual (stage) presence alongside Cyrano provokes a critical reaction to the "ultimate" meanings of both texts. First the students are forced to hypothesize whether the two characters could meaningfully come together. Then, after an attempt to better understand not simply who the characters really are, but more important, *who they can be and what they can mean*, the students help recover a new, meaningful context. In the presence of a mortally wounded Cyrano, they are obliged to rethink Sganarelle's famous line "I am the most unfortunate of men" and correct it to "Ah, yes. We two are the most unfortunate of souls!" And when Sganarelle asks Cyrano if by chance he could use a good valet, the second-degree authors of this text are more likely to reflect on the fact that in the context of his original story, Cyrano does not have a valet. Indeed, before Christian, Cyrano has no one in whom to confide. Why not? Is Cyrano more of a loner than Dom Juan?

Retrospectively, what about the relationship between Juan and Sganarelle, a relationship whose complexity becomes more evident to students when performatively juxtaposed and integratively compared with the *Cyrano* text? Characterization, dialogue, and action of the rewritten text all contribute to "re-create the creative principle of things created" (Boal), to regenerate the creative principles of the two plays. The students have witnessed and participated in creative, analytic, and conditional performance responses to subjunctive questions such as "How would Cyrano react if he happened upon Dom Juan's fall into hell?" and "What would Sganarelle do if given the opportunity to have Cyrano as a master?".[52]

The nature of performance such as it is, the "acting out in space" of the rewritten text that begins with rehearsals, truly consummates the subjunctivity of the integration. The linkage of dialogue, action, image, and characters was extended, reinforced, or reinvested during the performance rehearsals. An additional character transplant was realized during one of the final rehearsals. We decided that the Spectre, a supernatural, veiled woman who delivers to Dom Juan the final warning to repent (by phone, of course, in our play), should have a place beside Roxane at centre stage during the Cyrano portion of the final act. Her presence would replicate – or, more precisely, as the French would say, "send into abyme" (*mettre en abyme*) – the idea-image of the abandoned, cloistered female love object-subject. This performative integration of the two separate feminine discourses from the two different works – one in which the female is over-loved, one in which she is under-loved – forces a close-up comparison and raises questions about the disparate ways in which the female love object can be objectified and victimized in a patriarchal society; it also generates insight into the ways in which authors inscribe these discourses into their texts.

Finally, I focus on a purely spatial point of view toward the *mise-en-scène*. The scenic architecture that graphically underwrites the transformation of the two separate texts into an integrated performance provides a spatial metaphor for our reading of the text(s) as cultural process. On our open stage, there were no wings, no back-stage areas; the actors were at all times visible to the audience. Our first decision, then, was to establish a visible offstage area divided from an onstage area, or more precisely, an area where the audience would perceive the actors as being present but offstage: that is, as becoming offstage (instead of onstage) spect-actors. We decided to make use of the multilevel aspect of the stage for this purpose. Since the semicircular stage area consisted of four distinct tiers – the lowest tier being no more than a kind of step – the wide top tier would serve as offstage. Spatially, the play begins with the well-defined segregation of the two camps of players: those mostly involved with *Dom Juan* roles on the upper level of stage right and the *Cyrano* camp on the upper level of stage left. In other words, the remnants of the two original, classical texts are separated physically. When the action begins, the two camps alternate their occupation of the playing field – the central stage space. In this respect, the performance still supports the indicative mood of the original texts and their illusion of textual authority. As the action progresses, however, the indicative mood is bombarded by a series of verbal exchanges between the two camps, and there is a breakdown in clear-cut transitions from the action of one play to that of the other – such as the exchange between Cyrano and Dom Juan in the *Dating Game* scene, as noted above. Finally, in act 5, we see a structural reversal of the human component of the scenic architecture as it was displayed at the beginning of the play. The offstage area is progressively abandoned; the characters of both plays, who were all (except Sganarelle, the co-narrator) offstage at the beginning, come together onstage, representing a spatial metaphor for the fusion of the two stories. In the grande finale of the performance, Cyrano's rancorous farewell to the world, all the

Fig. 16. "Dom Juan–Cyrano." "Dom Juan" meets "Cyrano." Scott Taylor, Pat McCoy, Noelle Wynne, Justin Martin, Karen Boehm, Anna Andrews, Jennifer Coffin, Paul Cate, Justin Armstrong, John Gullion. Carousel Theatre, University of Tennessee, Knoxville, TN. Photo by Les Essif.

actors form a semicircle to background Cyrano and the two female figures, Roxane and the Elvire-Elvire (see fig. 16). The players have moved from an offstage area, where textual authority segregated one story and its characters from another, to an onstage area, where cultural process and creative reception have negotiated a new integrated and contextual meaning for the themes of passion instigated by the original texts. My actors have helped guide the canonic characters out of textual bondage into an adventure in creative performance, an adventure that responds to Brecht's challenge to find solutions for "the increasing difficulty of reproducing the present-day world" (see "Introduction").

This project was only a beginning, an effective prototype for the subjunctive art of combining texts. Instead of focusing on the interpretation of one canonic story, through the process of textual confrontation we have induced a meaningful (subjunctive) performance *event*, one which is not as inconsequential or ephemeral as it may appear at first.[53] At the outset, neither I nor any of my students could foresee where the combining of the two hitherto self-sufficient and sovereign texts would lead in terms of a theatrical performance. Together, we made discoveries about textuality. With every day of rehearsal the integration grew, expanding our insight into how texts work and how they can and cannot work. Instead of searching for normative answers to the critical question of why Cyrano seems to be more of a loner than Dom Juan by using such ideas as romanticism versus classicism, we responded inductively to the question by creating a visible, interrogatory realm of intertext. Continued rehearsals would have dissolved additional borders between the two works, implying critical investigation into creative ways to dissolve those borders, to expand the intertext. What began as a performative textual reading, which was guided by a dialectical contract giving negotiatory power to the reader, continued into a writing exercise based on the same dialectical and performative point of view; eventually it was liberated altogether from the page in its transition to stage. Even during the three days of the three public performances, some of the *mise-en-scène* was subtly adjusted in the direction of fusion.

7.2 REINTERPRETING THE ABSURDITY OF CRUELTY THROUGH THE CON-FUSION OF CHARACTER IDENTITIES IN IONESCO'S MACBETT

The re-creative strategy of combining texts might be the most evident and aggressive path to instructive textual hybridity, but it is not the only path. Through the strategies of rewriting the text, combining texts, and role sharing, my productions have led to hybrid forms of identity (of character and space), art, and cultural artefacts. Character identities can be considered a focal point of textual hybridity insofar as they represent a kind of text within the text itself. In the act of rewriting classic dramatic texts, my students and I simultaneously and necessarily engage in the re-creation of formerly fixed character identities. Characters in *Exercices* become infused with identity traits belonging to *Ubu* characters; characters like Bordure and Bougrelas of *Ubu*, played by the same actor manipulating life-sized marionettes, assume new resemblances; at the end of the story of Dom Juan-Cyrano, Sganarelle must adjust his identity to the demands of our re-created text's new situation, conforming his "Dom Juan" traits to the demands of his new master, Cyrano. In this section, I'd like to discuss a rather remarkable and radical example of how one of our projects took the con-fusion of character identities to another level, that is, to the level of a conscious strategy to further regenerate text in our pursuit of the subjunctive mood of performance.

In 1998, we set out to perform another classic tale, the Macbett story. This project too was something of a combination of texts, since it began when my students read and discussed the French translation of Shakespeare's *Macbeth*. In fact, the first-day re-creative exercise was based not on Ionesco's text at all but on the witches scene from Shakespeare's play. However, after a week of Shakespeare's *Macbeth*, we shifted our attention to the primary text for the project, Ionesco's *Macbett*, a text that in itself can be described as a version of the Shakespeare play that Ionesco re-creatively updated in the "absurdist" tradition of the sixties. Ionesco's absurdist strategy foregrounds the universalizing metatheatrical conversion of the dramatic character (character *as* a theatrical function), which challenges the naturalistic and naturalizing concept of an individualized character identity. While our Macbeth-Macbett project was to some extent a confrontation-combination of the two texts, I want to focus on one particular result of our re-creative effort to reinterpret for our times and our milieu Ionesco's reinterpretation of the Macbeth story: the way in which our re-creative method took to a higher metatheatrical level the con-fusion of character identities that Ionesco designed in his play *Macbett*.

Let me quote Banquo in act 1, scene 3 of Shakespeare's *Macbeth*. You will remember that the witches set the supernatural tone of the play by evoking their astounding prophecies of kingship and quasi-kingship to Generals Macbeth and Banquo. This done, the witches disappear into thin air. Banquo attempts to allay Macbeth's bewilderment and his own with the following observation: "The earth hath bubbles, as the water has, / And these are of them: Whither are they vanished?" This ostensibly pragmatic explanation of the supernatural adds the necessary zest to the theatricality of Shakespeare's text: witches and bubbles are in the hearts, minds, and lines of all the principal characters throughout the action of the play. A few centuries later, rewriting Shakespeare for a more self-conscious historical period, Ionesco emphasizes not so much the supernatural itself as the theatrical effect of the supernatural. He was aware that the theatricality of his own dramatic works is like the bubbles of the earth (or the bubbles of champagne or of a cold soft drink, for that matter). If we ignore the dramatic text's underlying potential for and tendency toward effervescence (toward the re-creation of its creative principle), if we don't allow the bubbles of the theatrical medium itself to form and vanish – generating a potent trace memory of artificial effect – the meaning of the dramatic character might remain as flat as "indicative" reality. In Ionesco's works, however, the theatrical subsumes the supernatural. He stirred up the mass of the Macbeth story to create a fresh set of bubbles, bubbles that become not simply more theatrical but more conspicuously metatheatrical than supernatural.

Shakespeare has long fascinated the French. The nonrealist theatre of France manifests a particular interest in Shakespeare's story of Macbeth, in which, prodded by his wife, General Macbeth assassinates King Duncan and takes over the throne of twelfth-century Scotland. In fact, *Ubu Roi* is a parody loosely and absurdly based on this story: Ma Ubu persuades Pa Ubu to kill the king and steal the throne. Furthermore, as we have seen, Ubu's character is by no means individualized. Rather, it is a repository of instinctual traits referring to human nature in its rawest state, traits that have been exhibited to one degree or another throughout the history of theatre within a theatricalized space where the characters have free rein to exaggerate their behaviour. Thus the notions of character, character identity, and authenticity are perpetually challenged by and for the medium in which they are constructed. More than half a century after Jarry's *Ubu*, Ionesco's re-creation of the Macbeth story, its actions and characters, illuminates the essential (and usually unacknowledged) absurdity of Shakespeare's story while revalidating it for the late twentieth century.

There are many changes in the Ionesco version, most of which undermine the realism and individuality – in other words, the subjective realism or realist subjectivity – of the characters while bolstering their theatrical and metatheatrical functions: that is, the characters' ability to remind the audience that they are part of a highly creative, super-referential world created by a number of overlapping, sometimes collaborative sometimes competitive, sign systems. The play doesn't begin like the Shakespeare play with the witch scene and its final phrase, "Hover through the fog and filthy air," before the three witches disappear. There are, moreover, not three but a *pair* of witches in Ionesco's play, the notion of the couple being important to the work and to the structuring of the con-fusion of character identities.[54] The role of the witches becomes increasingly determinant for the story, or more to the point, for the metatheatrical bubbles of the story. An array of unusual secondary characters is added to the cast. The "real" Lady Macbeth seems to have only a bit part at the end of the work, while Lady Duncan, wife of the king, is really a metamorphosed witch who charms Macbett into killing her "husband." (This witch also becomes, very briefly, a curious version or facsimile of Lady Macbeth when she marries the newly crowned Macbett.) Finally, Ionesco defers the King Duncan assassination itself until about the last

Fig. 17. "Macbett." Witches and Limonadier plot the story. Balaam Long, Dawn Livesay, Pat McCoy, Noelle Wynne, Kristin Matheny, Jason Osborne, Alistaire Tallent. Carousel Theatre, University of Tennessee, Knoxville, TN. Photo by Les Essif.

quarter of the text. This deferral allows the dramatist the time and space to con-fuse the identities of his characters and to stir them into the bubbling cauldron of cruelty, so to speak. By the conclusion of the play, the process of con-fusion has altered our receptive sensibility enough for us to accept a supercharged synthesis of megalomaniacal cruelty in the form of the tyrant Macol. After killing Macbett in the final fight, extreme Macol announces his new reign of terror as the "Emperor of All Emperors" (an allusion to Malcolm's crafty scheme to feign treachery in order to test MacDuff). Thus, Ionesco's play brazenly and absurdly reverses the triumph over evil that concludes the Shakespeare story.

Let me now explain how our re-created performance of the Macbeth story, titled "Macbeth-Macbett: moitié-moitié" ("Macbeth-Macbett: Half and Half"), pushed the envelope of theatrical self-consciousness by intensifying the con-fusion of characters and their stories, and how this technique contributed to the subjunctive art of textual regeneration. Our version literally set the stage for theatrical subversion at the very beginning of the performance. We borrowed the famous refrain from the witch scene at the beginning of Shakespeare's act 4 ("*Double, double, peine et trouble! / Feu, brûle; et, chaudron, bouillonne!*" – "Double, double toil and trouble; / Fire burn and cauldron bubble"), lines that do not appear in the Ionesco text. To begin the performance, all our actors, approximating the character-function of a group of seven witches, form a circle and dance in alternating directions chanting this refrain. Six actors are dressed only in their black body suits, and the actor playing the Narrator-Limonadier is distinguished from the rest of the group by the vest and hat that she wears (see fig. 17). The chanting increases in volume up to the point at which the Narrator-Limonadier separates from the group and, pointing to a copy of the program where the refrain is written, she gets the audience to join in the chanting. Then the actor who will play the role of the First Witch separates from the group of chanting witches. She advances toward the Limonadier and, with a gesture, signals to her to play a game of "Heads or Tails." The Limonadier takes a coin from her pocket and they say "*moitié-moitié*" ("fifty-fifty"), a phrase that recalls the title of the play as it prefigures the theme of duplicity, and one that is immediately echoed by the group of witches before they all beat a rapid retreat from the stage. With another nod to the Limonadier, the First Witch follows the group into the "offstage" area. The Limonadier picks up her basket and begins to hawk her merchandise: "*Limonade! Limonade bien fraîche!*" ("Lemonade! Fresh lemonade!"). Thus, our story begins with a re-created reference to Shakespeare's text, with a scene that greatly expands the theme and the function of sorcery, emphasizing its link to theatrical illusion. This to some extent combines Shakespeare and Ionesco but primarily to the extent that our story adhered to Shakespeare's emphasis on the multiplicity of witches and witchcraft.

This initial emphasis on witchcraft and its theatrical effect led to four primary dramaturgical twists in our version of the story. First, Ionesco's text has a large number of auxiliary or secondary characters who weave a comic reality effect through the action of the play. Three such characters are the Lemonade Hawker (*Limonadier*), the Ragman, and the Butterfly Chaser. In our play, the Limonadier assumed a principal role. She became a liaison with the audience, commenting on the action of the play in French and in English; she also played the roles of the other auxiliary characters mentioned above. Thus, with the addition of an article of costume (sometimes no more than a scarf wrapped around her head), the Limonadier, a role in itself, toys with a plethora of additional roles. At the end of the play, the full metatheatrical significance of her metamorphic character-function becomes (retrospectively) clear, as we will see.

Second, Ionesco's text con-fuses ("con-fuses" in the sense of bringing together and blending and blurring the individual identities) the roles of Macbeth (now Macbett) and Banquo (now Banco). In an early scene, Ionesco has Macbett soliloquize on the cruelty and the normality of war (war is cruel and this is normal): his line "The blade of my sword is all reddened with blood..." is followed by "That's funny, despite my effort in battle, I don't have much of an appetite." Ionesco immediately follows this scene with an equally lengthy soliloquy by Banco that is quite nearly

Fig. 18. "Macbett." Macbett and Banco declaim in tandem. Balaam Long, Jason Osborne. Carousel Theatre, University of Tennessee, Knoxville, TN. Photo by Les Essif.

Fig. 19. "Macbett." Witch-Babe revealed. Balaam Long, Alistaire Tallent, Noelle Wynne. Carousel Theatre, University of Tennessee, Knoxville, TN. Photo by Les Essif.

Fig. 20. "Macbett." Witch/Lady Duncan and Limonadier behind the marionettes. Alistaire Tallent, Noelle Wynne. Carousel Theatre, University of Tennessee, Knoxville, TN. Photo by Les Essif.

the reproduction of Macbeth's. Our re-creation of this scene further confuses the identities of these characters by weaving the two monologues into one. With background music of Phillip Glass, the two generals circle around the half-lighted stage, stopping at alternating intervals to give a line of text (see fig. 18). This transforms Ionesco's separate but similar speeches by Macbett and Banco into something of a synthesized (con-fused) soliloquy.

Third, about halfway through the Ionesco play, Macbett and Banco meet the two witches who make the fantastic predictions that Macbett will be king and Banco will become the founder of a line of kings. The witches persuade Macbett that he'd make a great king, and then, *coup de théâtre!*, they reveal their true identity to a charmed Macbett: under their witches' rags, they're both "beautiful young women" , and the First Witch is Lady Duncan herself, who strips down to a "glittering bikini" (*Macbett* 83). In our version, however, we have reduced Shakespeare's trio of witches still further to only one witch, or more precisely, one "witch-babe" (see fig. 19). More con-fused still, the witch/Lady Duncan takes over the role of Macbett through the use of a life-sized marionette. And the Limonadier advances from playing mere secondary roles to the role of Banco, also with a marionette (see fig. 20).

The fourth of our dramaturgical twists is really a group of adjustments, re-created versions of the final twists of Ionesco's revisionist work. Quite late in the Ionesco text, the three co-conspirators – Macbett, Banco, and Lady Duncan – assassinate the king. Subsequently, Lady Duncan, who is really a witch in disguise, marries Macbett, becoming Macbett's queen – that is, Lady Macbett. Immediately following the marriage ceremony, Macbett voices his trepidation over the prophecy of the witches and he precipitously kills Banco; in the next scene, the new Lady Macbett (formerly Lady Duncan) and her servant transform back into the First and Second Witches and make their final departure from the stage and the action of the play.

In the final scene of Ionesco's work, the victory celebration in the Great Hall of the palace, Macbett and his guests are confronted by the ghost of Banco, the ghost of Duncan, and the "real" Lady Duncan, whom the First Witch had locked in a prison in order to accomplish her dastardly deeds. In accordance with the witches' prophecies, however, the play concludes when Macol appears. Strangely descended from the Banco line with a little help from witchcraft, he exterminates the depraved Macbett. All is not won, however. To the utter despair of the people who proclaim him a hero, Macol consummates the diabolic, hopeless conclusion of the play with this megalomaniacal line: "An empire, I'm an emperor. Super-Highness, Super-Sire, Super-majesty, emperor of all emperors" (149).

Thus, Shakespeare's text constructed an *ambitious* Macbeth exploited by the *cruelty* of his wife, Lady Macbeth.[55] Ionesco's text suppresses the character-function of a true (clearly individualized and identifiable) Lady Macbett, replacing her with a supernatural witch, who represents a more

Fig. 21. "Macbett." Macol-Marionette, emperor of all emperors. Noelle Wynne, Dawn Livesay, Kristen Matheny, Pat McCoy. Carousel Theatre, University of Tennessee, Knoxville, TN. Photo by Les Essif.

fundamental, incontrovertible, awesome engineer of cruelty. This is the force that fuels the hypertheatricality and metatheatricality of the play: hypertheatrically, supernatural magic works hand in hand with performance systems and theatrical devices to transform the "persona" of the First Witch into Lady Duncan and vice versa; metatheatrically, the roles of the Witch and Lady Duncan, more than a simple role-within-a-role artifice, are inextricably con-fused.

In our re-created, trans- and con-fused version, we push the envelope of the post-war–absurdist dramaturgical model, moving the once subjunctive but now rather indicative mood of the Ionesco text toward new subjunctive terrain. In a sense, we regenerate the theatrical self-consciousness that inspires the Ionesco text, expanding the shift from the supernatural to the hyper/metatheatrical. The Limonadier, absent of course in the Shakespeare play and only a minor player in Ionesco's work, appears throughout our play as an *emblem of metatheatricality*. Having functioned throughout the work as a liaison with the audience and having worked his way up the ranks of character-functions, from auxiliary characters to Banco-Marionette, for the conclusion of the play he appears on stage manipulating the huge Macol marionette. As part of his tirade he explains his descendancy from Banco and a witch transformed into a Limonadier. He concludes by proclaiming himself, as Macol does in the Ionesco text, "*supra-majesté, empereur de tous les empereurs*" (see fig. 21). But the final collective cry issuing from the entire cast of characters is "Limonade!" This represents a con-fused character identity in the extreme.

In a book chapter titled "Interpreting Drama," Umberto Eco discusses the transformation of human bodies, objects, and space into sign systems. He says that "framed within a sort of performative situation

CHAPTER SEVEN: COMBINING TEXTS   171

... anything can happen – Oedipus listens to Krapp's last tape, Godot meets La Cantatrice Chauve, Tartuffe dies on the grave of Juliet" (110). These intertextual collisions are just a small part of the "anything" that can happen on the stage. Let's get this straight, "anything" can not happen in a novel or on a canvas, or even on a screen, because the operative word here is "happen," suggesting the authentic, "live" event of theatre. The "live" theatrical event can create the illusion of the referential world or it can break this illusion – and, in a sense, become even more resolutely and emphatically "alive" – by allowing the mysterious supra-referential bubbles to form, to happen. To use Anne Ubersfeld's terms, we can (re-)produce the transparent theatrical signs of referential, naturalist theatre, or we can experiment with the effects of "opacification" by emphasizing "opaque" signs, the ones that force the spectator to confront the theatrical sign as a theatrical sign and the global performance as an amalgam of sign-making systems.[56] By saying "theatre" instead of "world," by resuscitating the creative principle of not one but two classic texts (both of which are to varying degrees re-creations of a classic story but the second of which prominently asserts its re-creative status), and by re-constructing character identities through the medium of theatre and before the very eyes and ears of spectators and spect-actors alike, my actors and I resist many of the pitfalls of our referential world, the powerful temptations to romanticize and psychologize a given story. Perhaps more than any other art, theatre exists to allow us to see through the illusion of convention and to understand it for what it is, and also, as Brecht hoped, to visualize and hypothesize alternative conventions and codes.

7.3 TAKING COMBINATION AND CONFUSION TO ANOTHER LEVEL
"Dom Juan, Ubu, Hamm: Quelque chose suit son cours" ("Dom Juan, Ubu, Hamm: Something Is Taking Its Course")[57]

For more than a dozen years now I have not changed my mind about my somewhat radical and perhaps controversial approach toward doing theatre with students. On the contrary, I continue to experiment with re-creativity. In spring 2003, the experimental bent of my project entailed several adjustments to my approach, including the reading of multiple classical texts, more independence for the students with respect to the rewriting of the original texts, and the integration of three rather than two texts in the final production. The group of twelve students consisted of four graduates and eight undergraduates. Reading and analyzing a greater number and variety of texts would provide the students with a broader, more comprehensive look at the history and the art, the subjects and the styles, of French theatre. But this came at a price: we would have to spend almost twice as much time reading, discussing, and reductively and re-creatively performing the actions, images, and characters of three texts from three different centuries: *Dom Juan*, *Ubu*, and Beckett's *Fin de partie* (*Endgame*), the one text that I had never before included in any of my projects. These texts also represent three different aesthetic philosophies – three different worlds, in effect. Despite the texts' disparities, however, they share many of the same themes, structures, and creative principles, insofar as they all deal with an unorthodox pair of human individuals in a world controlled by absurd and mysterious forces. The exploding Palotins of the Ubu story could stand as the late-nineteenth-century equivalent of the walking, talking statue of the Commander, conceived by Molière for *Dom Juan* two centuries earlier. After the twentieth century's two world wars and its surrealist revolution in the arts, an artistic endeavour equivalent to the creation of Monsieur Ubu and the eccentric space he inhabits might well be to concentrate the meaning of an entire metatheatrical world within an "empty figure on an empty stage," a character like Hamm who wonders "We're not beginning to… to… mean something?" (*Endgame* 32), and a stage representing no more than a (hollow) "cell."[58]

In what might be deemed a further break with tradition and its adherence to the conventional notion that literature and art evolve in a linear fashion, I made the decision to study the three texts out of the usual chronological order of their time periods. We began instead with the late-nineteenth-century *Ubu* and its dynamic thrust of extreme characters in extreme situations, before proceeding to the seventeenth-century *Dom Juan* with its lengthy dialogue yet very active and mysterious cast of characters and finishing with the study of our post-war, *nouveau théâtre* world of Hamm and Clov. We spent approximately two weeks examining and re-creatively performing each of the three texts. In addition to reading these texts, we devoted one class session to the semiotic analysis (with Pavis's questionnaire) of the campus theatre's performance of Wole Soyinka's *Bacchae*. To further widen the students' understanding of French and francophone theatre history and theatrical styles while increasing their comparative point of view, I also (casually and briefly) introduced short excerpts from other texts, like Racine's *Phèdre, Cyrano*, Ionesco's *Le Roi se meurt*, and Aimé Césaire's *Une saison au Congo*. As I do with all my courses, we began the study of each new text by comparing it with the text(s) we had previously studied. I asked the students to propose differences in the texts' stories, structures (external and internal), themes, spaces, characters, actions, time (including rhythm), and language (including dialogue and didascalies), as well as the implicit and explicit use of costumes and objects.

Although I started the project with the intention to bring these texts together on a stage, somehow the texts' stories, actions, and characters began to insinuate themselves on one another – first more subtly, then more obviously – in class discussions as well as in the re-creative sketches. Furthermore, when we completed our study of *Dom Juan*, for the next re-creative sketch I instructed the groups to create a crossover and bring this story together with *Ubu* – something like Dom Juan and his valet Sganarelle meet Ma and Pa Ubu, or perhaps, the spaces of the Dom Juan story invade those of the Ubu story. Though time was running short, my plans to have the students integrate three prewritten texts for the final performance were well underway.

We began to read *Fin de partie* on March 6, more than seven weeks into the semester. Usually at this point of the project the students and I would have collaboratively rewritten one single text or rewritten and combined two texts into one integrated text for performance, roles would have been assigned, and we would have achieved a rough blocking of the full rewritten text. The students would have left for spring break (March 15–22) with their texts in hand, prepared to memorize their lines. Not so with this experimental project: a preliminary re-created text was not yet clearly in sight, at least not for the students. The students did a re-creative sketch of a designated part of the *Fin de partie* text and, on the last day before spring break, another sketch in which each group invented a "post-conclusion" scene – a hypothetical scene that could take place after the conclusion given in Beckett's text. So we finished examining

Endgame on the last day before break. Instead of working on their roles for the final production during the break, the students would continue with the textual-performative analysis component of the course and read and re-create two other texts.

Originally, I had planned to make the following assignment for the Tuesday after the break: each student would read Beckett's very short *Act without Words*, which has only one character and consists entirely of stage directions with no monologue; individually they would then re-create the text and perform it in class, adding words and reducing the text to a mere three lines at precise moments of the action. But in the interest of time I withdrew this text from the program. Instead, I assigned the first act of *Cyrano*, which the students in groups re-created in two short tableaux.

Concurrent with this textual assignment, we began the comprehensive, definitive re-writing work. On the Tuesday after spring break, I distributed the guidelines for re-creating our final performance project. Many of these guidelines resembled those for previous projects: themes and styles, as well as a reminder of tips and techniques that would help the actors enhance the theatrical opacity of the play (see appendix E, "Textual Re-creation: Guidelines for Ubu 2000"). However, the structure of this final performance would be substantially different from the others I had done, so I decided to assign the re-creative writing in two steps. First, having divided the actors into one group of three and two of four (by this point in the semester, we had lost one graduate student because of an irresolvable conflict), I asked each group to produce a rough sketch of a short but comprehensive text for the performance. I gave them the following sample structure to consider: 1) an introduction with a narrator who is either outside the framework of the three plays we have read or whose function is assumed by one or more of the principal characters from one of the works; 2) three tableaux representing a key moment that covers one or two scenes from each of the texts and takes place in a specific space with specific primary and secondary characters; 3) intervention of the narrator (or narrators) between each tableau and perhaps within the action of a tableau, attempting to help connect the stories and guide the audience; and 4) the integration of other theatrical devices into the action to help connect the stories – devices such as songs, chants, objects, and costumes.

CHAPTER SEVEN: COMBINING TEXTS 175

Once these very preliminary texts had been written, distributed, and read by all, we discussed them in terms of their ideas, strategies, and potential to produce a creative integrated text. As usual, each writing group performed an excerpt from their proposed model. These discussions and sketches led to the decision that we could do the play in three essential parts: we could begin with a simple three-step re-created summary of each play, which would lead to a more substantially integrated second part of the play, which in turn would be followed by a short but sweet conclusion and grand finale. Based on this idea, I produced a second set of guidelines for an even more definitive version of our play. This included, for the first part of the performance, preliminary assignments of principal roles for each of the stories and suggested assignments for secondary roles. I distributed these guidelines to the groups and they returned to the drawing board to rework their original ideas according to the new plan. One graduate student would become the principal narrator of the first part. First she would introduce the performance itself and the three plays that would come together to form a part of the whole: "*Voilà trois des plus grandes histoires théâtrales*" ("Presenting three of the greatest theatrical stories ever told") or "*Voilà les trois couples les plus théâtraux de l'histoire*" ("Presenting the three most theatrical couples in history"). Then she would intervene during the transitions from one story to another and at select points of each of the stories in order to engage and enrich the metatheatrical quality of the performance and to guide the spectators in the understanding of the stories. She would also do caricatural impressions of each of the characters. The second part of the performance would consist of an amalgamation of the three separate (and already re-created) stories that played in the first part. I assigned a new principal narrator (an undergraduate) who would begin the second part with a phrase like: "Voilà que ces histoires et leurs personnages se rencontrent «par hasard» sur la scène..." ("Now these stories and their characters meet 'by chance' on the stage"). I did not assign any other roles for this part of the play; instead I encouraged the actors to rotate the principal roles in each of the stories to different actors. Finally, they had to come up with an effective conclusion to the production.

Thus, this project became an even more dynamic, ever-evolving process of renewal than my earlier ones, according the actors a much larger stake in the text and structure of the final product. The two narrators

Fig. 22. "Dom Juan, Ubu, Hamm." A "chance" meeting of legendary theatrical figures. Keith Moser, Carissa Stolting, Melissa Richey, Stephanie McCullough, Holly MacDonald, Scott Sherrill, Amy Bertram, Joe Caldwell. Carousel Theatre, University of Tennessee, Knoxville, TN. Photo by Les Essif.

took the lead in supervising the scripting of the final re-written text. All the actors played a role in directorial decisions that honed the final version of the play. Given the circumstances of this project – the multiple texts, the lateness in producing a clear design for the final performance, my decision to allow the actors to produce the final text, and the reduction of the rehearsal phase to less than two weeks – the actors were forced to come together and propose performance solutions on their own. In effect, my role was reduced from that of a director to more of a dramaturg and a resident critic of the work. I can't say I was free of doubt, especially at the beginning of the rehearsal phase. But I'm happy to say that in a surprisingly short time the re-creative principle and the semester-long re-creative and collaborative training and practice succeeded in galvanizing the talent and good will of the actors. Though probably a bit less polished than my other productions, the final performance gave pleasure and reflection to the audiences and a warranted sense of achievement to the actors. As other groups had accomplished with the "Dom Juan-Cyrano" and the "Macbett-Macbeth" projects, this group had constructed critical, conceptual, and metatheatrical bridges, connecting three centuries of French theatre and characters from seemingly very different walks of "life" (see fig. 22).

In order to bring the reader up to date on the evolution of my re-creative experiments and experiences, let me conclude this chapter with a brief account of my most recent play project, "Le Bombardement humain" ("Human Bombing," spring 2005), which I mentioned briefly in the prologue. After reading a selection of short pieces from the collection *Les Courtes* by Jean-Claude Grumberg, my five actors set to work to re-create and assemble four of the plays into a kind of performance medley.

CHAPTER SEVEN: COMBINING TEXTS 177

One of the plays, *Les Vacances* ("On Vacation"), is about a rather dysfunctional and chauvinistic French family – a mother, a father, and two teenage sons – who lunch at a restaurant while vacationing on a tropical island. We divided this text into a series of scenes subtitled *"On s'installe," "La Carte," "La Commande," "La Crise"* and *"L'Addition/Conclusion."* Then we expanded and compounded the piece by alternating each of these French-language scenes with scenes depicting a vacationing American family (of four) dining in a Parisian restaurant. These scenes were written largely in English and were given the following subtitles, which are more or less equivalent to the French subtitles listed above: "Finding a Table," "The Menu," "Placing the Order," "The Crisis," and "The Conclusion." So the newly titled "Les Vacances/On Vacation" piece began with the first French-language scene "On s'installe," which was followed by the mostly English-language scene "Finding a Table," followed by "La Carte," and so on. Given the considerable cultural differences between the Americans and the French, especially as concerns culinary habits and family structure and relationships – differences that my actors came to appreciate in a new light – the dialogue for the "Americans in France" scenes were more original than re-creative, more written than re-written. In the Paris scenes, for example, second-hand smoke and meagre portions of food and drink became serious issues.

In addition to this "vacation piece," we re-created three other Grumberg shorts to form the medley. The piece that preceded "Les Vacances/On Vacation" and began our performance was *Michu*, a very short play about a strange husband and wife and the husband's even stranger office colleague who convinces the husband he is first a homosexual, then a communist, then a Jew (which became a terrorist in our version), accusations that eventually cause the wife to leave the husband. Following "Les Vacances/On Vacation" came a re-creation of *Hiroshima Commémoration* (which we retitled simply "Hiroshima"), a play in which a talk-show host (two hosts in our play) brings together for the first time two guests who the host believes are ripe for confrontation: a Catholic Japanese nun who, as a child, had survived the atomic bomb attack but lost her family, and the American Army officer who had triggered the bomb. The final piece we re-creatively played is unusually but closely linked to *Hiroshima*: *Nagasaki Commémoration*, which became simply "Nagasaki" in our version. In the original version, an escaped patient from a mental hospital holds up the Japanese-American owner of a convenience store. In our version, "Nagasaki" became a subsequent episode of the same "reality" talk-show of the preceding piece, and the host-reporter is unexpectedly caught in the hold-up of the convenience store, which we located in a small Louisiana town, in part to justify the mental patient's use of some broken Cajun French.

At this point, only a couple of months from the final stages of the decision-making process and from the staging of the (un)finished product, I have not had sufficient time to reflect on this production. But I can say that it broke new re-creative ground, despite the fact that, except for the last two pieces ("Hiroshima" and "Nagasaki"), there were not as many evident cross-overs between textual or material aspects of the formerly unconnected play material composed by Grumberg and re-composed by us. We did find that each of the pieces contributes in one way or another to a common theme of "human bombing," as ambiguous as this title may sound.

I am at a loss to predict the re-creative territory into which the next play project will lead us.

Conclusion

I begin this conclusion by apologizing to those readers who might have felt discomforted by the theoretical-analytical bent of the last chapter. Having intended this book as a multipurpose work that can accommodate a wide variety of interests, tastes, and needs, I realize that not all readers will respond equally to the theoretical underpinnings of my re-creative approach, or to my efforts to flesh out the instructional and critical utility of re-creative analysis of text and performance, or even to my efforts to merge theory, analysis, pedagogy, and art by signalling the artistic merit of the play project and recommending it as an artistic endeavour as much as a pedagogical one – or at least as an artistically enhanced instructional enterprise. I hope I've done enough to articulate the validity of these less practical, less functional components and their interconnectedness with and relevance to the practice of doing foreign-language theatre with students.

Overall I hope this book will inspire deeper conceptual, practical, and artistic understandings of theatrical texts, performances, and production. It should provide helpful guidance for many teachers, practitioners, students, and other readers who look forward to building a play production. It should also provide fresh food for thought and new tools for action to already active producers of theatre. Beyond these expectations, I hope the book will inspire a number of readers, whether they are theatrophiles or not, to become active producers and more engaged spectators of theatre. But at its most essential, I hope this book will guide teachers of language and literature, especially those who teach foreign-language literature, toward a re-creative analysis and production of plays.

There is no better way to rouse the creativity of an individual-in-a-collective – the typical classroom situation – than by way of theatrical performance, except, of course, by way of doing re-creative theatre. "Enough with theatre that does no more than interpret reality," says Augusto Boal. "[T]heatre must transform reality!" (*Jeux* 19). Likewise, we've all had enough of instructional methodologies that do no more than interpret and "teach" reality's strange bedfellow: art. For Boal, interpretation is simply and rather passively "performative," whereas re-interpretation, or re-creation, is complexly and actively transformative. To recall my introductory remarks to this book, I approach theatre as the "presentation of a transformation," transformation meaning so much more than the spatial, material, and physical interpretation and rendering of a written text. Accordingly, this book is a presentation of how I orchestrate the transformation processes that constitute theatre.

My artistico-pedagogical approach to transformation serves the essential principle of theatrical art, *resistance!*, which is also the essential principle of art in general. Art is, after all, a product of resistance, a challenge to and subversion of the routine and familiarity of reality and its facile reproduction: there is no mimesis like re-creative mimesis. True art is never business as usual, and the usual business of play production is a level of adherence to the written text – its story, its words, its inscripted guidelines, implicit as well as explicit – for its production. My resistance to doing theatre as usual, to the traditional practice of interpreting and representing (or even "re-presenting," in the sense of an innovative approach to production, with an anachronous use of contemporary costumes or setting, for example) the dialogue and the directions of the original classical text, contributes to the validity of my projects as genuine theatrical art. The uniqueness of the theatrical genre is owed largely to its collaborative and polysemic production practices: individuals (minds and bodies) collaboratively communicate within a veritable cauldron of supporting (collaborating and/or competing) sign systems, including costumes, setting, objects, lighting, sound, language. Not only meaning, but resistance too can become multidimensional.

To be sure, the authors of the greatest drama throughout history resisted to varying degrees – depending on the historical period – the conventions governing the theatrical construction of a given "story," from the sacrilegious overtones of Molière's *Dom Juan* to the absurdity of Beckett's *Godot*. In the twentieth century, the resistance extended increasingly to the transposition of the classical text to the stage, to the performance side of the art.

A poster designed by Peter Schumann's alternative, dissident, and supremely collaborative Bread and Puppet Theatre troupe reads, "A resistance of the heart against business as usual." Most of us, of course, feel in our hearts that we do resist, and many of us even feel like revolutionaries when we dress a classical male character in drag or have a character make a lewd gesture to the audience. But, make no mistake, resistance is more difficult and less frequently achieved than we think. That is why we need strategies to attain and sustain it – conscientiously. No matter how radical the *mise-en-scène*, the choice of the text usually prescribes a great degree of submission to much of its once subjunctive but now antiquated language and a bit of reckoning with many of its most problematic, obscure, and esoteric cultural references. Sometimes a nod to (our idea of) period authenticity is valid, but often it is not.

As I pointed out in the introduction to this work, I believe that my re-creative approach to the production of texts follows the advice and the wisdom of a great number of resistant celebrity theorists of theatre who knew that the objective of producing art was not mimetic re-presentation, but poietic renewal, which could only be attained by a resolute resistance to the status quo. In addition to resistance in the form of subjunctive liminality (Turner), in the form of a call to recreate the creative principle of a given work of art (Boal, Brecht) or in the endorsement of an approach to theatrical art that is radically absolute and "cruel" (Artaud), the writings of Theodore Adorno remind us that radical, unrealistic art forms, those that challenge established sociocultural constructs – including, of course, processes that re-create established, classical dramatic texts – are by no means to be considered antisocial or even asocial. On the contrary, these subversive processes tend to become all the more socially viable and effective:

Art, however, is not social only because it is brought about in such a way that it embodies the dialectic of forces and relations of production. Nor is art social only because it derives its material content from society. Rather, it is social primarily because *it stands opposed to society*.... What [art] contributes to society is not some directly communicable content but something more mediate, i.e. resistance. Resistance reproduces social development in aesthetic terms without directly imitating it. (*Aesthetic Theory* 321; my emphasis)

By reproducing social development, resistance can achieve an excellent learning experience.

Are we sufficiently determined and driven to resist mimesis, classical authority, and convention, really? My basic strategy for resistance comes in the form of a motivated and prescriptive re-invention of an existing cultural icon (story), and since the re-invention is collaborative, it's more of a renegotiation of the text's original "meaning." As a result of the re-creative template for performance, my play productions, while based to a significant degree on classical texts/stories, have been, shall we say, "different," especially when you consider that they emanated from the foreign-language classrooms of a public university and not from any avant-garde theatrical milieu. If they weren't different, they wouldn't be art ... and I wouldn't feel like an artist.

I dedicate myself to the task of foreign-language play production, not only because I want to be an effective teacher but equally because I want to experience first-hand the uniqueness of genuine artistic production. I tell my students that I wouldn't do theatre production if I felt my role in it were merely as a teacher, as a scholar, or even as a simple "practitioner" (one who simply "practices" it). I must feel creative in the full, the radical and artistic, sense of the word. The fact is, I feel like an artist: the artist as the true heretic.

True art is never altogether or ultimately incomprehensible, but it always contains mysterious elements that generate an interrogative response. So my students and I are encouraged by the many questions about staging decisions from spectators and from colleagues: Why the centre-stage pairing of Done Elvire and Roxane in the combined story of Dom Juan and Cyrano? Why is chocolate so important in the Candide story? And why the musical reference to the film *Psycho* and the even more obvious and elaborate reference to the Wizard of Oz? Why the leather jacket and the red wig on Joan when she becomes a warrior? Why the flashy green, sausage-shaped necktie on Père Ubu? Why does Macbett smoke a cigarette? Why the marionettes? Why have more than one actor play the same role? Why?... Why?... Why? – I think we're on the right track. Perhaps our experiments with increasing the "radicalization" of the method (see chapter 7) were not intended for immediate consumption and digestion by the student-actors, the audience, or me. Perhaps we should approach them instead as a legitimate encounter with the mystery of art and its provocative nature – within limits, I guess. The comprehension of art has as many degrees as it has levels, and curiosity

CONCLUSION

is a clear indication of interest. Spectators and readers still inquire about the unfamiliar places, characters, and actions of Jarry's drama. And – why does Dom Juan defy Heaven the way he does?

I find comfort in the questions about our performances, to which my students usually provide analytical responses in their final critical papers. The decisions that I make with students are often as intuitive as they are rational. They are made to some extent for their challenge to the conventions of the text and the conventions of world, but, in retrospective analysis, we invariably discover that the signification is more complex than anyone had figured, often on the edge between signification and chaos. Consequently, our processes and our productions are full of metatheatrical quotation marks, and their conclusions flaunt rather prominent question marks. Process and product signify theatre rather than world, meaning is clearly rooted in performance rather than text, text is absent, performance is present. Our theatrical art is not business as usual – and I/we also think it has the potential to inspire social redemption. (Not to mention that we seem to have diverted our spectators' attention and our own from the foreign-language medium!)

As I said at the very beginning of this book, theatre is a survivor. It survives not so much because all the world is a stage, but because the stage presents a very special *transformed* part of the world: the stage is that concentrated and enchanted location of civilization where languages, cultures, and subcultures coalesce in order to create, to learn, to teach, and, most importantly, to simply evolve.

When the time comes to prepare for our next production, I will have absolutely no idea of the resistant "statement" that my students and I will make, or of the semiotic systems we will use to make this statement: How will our re-creation of the text be structured? How will the cast be assembled? What costumes will the actors wear? What props and set materials will we use? However, since I have used and continue to use the theatrical medium in my own (instructionally and artistically) re-creative way, I have no doubt that the production will be the presentation of a transformation, one that is different from all the others I have mounted, leading me and my actors to and through new enchanting territory on our way to the stage. There is no doubt that many readers of this book will build a similar experience: *Mer-dre!* (Break a leg!).

Appendices

APPENDIX A:
SAMPLE COURSE DESCRIPTION AND SYLLABUS

Short Course Description for Promotional Purposes

430 Theatrical French (*4 credits*): DR. ESSIF, SPRING 2003

> *(Please note: this course is 4 credits and will meet TR, from 3:40 to 5:30. If you have any questions, please contact the instructor: [telephone number and email address])*

More than a lecture-type class or simply a play project, this workshop serves as a comprehensive introduction to theatrical production and performance in French.

It teaches students:

1) to understand the complex structures of the dramatic text and their relationship to theatrical performance and
2) to express and *perform* French with a passion (students learn to "feel" their speech and concentrate their listening).

All activities stress creativity, collaboration, and total participation.
In the first half of the course, we will learn basic performance techniques and read a variety of classical French dramatic texts using primarily a "performative" and "re-creative" approach.

In the second half of the course, we will collectively and collaboratively design a performance text based on the stories and characters from one or more of the plays we've read, and we will rehearse and perform our original French-language production for an audience at the end of the semester.

All students will have significant acting parts in the central project. They should have a reasonable grip on French grammar, vocabulary, and pronunciation, but are *absolutely not required to have any prior acting or theatrical experience*. The principal requirement for this truly collective enterprise is high motivation. The "official" prerequisite for the course is one French lit class (300-level or above) or the permission of the instructor.

The rehearsal and performance schedule will be announced during the first week of class. (Short road trips to area high schools and a community college are probable again this year.)

Written work includes the keeping of a journal, short exercises on the analysis of written texts and corresponding performance activities, and a conclusive analysis of the project and the production. Grading is based on written work (30%), in-class contribution to creative-critical activities and discussions (30%), and performance of role (40%).

Graduate Students

Graduate students will learn techniques *to analyze* and *to teach* language, theatre, literature, and culture "performatively." In addition to the journal, a term paper will be required. This will take the form of a critical evaluation of the course project based on critical texts selected from a short bibliography provided by the instructor.

Place au théâtre!

****

Sample Course Syllabus

FRENCH 430: THEATRICAL FRENCH, SPRING 2000, 4 CREDITS, T-R, 3:40-5:30, HSS 68

Instructor:
Office:
Office Hours:

Principal texts: Alfred Jarry's *Ubu Roi* dans *Tout Ubu*; supplementary "texts" include photocopied materials as well as audio and video recordings, which the instructor will provide or place on reserve at the library.

[Or, for a project that undertakes the study of several full-length plays, such as my spring 2003 project: Alfred Jarry's *Ubu Roi*; Molière's *Dom Juan* (Bordas); Beckett's *Fin de partie*; another full-length text (to be determined); excerpts from a number of other dramatic texts; and other supplementary "texts," including photocopied materials and audio and video recordings, which the instructor will provide or place on reserve at the library.]

Course Description

More than a lecture-type course or simply a play project, this workshop serves as a comprehensive introduction to theatrical analysis, production, and performance in French. It teaches students 1) to understand the complex structures of the dramatic text and their relationship to theatrical performance, and 2) to express and *perform* French with a passion (students learn to "feel" their speech and concentrate their listening). Since theatrical performance demands "whole" speech – i.e., natural expression that thoroughly engages the body – this course can greatly assist the student's oral competence in French, especially as concerns the psychological and physical ability to communicate.

All activities stress creativity, collaboration, and total participation, and all participants will have significant acting parts in the end-of-semester performance.

Prerequisites

The student is expected to have a reasonable grip on grammar, vocabulary, and pronunciation, but you are *absolutely not required to have any prior acting or theatrical experience*. The "official" prerequisite for the course is one French lit class (FR 352 or above) or the permission of the instructor. The principal requirement for this truly collective enterprise is high motivation.

This collective-collaborative project demands a serious contribution from each of the participants, who will generously submit to some form of collective- as well as self-criticism. Participants must be exceptionally devoted to this project, keeping up with all reading and writing assignments, attending every class session, and making themselves available for group meetings outside regular class hours. One person's absence, laxity, or inflexibility can adversely affect all others involved.

For the motivated student, this will be an unforgettable experience: *GA-RAN-TI*!

Structure

There are essentially three interdependent and overlapping components of the theatrical project. The first will focus on the relationship between the written dramatic text, the "world" it reflects, and the performance it engenders. It will cover the analysis of dramatic texts from a primarily theatro-historico-cultural point of view. What aspects of the texts lend themselves to an original, contemporary, creative expression on the stage? What do the texts say about the world, society, and human behaviour in terms of the visual (material and corporal) image and physical sensation and/or expression, including the production of speech? The second component will cover performance techniques, including dramatic activities and games and short sketches in the form of performance responses to the texts we study. Finally, these intellectual, artistic, and practical exercises will lead to the production of a 60-minute *spectacle* that we will collectively create by re-creating (rewriting) either one particular dramatic story or selected scenes from a number of texts and weaving them together into some sort of comprehensive package. (One of the criteria for altering the story/text will be to increase its appeal to a contemporary audience with a wide variety of competence in the French language.)

In the first half of the course, we will learn basic performance techniques and study plays using primarily a "performative" and "re-creative" approach. In the second half of the course, we will focus on the creation of the final production and the rehearsals it will entail.

Academic Responsibilities and Grading

For the written work you will keep and regularly update a journal (in French, with maybe a smattering of English), which the instructor will collect for review, usually on a weekly basis, every Tuesday, to be returned on Thursday. Entries will concern all aspects of the project, including analysis of the dramatic text, evaluation of performance exercises, and evaluation of the development of the performance project. At the end of the semester you will provide a detailed analysis of some aspect of the completed *mise-en-scène* and its relation to the original text.

Grading is based on written work in the form of a journal and includes the final analysis of the production and the project (30%), in-class participation and contribution (40%), and performance of role in final production (30%).

Graduate students will learn techniques *to analyze* and *to teach* language, theatre, literature, and culture "performatively." In addition to the journal, a term paper (10–12 pages) will be required. This will take the form of a critical evaluation of the course project (and its relation to the original dramatic texts) based on critical texts selected from a short bibliography provided by the instructor.

Place au théâtre!

Program

13 January – 3 February:
> introduction to the project, study of texts, performance practice. Analysis of play presented by the UT Theatre Department.

8 – 17 February:
> creation of our text. The weekend of February 11–14 all participants must be available to meet in small groups to rewrite the text.

22 February – 16 March:
> initial (in-class) construction of our play; supplementary rehearsal time (see calendar).

20–24 March:
> spring break

28 March – 11 April:
> *mise-en-scène* at theatre

12–14 April:
> performances at on-campus theatre. BRAVO! BRAVOUILLE!

17–26 April:
> road trips.

27 April:
: post-performance assessment of the project; discussion of final written analysis.

5 May:
: deadline for final paper.

APPENDIX B: SAMPLE INTERACTIVE DRAMATIC GAMES AND EXERCISES

This category of exercises usually follows the warm-ups and precedes the *petites mises-en-scènes*. There are, of course, abundant published sources for this type of activity, and many instructors will have ideas for modifying or expanding games endorsed by other practitioners or even ideas of their own for developing interesting games. Whatever the case may be, the instructor's choice of which games to do and when and how to do them is by no means arbitrary. The choice, timing, and manner of execution will be critical for the accelerated apprenticeship of the actors and for the attitude of these actors toward the project and the project's director. So the instructor chooses exercises that she can execute comfortably and with precision, exercises that the actors can successfully accomplish and whose value and usefulness they can easily recognize. Further, the instructor always seeks ways to customize the exercise to the group and to the project's format and its subject matter.

I have two primary sources (or sources of inspiration) for these exercises: 1) Augusto Boal's *Games for Actors and Non-Actors* (*Jeux pour acteurs et non-acteurs*) and 2) theatrical workshops and classes in which I have participated (see, for example, the Monod/Ryngaert and Jango Edwards workshops, listed in the Works Cited). (For additional sources, see note 21.)

Boal's *Games* is one of the best sources for this type of exercise in this type of course, not only for the quantity and variety of effective exercises and for the quality of their descriptions, but also because the book has been so widely translated, making the exercises available in a great number of languages, including French, Spanish, German, and Italian. The Boal exercises I use issue from the section titled "Five categories of games and exercises" (*Les cinq catégories de jeux et d'exercices*), though I don't generally pay close attention to the classifications Boal provides for them, such as "Feeling what we touch" (*Sentir tout ce qu'on touche*) or "Integration games" (*Intégration*). Though I use the French translation of the text (translated from the original Portuguese), in order to facilitate and widen access to the original source of these exercises I will list the references first to the 1992 English edition (a second edition by the same translator was published in 2002) and then to the French edition. Exercices I use with some regularity and with little or no modification are "Joe Egg" (67) (*La bouteille saoule* 84), "Pushing against each other" (65) (*Se pousser l'un l'autre* 89–90), "Slow motion" (73) (*Au ralenti* 91), "The bear of Poitiers" (79) (*L'ours de Poitiers* 98–99), "*Rythme avec des chaises*" (99) (not available in English version), "The orchestra and the conductor" (96) (*L'orchestre et le régisseur* 117), "The president's bodyguards" (97) (*Les gardes du corps du président* 118), "Walk, stop, justify" (98) (*Marchez! Stop! Justifiez* 118), "Crossing the room" (100) (*Traverser la salle* 120), "The magnet – positive and negative" (109) (*L'aimant négatif et l'aimant positif* 127); "Find a convenient back" (115) (*On cherche un dos convenable* 131).

For other exercises from *Games* I make minor adjustments that I feel will enhance their fit for our project. For example, with "The machine of rhythms" (90) (*La machine à rythmes* 113), in which the actors become a moving part in a complicated machine, I ask the participants to vocalize a two- or three-syllable French sound or word to accompany the movement, instead of simply using just any sound. In "The smell of hands" (112) (*L'odeur des mains* 128), the five or six players of a group approach one-by-one a blindfolded comrade. Each player states her name and extends her hand to smell. After the first round, they approach the blindfolded person again and she must identify each player by their smell. In my version of the game, instead of stating their name, each of the players must produce a short phrase or sound (usually associated with a text we are studying), which the blindfolded person must repeat instead of the name of the player.

Perhaps my favourite exercise from this series is "The wooden sword of Paris" (81) (*L'épée de bois parisienne* 100). I usually introduce this exercise in its simple form, more or less as it appears in the text. Two groups face each other, with a leader in front of each group, and they "fight a duel as if they had wooden swords in their hands" – that's why I prefer to call this game "*L'épée imaginaire*" ("The imaginary sword"). Each leader is limited to choosing one of six possible strikes (to the head, to mid-body, to the left, to the right, to the legs, and a forward thrust). The workshop director instructs each group leader alternately to render a single strike. When the group leader strikes, the opposing team reacts (more or less in unison, as I understand it) to evade the strike. This is an excellent exercise to get each group of actors to work together with a common rhythm and a common purpose. So, first I introduce the actors to this preliminary exercise by instructing them to execute all movement in slow and steady motion and with a well-defined and highly stylized gesture.

After the initial experience, I increase the exercise's complexity and the demand for intimate co-operation among the participants. First I eliminate the group leader and ask the two groups of adversaries to seek a common rhythmic motion to serve as a context for the duel, as a source and a base for the strikes. This might be a circular or forward and backward movement of their bodies, where the collective body of one group harmonizes with the motion of the other. To facilitate and enhance the "dance," I play music, such as Ravel's *Bolero*. From the communal motion, one member of one group intuitively takes the initiative to execute the first strike against the entire opposing team, a strike that will be followed by the entire team of that individual. The opposing group reacts in unison and, once the response is complete and the basic rhythm is restored, a member of the opposing group executes a counter strike. At another point, perhaps in the second or third session in which we practice this exercise, the groups close ranks into a tightly knit "dueling machine" and I tell them that alternately one player must add a two- or three-syllable word or sound while executing the strike (always in slow motion!), requiring all their teammates to join in the utterance of the sound (*Fan-fa-ron!*, for example). In response, the adversaries repeat the final syllable of the sound while they move – in unison – to evade the strike ("*On!*" /Ō/), and then they respond with their own strike and their own utterance, and the opposing team responds in kind. I constantly remind the participants that slow motion is key, especially in the initial phase of practicing the exercise.

With these modifications, this exercise becomes so comprehensive and effective that we have integrated it into the battle scenes of a number of our productions. Readers will want to read through the entire series of exercises that Boal proposes in order to choose exercises that they can use as is, expand, or otherwise modify to suit their own needs, interests, and abilities.

Other exercises that I use in the course are less clearly traceable to one source. Those I list below are either of my own design or a considerably modified version of some exercise used at one of the classes or workshops I attended in France. I list them in order of their complexity and their chronological placement in the project.

1. *Keeping the ball in the air* (*La petite pelote dans l'air*). In this very simple exercise, a group of five or six actors form a circle. One member of the group calls out the number one in the foreign language (*Un!*) as she gently hits a ball (or balloon, or ball of wadded paper) into the air in the direction of another actor. The other actor calls out the next number in succession (*Deux!*) as she hits (or tries to hit) the ball into the air toward another player (*Trois!*), and so on. The group tries to maintain the ball in the air as long as possible without it hitting the floor. Once the group reaches a certain number, say ten, the instructor issues an order to switch to counting by tens (*dix, vingt, trente,* and so on). To expand the use of language and to enhance the cultural component of the exercise, eventually the group can "count" by the days of the week (*lundi, mardi...*) or the months of the year (in succession, of course), or, without repeating the same name twice, French names for women or for men, names of French and francophone cities, celebrities, or monuments, and so on.

2. *Face to face* (*Face à face*): actors pair up, one facing another. (In the case of an odd number of total participants, this can be done with two actors facing one.) The director proposes a word or a phrase from the play being studied (for *Ubu*, "*Cornegidouille!*" or "*De par ma chandelle verte!*" or "*Bougre de merdre et merdre de bougre!*"; for *Dom Juan*, "*Sganarelle, le Ciel!*" or "*Coeur de tigre!*" or "*Un feu invisible me brule!*"). Then, on the director's cue, each actor takes a turn at performing the phrase to her partner in a variety of tones and with an appropriate gesture: happy, ecstatic, sad, perplexed, angry, and so forth.

For another version of this exercise, I have the actors sing with varying intensity the refrain of a French or foreign-language song to their partners. I use songs that are well known and popularly respected, like "*The Marseillaise*," and songs that are more youthfully playful and phonetically challenging, like "*La Soricière Carabistouille*":

La Sorcière Carabistouille
Préparait des ratatouilles
Pour son vieux crapaud crapouille

Qui ne voulait que des nouilles.

One actor might begin by singing the refrain softly and descrescendo. Her partner repeats it by either increasing or decreasing the intensity, tempo, and volume. Once the group has practiced a variety of renditions, the director has all the actors come together to articulate the softest possible articulation of the refrain followed by the most intense, both renditions accompanied by an appropriate gesture.

3. *Communal brawl (Bagarre générale)*. Whenever the tempo of a session seems too slow and the group's energy level ebbs, on the spur of the moment, the director can call for a "Fight!" At this cue, all the actors spontaneously switch focus from whatever activity they are involved in and begin a fake fight with the individual who is nearest to them. The first time in the semester I introduce this impromptu exercise, I shout "*Bagarre!*" ("Fight!") and rambunctiously incite the actors to perform a general rumble, instructing them to do it in slow motion with well-defined, extravagant, and stylized gestures, reminding them that they must act both defensively and offensively, reacting to blows as well as doling them out. As with the imaginary sword exercise, after we've done this exercise once or twice, I instruct the actors to pronounce a two- to three-syllable word or sound when giving and receiving a blow. At some point, I also add some complexity by informing the actors that the fight takes place on a surface of ice or in the water.

4. *Sculptor-sculpted (Sculpteur-sculpté)*. The class divides into groups of four or five. One member of each group is designated the sculptor of the group. Each group decides on a specific emotional state, such as frustrated desire, sudden shock, disguised jealousy, or emerging anger. (Other than an emotional state, this could also be any one of the themes listed below under "tableau vivant.") With the groups isolated from one another, in five minutes or less, each sculptor moulds and shapes the human bodies belonging to her group into a living sculpture based on the chosen emotional state. The sculptor must include herself in the work. When their time is up, the groups return to the classroom. Taking turns, one group sets up its "sculpture," and the other groups guess as specifically as possible the emotion created. As a final, analytical, step, the actors may discuss the following questions: Why did the sculptor choose this particular scene and what was the purpose of some of the elements

in the scene? How did the actors feel about their respective roles in the composition? How exactly did the "audience" view the piece?

For another step in this exercise, after the groups have had their turn at guessing the other's emotional state, members of one group return to their positions in the work while members of the other group examine in detail the composition and, with the assistance of their sculptor, attempt to reproduce the same scene, each member assuming the role of one of the members of the other group. Once they are satisfied with their reproduction, I instruct them first to articulate a word or a sound associated with their "role" in the scene and then to vocalize their "role" in the scene while maintaining their position in the composition. Finally I tell them to become progressively animated in the represented scene, acting it out to the extent possible.

5. *Tableau vivant* (*The living tableau*). A number of practitioner-teachers include some version of this exercise in their performance training and performance-based instruction. (For a clear and precise explanation of one version of "*le tableau vivant ou le théâtre-image*," the living tableau, see Daniel Feldhendler's "Expression dramaturgique," 47–48.) The class is divided into groups of four to six, and members seat themselves on the floor in a circle. We decide on a theme, which could be a situation, an event, an institution, a tradition, a practice, or even an emotion or a moral trait or mannerism. Usually the theme relates in some way to the story being studied. During the Ubu project, for example, one of the themes I used was gluttony. As a first step, whenever an actor feels ready, she moves to the middle of the circle (the designated playing area) and assumes a fixed position and an attitude expressing or suggesting the idea or practice of gluttony. Next, as soon as a second actor feels the desire, she enters the playing area and takes up a fixed position and an attitude, one that may be related or attached to the image of the first or that might be completely independent. Then, based on the (partial) image (or images, if the two have initiated separate scenes) of these two actors, if and when any of the other actors feels ready and willing, they enter one by one to either complete, reinforce, transform, or expand the scene or scenes represented in the playing area (or connect one scene with the other). When any actor, whether she be inside or outside the playing area, feels that a given tableau is complete, she calls out "Tableau!" This completes the construction of the tableau in question, and the incor-

porated actors remain fixed in position. The non-participating actors examine the scene. They identify the key characters in the composition, comment on specific elements, and assign the scene a specific title, such as "Sneaking the Picnic Lunch" or "Some People Never Get Enough" or, more referentially, "Ubu Pigs Out While Others Starve." I give each of the in-tableau actors the opportunity to individually and momentarily disengage from the tableau to view the comprehensive scene of which they are a part. Then I instruct the in-tableau actors to close their eyes and imagine as vividly as possible the scene they are in. They think of a word or a phrase associated with their respective roles in the scene, an utterance they present when I touch them on the shoulder. Next I give the signal for the scene to become animate, and the in-scene actors begin to move in slow motion and without voice. At a given moment, when I feel the scene has sufficiently evolved, I tell them to freeze. Once again, I ask them in turns (when I touch them on the shoulder) to utter a sound, word, or phrase that corresponds to their new position in the scene. Finally, I cue them to do and say whatever they feel as their character in the scene, acknowledging the other characters in the scene and interacting with them if they so choose. If the scene develops dynamically, I ask other non-participating actors to join in as they like. When the scene winds down, we stop. As a final step, we discuss the exercise – its development, its potential, its problems, and its lessons.

I introduce the following games in the second half of the project. They help the actors develop more sophisticated techniques of role interpretation and character analysis:

6. *Exercise in style* (*Exercices de style*). I base this exercise on Raymond Queneau's *Exercices de style*. It complements the exercise I use to introduce the semiotics of style (see chapter 2, "Introducing the 'Systems' of Style, Costume, Prop, and Music"). To demonstrate the power of style, the authority of style over content, and its consequent control and production of meaning, Queneau recounts in ninety-nine different styles a very banal and somewhat pointless anecdote. But he does this in writing, a form of (or a step in) communication that represents only one dimension of meaning, a preliminary step in a meaningful process: the production of meaning. Thus, it's not surprising that Queneau's work has had significant and continued success in its transposition to the stage.

For this game, I select "styles" that are more or less readily apparent and familiar, and those that are based more on presentation and delivery than on vocabulary and written form, such as "Onomatopeia," "Geometric," and "Past Tense" – though it's clear that the performance can play a significant role in defining these styles as well. For a group of twelve actors, I select about a dozen or so styles, such as "Exclamations," "Interjections," "Philosophical," "Telegraphic," "Peasant," "Precious," "Clumsy," "Hesitation," "Impotent," and "Dreamy." We then reduce the pool of styles to six, and I assign two actors to each style in order to add a comparative aspect to the exercise. I give the actors at least two days to re-create individually their style, reducing the verbal text of Queneau's version (usually about a ten-sentence paragraph) to about three or four short sentences. For the class exercise, each actor works for five to seven minutes with a partner (who is not presenting the same style), who helps her develop the *mise-en-scène* of her style through language (rhythm, volume, tone), physical expression (corporal and facial gestures), physical positioning, and movement. Each actor performs her version of one of the styles, say "Precious," followed by the second actor assigned the same style, and the audience compares and critiques the two different performances of the same style, commenting on the re-created text and on what it takes to create and interpret a style. All actors present their styles.

7. *The perfect impression* (*L'impression parfaite*). Together we view very closely a videotape of a very brief (perhaps ten to twenty seconds long) excerpt from a well-known French film, usually a scene that is key to defining (in terms of voice, expressions, gestures, and actions) two prominent characters. Over the years I have used scenes such as the following with great success:

In *Le Retour de Martin Guerre* (*The Return of Martin Guerre*), Martin (Gérard Depardieu) is taken into custody by the judge. Under arrest and with his hands bound, he is being escorted out of the village when his uncle (Maurice Jacquemont) accosts him:

Uncle: Tu vas avoir ce que tu mérites. Tu es un imposteur. Tu nous as tous trompés.
Martin: C'est vous que la justice saisira. L'imposture ne vient que de vous.
Uncle: Tu nous as tous trompés pour t'emparer de notre bien.

In *Diva* (*Diva*), the two drug-dealing hatchet-men, played by Dominique Piñon and Gérard Darmon, have Jules, the courier, in an elevator with a knife to his throat. As the elevator ascends toward the courier's converted apartment in a warehouse, they have the following terse conversation:

Piñon: J'aime pas ça.
Darmon: (chewing gum) C'est beau un garage.
Piñon: J'aime pas les ascenseurs.
Darmon: T'aimes rien, toi.

In *Les Visiteurs* (*The Visitors*), I have used a number of different scenes, such as the scene where the count (Jean Reno) and his valet, Jacquouille (Christian Clavier), first awaken in the late twentieth century. For a more complicated scene with more spoken text, I do the scene where the count meets the countess (Valérie Lemercier), his extremely distant descendant, for the first time. (For this scene, the actors must do a bit of reductive re-creative work in order to memorize the text and master the characterization in the short time alloted.) The countess has been called to the church rectory by the priest to see if she can identify him, but the count mistakes her for his fiancée from the eleventh century:

Count: Ma promise... Ma promise! Vous ici, Frénégonde? *(He rushes toward her and takes her into his arms.)*
Countess: Non, mais, lachez-moi! Vous me faites hypermal.... Mais, calmez-vous, espèce de brute!
Count: Mais, c'est moi!
Countess: Je ne vous reconnais pas!
Priest: Ecoutez, Monsieur, Madame la comtesse ne vous reconnaît pas. *(This role can be omitted, and the dialogue adjusted accordingly.)*
Count: Ca suffit, l'abbé. Je n'ose comprendre. Cette jeune demoiselle n'est point mon amie, mais ma descendance. Mille ans nous séparent.
Countess: Oui, certainement.

For all of these scenes, I divide the actors into groups of three: two actors will assume the two prominent roles in the scene and the third will direct them in perfecting their roles. I run the clip at least an additional four to five times, until the actors feel they have a good grip on the personal style of the actors they will represent. Then, with the help of the directing actor, the student-actors attempt to build an impression of the actors on the screen by reproducing and mimicking exactly every detail of Gérard Depardieu's performance in a scene from *Martin Guerre* or Jean Reno's or Valérie Lemercier's performance in *Les Visiteurs*, including the slightest movements, gestures, and intonation of voice. (Once the actors begin to rehearse, they usually ask to see the clip two or three more times.) After about four or five minutes of rehearsal, each group presents their "perfect impression" of the scene, and we discuss and compare the details of each interpretation. In this exercise, I encourage some competition, asking the class to choose the best of the impressions performed.

Another French film I use is the contemporary silent film *Le Bal*. I play the first long scene, where the characters enter the ballroom in their highly individualized, stylized, affected, and overacted manner. Then I ask each actor to recreate the entrance of one of the characters, mimicking the totality of their carriage of their head and torso; their walk, postures, manners, comportment; and the slightest of their gestures.

8. See also appendix G, "Instructions and Suggestions for Activist Promotion" and "The Traffic Accident," for more advanced types of dramatic games that I use to promote the play.

APPENDIX C:
SAMPLE STUDY AND PERFORMANCE GUIDE FOR A CRITICAL-CREATIVE-PERFORMATIVE APPROACH TO UBU ROI

Ubu Roi d'Alfred Jarry: mode d'emploi
Le Texte (et sa mise en scène)

1. *La critique sur la pièce.* Lisez les extraits des textes de Kleiger-Stillman, d'Abirached et de Béhar. Qu'en pensez-vous? Que disent-ils qui pourrait vous aider à mieux comprendre le texte théâtral et son rapport à la scène théâtrale? Qu'est-ce que vous ne comprenez pas?
2. *Structure/Action.* Quelle est la structure globale d'*Ubu*? Faites une liste des « moments théâtraux » dans cette pièce, ceux qui expliqueront le déroulement de l'histoire et de l'action. Quels « moments » vous semblent plus ou moins vraisemblables? plus ou moins invraisemblables? plus ou moins « théâtraux »? Notez-vous un certain « système » dans l'organisation du mouvement du spectacle? dans la mise en ordre ou dans l'enchaînement des divers types d'action (violente, grossière, « classique », normale, anormale, fantastique, « absurde », etc.)? dans le rythme/la rapidité du texte?

    A quoi sert l'action « rapportée » du texte? (Voir, par exemple, 2.3)
3. *L'Espace.* Dans quelle sorte de théâtre doit-on monter cette pièce? Pourquoi? De combien d'espace a-t-on besoin pour monter cette pièce? Quel rapport devrait-on établir entre le public et la scène (l'action et les personnages)? Voyez-vous facilement les divers espaces de ce texte? Voyez-vous facilement le rapport entre ces multiples espaces et la scène? Comment les transitions d'un espace à un autre s'effectuent-elles? Donnez-en un exemple précis. Quelle est la *couleur dominante* dans *Ubu*? Pourquoi? Y a-t-il des variations de couleur d'un acte (ou d'une scène) à l'autre?

    "Pologne ... Nulle Part"?

    Pouvez-vous penser à un autre type d'espace qui puisse s'intercaler dans le texte? Comment et où pourriez-vous le mettre dans l'enchaînement spatial?
4. *Personnages.* Y a-t-il un « système » (groupement) de personnages? Y a-t-il des personnages qui se ressemblent? Pouvez-vous classer les personnages à partir de leur fonction? de leur vraisemblance? de leur langage? de leur rapport avec les autres personnages? de leur capacité d'évoluer? d'une autre qualité? Personnages stéréotypés?

Père Ubu est-il vraiment le personnage principal? Pourquoi? Peut-il exister sans la Mère Ubu? Que pensez-vous du couple Ubu? Peut-on parler de complémentarité dans ce couple? Quelle sorte de complémentarité?

Pensez à un autre personnage (hypothéthique) qu'on pourrait intégrer dans la distribution de cette pièce. Expliquez son rôle, sa fonction et son rapport avec les autres.

Discutez le rapport espace-personnage dans *Ubu* en tenant compte des citations suivantes: « le personnage se déshumanise, inversement l'objet s'anime »; « Les personnages sont tout aussi schématiques que l'intrigue. C'est de là qu'ils tirent leur puissance théâtrale ».

5. *Langage*. Absurde? Comment? Comique? Comment? Invraisemblable? Comment? Concret ou abstrait? Comment? (Soyez précis et donnez des exemples!)

Quel rapport entre le langage et l'action? Rapport direct? (On fait ce qu'on dit?)

Quelles différences entre les « langages » de chaque personnage? (Dans la forme et dans le contenu) Vocabulaire? Registre? Grammaire? Longueur de phrases? Style?

Commentez cette citation: « [Dans Ubu] le mot devient ... objet concret, opaque, en tout cas peu susceptible d'une traduction 'en clair' »

Les indications scéniques de Jarry, dans quelle mesure contribuent-elles à la création de l'espace scénique? Et les répliques des personnages? Celles-ci portent quelles informations explicites et implicites sur l'action, la gestuelle et l'espace?

6. Commentaire sur le bruitage (les sons) indiqué dans le texte (bruitage implicite et explicite)?

7. Quel est le moment (image, action, langage) le plus fort, le plus théâtral de cette pièce? Pourquoi?

Le Journal (à remettre les mardis 28
jan et 11 fév, et ainsi de suite)

Undergrads, 1 à 1 1/2 pages *par semaine*; grads, 1 1/2 à 2 pages.
Mettez la *date* (le mardi 14 janvier, etc).
Commentaires critiques/analytiques sur:

APPENDICES

1. *Les exercices et les jeux dramatiques* du cours. Vous devriez vous concentrer sur un exercice en particulier, ou même un seul aspect d'un exercice: Qu'avez-vous fait/dit? Qu'avez-vous ressenti en faisant cet exercice? Quels effets avez-vous vus chez vos partenaires? Quels rapports avez-vous établis avec eux? Etc. Soyez créatif et critique!
2. *Les petites mises en scène* (PMS) que nous avons faites. A quel point y avez-vous participé? Et vos partenaires? La transposition du texte à la scène: que vous a-t-elle apporté? Qu'avez-vous appris? Est-ce que cet exercice vous a éclairci un certain point ou procédé du texte? Comment? Avez-vous l'impression que votre participation dans ces exercices évolue? Voyez-vous la progression vers le projet final de cet atelier? Et quelles sont vos impressions du travail de vos co-équipiers et des autres groupes?
3. *Commentez le texte*: Voir les questions ci-dessus.
4. *Devoir supplémentaire*: Réduisez à trois (petites) phrases la première tirade de Mère Ubu au début de l'acte 5 (« Enfin me voilà à l'abri.... »)

Petites mises en scène à prévoir

Dans *toutes* les PMS il faudra réduire le texte au maximum (à 2–3 petites répliques par acteur/personnage). Il faut apprendre les répliques par coeur, bien sûr.

le mardi 21 janvier. PMS: I, 4 *ou* 6.

le jeudi 23 janvier. PMS: la scène de l'assassinat (II,2): mêmes équipes que mardi dernier.

le mardi 28 janvier. La scène de la condamnation-exécution de toute la hiérarchie du royaume (acte 3). Trouvez le rapport spatial des personnages, le déplacement, les gestes et un ou deux *objets* pour communiquer l'essentiel de la scène. Jouez-la d'abord en scène muette et puis parlée.

le jeudi 30 janvier. Jouez la scène de bataille (acte 4). Jouez-la d'abord en scène muette et à trois acteurs-personnages; ensuite à trois personnages et parlée; enfin, à un seul personnage et deux *narrateurs*. Mêmes équipes que mardi dernier.

le mardi 4 février. Jouez la conclusion de la pièce de façon à entraîner le public dans l'action.

le jeudi 6 février: Chacun va re-créer (réinventer) et mémoriser un petit texte-clé (de 3–4 phrases) qui résume bien le caractère de *l'un* des personnages dans *Ubu*. Nous les jouerons individuellement en classe.

APPENDIX D:
PAVIS'S QUESTIONNAIRE

I reproduce below my two abridged and modified versions of Patrice Pavis's questionnaire, one French, one English. I used the English translation of the questionnaire (*Dictionary* 295–96) to translate my French adaptation of Pavis's original French version (*Voix et images* 318–19). To both versions I have added a question covering possible intercultural aspects of the staging (VIII, E). See also Pavis's more detailed version of the questionnaire in his *Dictionnaire du théâtre*.

French Version

Analyse du spectacle

I. Scénographie:
    A. Formes de l'espace urbain, architectural, scénique, gestuel, etc.
    B. Rapport entre espace du public et espace du jeu
    C. Systèmes des *formes* et des *couleurs*, leurs connotations et leurs dénotations
    D. Principes de la structuration de l'espace:
        1. Rapport du scénique et de l'extrascénique (espace évoqué hors scène, etc.)
        2. Lien entre l'espace utilisé et la fiction du texte dramatique mis en scène
        3. Rapport du montré et du caché (non-vu)

II. Système des éclairages

III. Objets: nature, fonction, rapport à l'espace et au corps/ au costume/ au public

IV. Costumes, masques, maquillage: leur système, leur rapport au corps/ au décor/ au public

V. Performance des acteurs (et le personnage dans le texte?):
   A. Gestuelle, mimique, maquillage, tics, démarche
   B. Voix, la voix et le corps, changement de voix, (femme/homme; façon d'exprimer les phrases-clées)
   C. Rapport de l'acteur et du groupe

VI. Fonction de la musique, du bruit, du silence

VII. Rythme du spectacle
   A. Rythme de quelques systèmes signifiants (échanges de dialogues, éclairages, costumes, gestualité, etc.).
   B. Rythme global du spectacle: rythme continu ou discontinu, changements de régime, lien avec la mise en scène.

VIII. Sens global de la mise en scène
   A. Principes esthétiques de la réalisation (réaliste, fantaisiste, mélodrame, etc.) (métaphorique? métonymique?)
   B. Rapport des systèmes scéniques
   C. Surprises? (Par exemple, l'action peut être plus ou moins violente que vous n'avez prévu; ou les objets et les costumes peuvent sembler plus ou moins artificiels ou naturalistes, etc.)
   D. Le texte dans la mise en scène: la mise en scène est-elle fidèle au texte? à quel texte? Quels éclaircissements du texte par la mise en scène?
   E. La/Les *culture(s)* dans la mise en scène: quels codes ou quelles structures interculturels ou multiculturels y reconnaissez-vous? Y a-t-il un *croisement* de cultures (le texte provenant d'une culture et sa mise en scène d'une autre; etc.)? Qu'est-ce qui marche ou qui ne marche pas dans ce croisement?
   F. Est-ce que la mise en scène a éclairci quelques ambiguïtés dans le texte?
   G. Qu'est-ce qui vous dérange dans cette mise en scène?; quels moments forts, faibles ou ennuyeux?
   H. Y a-t-il des problèmes? Comment résoudre les problèmes pour rendre le spectacle plus cohérent?
   I. Quelles images fortes vous restent de ce spectacle? *POURQUOI?*

English Version

Analysis of the Performance

I. Stage design
   A. Forms of urban, architectural, stage, and gestural space
   B. Relationship between audience space and acting space
   C. System of forms, materials, and colours, their denotations and their connotations
   D. Principles of organization of space:
      1. Relationship between what is on stage and what is off stage (offstage spaces referred to by actors, etc.)
      2. Connection between space used and fiction of play staged
      3. Relationship between what is shown and what is hidden

II. Lighting system
   A. Nature: its links to fiction, performance, actors
   B. Effects on performance reception

III. Props: nature, function, materials, relationship with space, body, costume, audience

IV. Costumes, makeup, masks: function, system, relationship with space, set, body, audience

V. Actors' Performances
   A. Relationship to character in the text
   B. Physical description of actors (gestures, mannerisms, facial expressions, makeup, movement); changes in their appearance, movement
   C. Voice: quality, relationship to body, effect on hearer, changes
   D. Actor's relationship with group: links to the whole, movements, trajectory

VI. Significance, nature, and functions of music, sound, silence

VII. Rhythm and pace
  A. Rhythm of signifying systems (exchange of dialogues, lighting, costumes, gestuality, etc.); relationship between actual duration and experienced duration
  B. Overall rhythm of performance: continuous or discontinuous rhythm, changes in pace, connections to *mise-en-scène*

VIII. Overall assessment of the production's meaning
  A. Aesthetic principles (styles) of the staging (realistic, fantastic, melodrama, etc.)
  B. Relationship among signifying systems on stage (stage design, lighting, props, performances, etc.)
  C. Surprises? (For example, the actors' performance could be more or less violent than you expected, or the props and costumes could seem more artificial or naturalistic, etc.)
  D. Text in performance: Is the *mise-en-scène* "faithful" to the text? Which text?
  E. The culture(s) represented in the performance: Do you recognize any cross-cultural or multicultural codes, structures, or intersections in the staging, such as a text that belongs to one culture and features of the performance that are grounded in another? Do these work?
  F. What elements, aspects, or points (moments) of the text did the production clarify for you?
  G. What elements, aspects, or points of the production bothered you? High or strong points? Low or weak points?
  H. Are there special problems? How could one solve these problems to make the performance more coherent or interesting?
  I. Which of the production's images are the most memorable for you? Why?

APPENDIX E:
TEXTUAL RE-CREATION:
GUIDELINES FOR UBU 2000

"Recréation" de textes théâtraux
Ubu Roi: Jouons ce « Nulle Part »

« *Nous ne connaissons vraiment que ce que nous sommes obligés de recréer par la pensée* » *(Proust)* ... « *et par le jeu* » *(Essif)*

I. Abreger, modifier, narrer (demystifier, interroger), actualiser, instruire, rendre plus comprehensible et accessible a un "jeune" public et a un public non francophone, trouver les secrets profonds du texte pour l'artiste et le spectateur du 21ieme siecle – plaire et *se plaire* en (s') instruisant

II. Thèmes (encadrés par et esquissés dans ce monde fantastique):

moyen âge/féodalité
pouvoir/gouvernance
royauté
politique-propagande
nationalisme
guerre
histoire/mythe

trahison
loyauté
noblesse
bassesse
orgueil
jalousie
célébrité
gloutonnerie
extrême égoïsme
peur

APPENDICES

sagesse populaire
fanatisme populaire
inconstance populaire

cruauté à la légère
le meurtre et sa facilité
la simplicité de la vie

(il)logique de l'intelligence
logique de la bêtise systématique
l'esprit guidé par le « bas corporel »
« l'homme fait de contradictions »
rapport entre language et corps

le couple (mariage de deux égoïstes)
homme/femme
femme fatale
sensualité

surnaturel
destin

être/paraître
illusion/réalité

théâtralité de la vie
l'absurdité de la vie ETC.

III. Groupes de rédaction:

Groupe A	Groupe B	Groupe C	Groupe D
(Nom)			
(Nom)			
(Nom)			

IV. Structure de notre texte:

A. *Introduction*. Un/Une narrateur/trice (Un Palotin, le Roi Alexis, un autre personnage, ou peut-être un grand choix de personnages en alternance) prépare le public en résumant l'histoire et en présentant l'espace et les personnages.

Ensuite, avant chaque tableau, le narrateur récapitule l'action tandis que les acteurs jouent un moment-clé du tableau à suivre avant de le jouer dans son intégralité.

B. *Les étapes* de cette « més-aventure » des Ubu suivant à peu près (mais en version condensée) l'action de chaque acte: 1) le complot—> 2) l'assassinat et la fuite—> 3) la mise en place du gouvernement « décervelant » à la Ubu et le départ à la guerre—> 4) LA GUERRE (MU chassée; PU en fuite)—> 5) le couple réuni et relancé à l'aventure + conclusion (quelle sera la toute dernière image/parole du spectacle?)

C. Choisissez et intégrez des chants, chansons, récitations (assez compréhensibles, pertinants, entraînants et faciles à retenir) que nous ferons répéter par le public.

D. Mettez les indications scéniques au début de la scène (décor, situation, description des personnages, etc.) ainsi qu'incorporées dans le texte-dialogue (changement d'attitude ou d'état d'esprit, déplacements, etc.). Indiquez *un costume* pour chaque personnage, et créez *une liste d'objets* pour chaque tableau.

E. Chaque groupe rédigera 1) une ébauche ("rough sketch") de l'introduction; 2) une ébauche ou quelques extraits de deux ou trois étapes au choix; 3) une ébauche de la conclusion. Pour chaque étape il faudra indiquer *un titre et sous-titre* ET *le style* dans lequel vous voudriez jouer la scène.

Exemples de « styles »:

comique, sérieux, épique, music hall/cirque, théâtre classique/tragique/Hélas!, diabolique, liturgique/cérémonial/sacré, érotique, mélodrame, jungle/animal/zoologique, végétal, sauvage/primitif, ultramoderne, précieux, à la Beckett, dessin animé, marionnette, rock/heavy metal, Las Vegas, lyrique, réalisme à l'américain, Disney, à la Woody Allen, intello, universitaire, etc., etc., etc.

V. **Personnages:**

Personnages principaux	*Personnages secondaires*	*Personnages collectifs*
(Narrateur)	Venceslas	Toute l'armée – Choeur?
Père Ubu	La Reine	Les paysans – Choeur?
Mère Ubu	Le Roi Alexis	Le Peuple – Choeur?
Bordure	Nobles, Magistrats, Financiers	Un autre?
Bougrelas	Les Palotins principaux (Giron, Cotice, Pile)	
Un autre?	Cheval à finances	
	Machine à décerveler	
	Un autre?	

Prévoyez l'emploi de marionnettes: Y a-t-il des personnages particuliers que nous pourrions faire jouer par des marionnettes? Serait-il plus efficace de remplacer ponctuellement un personnage par une marionnette?

VI. Recréation de texte: mode d'emploi
- tenir compte de l'ensemble
- déterminer les personnages essentiels de chaque séquence
- puiser des idées et des répliques dans le texte tout en essayant de trouver quelque chose d'original
- essayer de trouver des moyens naturels et fluides d'intégrer des phrases en anglais à des moments critiques
- prévoir le rôle d'un/une narrateur/trice
- trouver des moyens d'entraîner *le public* dans l'action du spectacle et de l'inciter à répéter certaines phrases-clées; transformer le public en « peuple », en soldats, en Polonais, en nobles ou en « juges »?
- prévoir l'emploi de pancartes (« En Lithuanie », « La Mère sauvegarde le trésor », par exemple. Ou bien, le narrateur peut demander au public de répéter une phrase écrite sur une pancarte)
- trouver un titre (précis, concret, évocateur) pour notre pièce et pour chacun de vos tableaux (par exemple: « La Guerre: Père Ubu en fait dans sa culotte »)
- (débuter l'histoire *in medias res*? ajouter une séquence de rêve?)
- privilégier le comique mais éviter à tout prix le cliché dans le langage et dans le geste
- privilégier la théâtralité sur le « naturalisme »
- faire attention à la longueur, la théâtralité, l'efficacité et la compréhensibilité de chaque élément (début, conclusion, transition de chaque réplique et de chaque tableau-séquence)
- déterminer l'équilibre entre narration-dialogue-image-action
- essayer de faire ressentir un rythme dans votre texte (par exemple: le malheur [rythme accéléré] et le bonheur [plus soutenu, plus développé] et le surnaturel [au ralenti])
- penser à des traits distinctifs, des tics, des habitudes, etc., pour chaque personnage
- Père Ubu: fou? enfant? bête ou pas bête? naïf? violent?; Mère Ubu: rusée? sexualisée?; Bordure: professionnel? militaire?; Bougrelas: noble?; Les Palotins: automates ou individualisés? ETC.

- réfléchir aux besoins visuels et matériels (espace, décor, corps, déplacement, *costume*, maquillage, objets) et auditifs (texte-dialogue, bruitage, silence, pause et surtout musique: chant grégorien? Pie Jésus? Carmen? Enigma?, etc.)

- - à rendre le mardi 8 fév. en *8* exemplaires
- - - *petite mise en scène*: chaque groupe jouera un extrait de son texte recréé—en intégrant une marionette
- - - - Ce n'est qu'un début d'un processus de « recréation » qui se prolongera dans nos répétitions

APPENDICES

APPENDIX F:
SAMPLE EXCERPTS AND MATERIALS
FROM REWRITTEN PLAYS

Needless to say, no version of a dramatic text is ever final; nor is it ever a complete record of the performance it proposes. At best, it is like the blueprint of a custom-built house: like the architect, the reader of the text can merely imagine the finished project, and given the re-creative freedom built into our projects, our mounting of the rewritten play will entail still further modifications great and small, extending the text's creative principle.

Originally, I considered including our complete rewritten text for "Père Ubu" in this book, but I changed my mind, and not only because of the sheer verbal "weight" this text would add. I've already made clear that the text my students and I create is only a rather preliminary version – a very rough blueprint – of the resulting performance. So the rewritten text might not provide the reader with a satisfactory impression of our final product. Furthermore, instead of providing the reader with a ready-made text to produce, I much prefer to entice readers into developing their own personal re-creative approach to a classic text. Readers should have confidence in what their own theatrical community/workshop can produce by working directly with the original text. Consequently, I expect that a good taste of my work and a careful glance at some of my recipes will suffice to demonstrate the artistic potential and critical-instructional merit of the method.

Below, I provide the first and final tableaux for the Ubu 2000 performance, re-creatively and collaboratively titled "Père Ubu: roi de nulle part!," which has been the project of reference for this book. In addition, I provide samples of our "narrative interventions" that preceded each of the tableaux, titles of the tableaux, the casting chart, and finally for the Ubu project, the names and titles the actors proposed for the acting company we had become and for the play we had designed. Following the materials from "Père Ubu," I provide the introduction and the conclusion to one other project, the Jeanne d'Arc story (1997).

Materials from both of these projects represent the more or less "final" version of the written documents for each. This will give the reader some idea of the range of creative solutions we proposed to achieve our re-creative goals of making the play accessible to a wider audience without sacrificing either the creative principle and spirit of the original text or the necessity to provide a high level of (accessible) theatrical art for the audience. In addition, I include references to photographic images of performances of these plays, which should help convey some sense of their material realization.

First Scene of "Père Ubu: roi de nulle part"

TABLEAU 1A: MERDRE! – LE CUL SUR UN TRONE (**PU, MU, OURS**)

(« *A ta place, ce cul, je voudrais l'installer sur un trône* »)

> *Noir, et puis la scène s'allume. L'Ours au fond à côté d'un lecteur de cassettes. MU, côté droit, debout et retournée vers les coulisses. PU assis, côté gauche. MU et PU, tous les deux figés. L'Ours met un air d'opéra, l'écoute. Tous les acteurs hors-scène disent « Merdre ». Puis l'Ours se ravise et hoche la tête. Il explique au public:*

L'Ours: Ah non! Ze musique iz not for ze PU ant 'iz lov-e-ly wife (*geste indiquant ses gros seins*). Zé are such « cochons »! MU, she want ze PU, who iz on-ly a capitaine de dragons, to kill ze King Venceslas and take over ze trone. But ze PU iz so 'appy to manger 'iz andouille (*PU s'anime pour dire « de l'andouille »—geste*). 'Ow do you say "sausage"? Oui, she (*geste-"gros seins"*) wants 'im to put his cul (*geste*) sur le trône (*MU s'anime pour dire: « Je voudrais installer ce cul sur un trône ».*) Do you understand? Oui? Zhen why don't we moque zem and say eet togezer? (*Il montre la pancarte, et accompagne la phrase du geste*). What does she want to do? She want to "Installer ce cul sur un trône": Un-deux-trois, dites!... Non, non, like zis (*leur montrant le geste*). Voilà! "Installer ce cul sur un trône". Now I get la bonne musique. Ah, oui. Can you say "merdre"? (*geste*). Allez! Say eet! Un-deux-trois, dites!...Voilà!

> *Il met l'air de tango et puis reste sur le côté de la table, genre maître d'hôtel. Ambience de cabaret argentin. MU s'anime et commence à danser. PU s'anime mais reste assis à mordiller sa cravate. MU*

s'approche de lui, le séduisant par toute sa beauté. Elle le relève carrément, et ils commencent à danser. Chaque fois qu'ils passent devant/ derrière la table, PU essaie de s'emparer d'un morceau de viande.

PU: Merdre! (*il s'arrête et puis repart*)
MU: Merdre? (*elle s'arrête et repart*)
PU: Bougre de merdre! (*il s'arrête et repart*)
MU: Oh voilà du joli, PU. Vous êtes un fort grand voyou!
PU: (*prenant une casserole sur la table, il s'arrête*) Que ne vous assomme-je, MU! (see fig. 9)
MU: (*calme*) Ce n'est pas moi qu'il faut tuer. C'est un autre qu'il faut a-ssa-ssi-ner (*geste*), PU. (*ils restent sur place tout en dansant*)
PU: De par ma chandelle verte, je ne comprends pas.
MU: Comment, PU, vous êtes content de votre sort?
PU: De par ma chandelle verte, merdre, et bougre de merdre, madame, certes oui, je suis content. Me voilà capitaine de dragons, officier de confiance du roi Venceslas. Que voulez-vous de mieux?
MU: Comment! Vous vous contentez de mener aux revues une cinquantaine d'estafiers armés de coupe-choux, quand vous pourriez faire mettre sur votre caboche la couronne de Pologne (*gestes*)?
PU: Ah! MU, je ne comprends rien de ce que tu dis.
MU: Tu es si bête!
PU: De par ma chandelle verte, le roi Venceslas est encore bien vivant; et même en admettant qu'il meure, n'a-t-il pas des légions d'enfants?
MU: Imbécile, qui t'empêche de massacrer toute la famille et de te mettre à leur place?
PU: Ah! MU, vous me faites injure et vous allez passer tout à l'heure par la casserole.
MU: Eh! pauvre malheureux, si je passais par la casserole, qui te raccommoderait tes fonds de culotte? (*geste: elle empoigne ses fesses*).
PU: (*regardant sa main sur ses fesses*) Mes fonds de culotte – mon cul!
MU: (*retenant ses mains sur les fesses de PU*) A ta place, ce cul, je voudrais l'installer sur un trône. Si tu étais roi, tu pourrais augmenter indéfiniment tes *phy-nances*, manger fort souvent de *l'an-douille* et rouler carrosse par les rues (*gestes*). (see fig. 10)

PU: (*il réfléchit et cède aussitôt*) Bougre de merdre, merdre de bougre, je cède à la tentation. Si jamais je le rencontre au coin d'un bois, c'est le roi qui passera à la casserole.

MU: (*elle le reprend pour danser*) Ah! bien, PU, te voilà devenu un véritable homme. (*aussitôt, PU se ravise et se dégage d'elle*)

PU: Oh non! moi, capitaine de dragons, massacrer le roi de Pologne! plutôt mourir!

MU: Oh! merdre! (*haut*) Ainsi, tu vas rester gueux comme un rat, PU?

PU: Ventrebleu, de par ma chandelle verte, j'aime mieux être gueux que mort (*il va se rasseoir sur la table*).

MU: Et les *phy-nances*? Et *l'an-douille*? (*elle se retourne vers le public—à part*) Vrout, merdre, il a été dur à la détente, mais vrout, merdre, je crois pourtant l'avoir ébranlé. Grâce à Dieu ... et à moi-même, dans huit jours je serai reine de Pologne! (see fig. 11)

Final Scene of "Père Ubu"

TABLEAU 5D: EN ROUTE! (**PU X 3, MU X 3, L'OURS [MARIONNETTE?]**)

« *Quel délice de revoir bientôt la douce France* »

Sur le pont d'un navire (en carton) [ou bien, sur l'autoroute à faire du stop?], TOUS les acteurs en PU ou en MU. Ils tanguent de droite à gauche. Tous ont le mal de mer.

PU1: Merdre! Nous filons avec une rapidité incroyable!
MU1: On va où?
PU2: En Amérique, dans l'état du Tennessee!
MU2: Non, tout le monde est dégueulasse par là!
PU3: Justement! Nous, les hommes nobles, nous pouvons chiper pas mal d'argent dans les caisses de l'état.
MU3: Mais il n'y a pas d'andouille.

(*tous les PU réagissent:* « *Oh, non!* »)

PU1: Si on retourne en France donc?

APPENDICES

Fig. 9. "Père Ubu," act 1, scene 1: "I'll clobber you, Mère Ubu!" Josh Hopkins, John Gonsoulin, Diana Devy. Wesley Foundation, University of Tennessee, Knoxville, TN. Photo by Les Essif.

Fig. 10. "Père Ubu," act 1, scene 1: "I'd like to place your butt on a throne!" John Gousoulin, Diana Devy. Wesley Foundation, University of Tennessee, Knoxville, TN. Photo by Les Essif.

Fig. 11. "Père Ubu," act 1 scene 1: Mère Ubu appeals to Pa's superior instincts. John Gousoulin, Diana Devy. Wesley Foundation, University of Tennessee, Knoxville, TN. Photo by Les Essif.

MU1: Ah! quel délice de revoir bientôt la douce France, nos vieux amis et notre château de Mondragon!
PU2: Et moi, je me ferai nommer Maître des Phynances à Paris.
PU3: Ah! messieurs! si beau qu'il soit il ne vaut pas la Pologne. S'il n'y avait pas de Pologne, il n'y aurait pas de Polonais!

(on défile dans la salle en naviguant le bâteau – musique) (see fig. 13)

FIN DE L'HISTOIRE

Sample Narrative Interventions between the Tableaux of "Père Ubu"

A narrative intervention precedes all but two of the twenty tableaux (scenes). Following the Bear's long narrative introduction at the beginning of the play, other actors, in their various character-functions, took turns playing the role of narrator, presenting a brief summary of the forthcoming scene, mostly in English but with a smattering of French vocabulary and a dose of French accent. For most of the scenes, the narrators, armed with a placard displaying a key line from the scene, rehearsed the line and its accompanying gesture with the audience. The character who was to pronounce the key line in the scene was usually located in the offstage area visible to the audience. He/she presented "in character" the line and the gesture, and the narrator directed the audience to mimic them. The following selection of seven interventions shows the variety of characters, remarks, and devices used to guide and to communicate with the audience.

T1B (Tableau 1B, meaning first act, "1," second tableau, "B")
L'Ours: Oui, la MU iz certaine zat she can be queen of Pologne//Poland. She can persuade ze PU to kill ze king parce que he want to get ze "phynances" (geste) and eet plenty of ze andouille (geste)…Now she iz angry zat he eet ze veau, how you say "veal"? He 'az eeten ze veal. 'Elp! (geste). (MU le dit, et puis:) (l'Ours montre la pancarte) « Il a mangé le veau! Au secours! »

T2A

Reine/Bougrelas/Bordure [Reine/marionnette!] (narrated by the actor playing multiple roles and using marionettes): This is the big assassination scene – and my tour de force, in which my marionettes and I play most of the parts. The queen and the king's son, Bougrelas, (both played by me!) try to warn the king not to trust PU. But the king is pretty stubborn – and maybe even stupid – so, on Ubu's signal (PU: « Merdre! »), Bordure (played by me!) kills the king. MU knows what to do (MU: « Je suis reine! »). What does she say? (Qu'est-ce qu'elle dit?) (pancarte: « Je suis reine! »). Bordure and his army pursue the former king's family: « Sus aux traîtres! » (all played by me!).

APPENDICES

T2B

Soldat: All is lost for Venceslas's family. PU, Bordure, and their men chase after Bougrelas and his mother (played by her: *geste indiquant la reine*), and they trap them in a palace chamber. Bougrelas warns that he will defend his mother to the death (*pancarte*: « Vive Dieu! Je défendrai ma mère jusqu'à la mort! » [*à répéter/geste*]). He fights Ubu and Bordure, nicking Ubu's finger. He then sends his mother ahead and gives the longest and slowest melodramatic speech of the play. His father's spirit comforts him.

T3B

Jean: Lots of brutal violence in this scene. PU (no longer played by me – hélas!) calls in the nobles, confiscates their wealth, and condemns them all to death by the *machine à décerveler* – the de-braining machine (*pancarte*: « Condamné! A la trappe! » [*paroles/gestes*]). MU is extremely upset by this royal strategy (MU: « Quelle basse férocité! » [*phrase/geste*]). After dealing with the nobles, PU "re-forms" the justice system by condemning all the magistrates as well. Then he goes from village to village collecting taxes from the villagers. Finally, he hits the poorest of the poor, the lowest of the low: « Les pauvres citoyens! ».

T3E

Diana: Meanwhile, back at the Polish palace, a message arrives for PU. Reading doesn't seem to be one of PU's strong skills, so MU reads the message and tells PU that Bordure and the Czar plan to invade his territory, reinstate Bougrelas, and finally kill PU. She tells him that his only recourse is to go to war: « Il n'y a qu'un parti à prendre, PU: LA GUERRE » [*geste*]. He readies himself, finds the right horse, and leaves MU with the warning to stay clear of the treasury, or else.

T5A

Jean: What has become of MU? And what will become of PU? Can you believe it! MU, fleeing from Bougrelas, happens upon the same cave where PU has fallen asleep: *Quelle coïncidence!* When she discovers him in the midst of a dream about his greedy wife stealing all his treasures, she has a great idea: "Why don't I pretend I'm a vision in his dream, in order to persuade PU that his wife is really a very charming person." Unfortunately, PU discovers her scheme and inflicts the usual punishment on her: (*pancarte*: « Torsion du nez, arrachement des cheveux » [*phrase/geste*]).

T5D: LA GRANDE FINALE!
Josh: Soundly defeated, the Ubus ride off into the sunset. But they must decide which "sunset" will be the most suitable for them: MU1: « Ah! quel délice de revoir bientôt la douce France » (see fig. 13).

In addition to these regular transitional strategies, at the end of Tableau 3D, where Ubu condemns the nobles and the magistrates to the "debraining machine," two actors direct the audience and the rest of the cast in the singing of the "De-braining Song" (Chanson de décervelage), written by Jarry: « *Voyez, voyez la machine tourner,/ Voyez, voyez la cervelle sauter,/ Voyez, voyez les Riches trembler, /Hourra, cornes au cul, vive le Père Ubu!* » (see fig. 14).

Descriptive Titles of the Tableaux

The reader will note that the technique of providing (and devising) descriptive titles for each of the tableaux, generally based on a key piece of text within the scene, serves not only to energize the spectators and guide their comprehension of the foreign-language text, but also to help the actors themselves situate the essential movement of each scene.

1. « Installer ce cul sur un trône ».
2. « Il a mangé le veau! Au secours! »
3. « Vous allez tuer Venceslas? »
4. « Ce n'est pas moi. C'est la MU et Bordure ».
5. « Merdre! Vive le PU! »
6. « Je suis reine! »
7. « Vive Dieu! Je défendrai ma mère jusqu'à la mort! »
8. « Je ne lâcherai pas un sou! »
9. Père Ubu distribue l'or
10. « Bordure ne sera pas Duc de Lithuanie! »
11. « Condamné! A la trappe! »
12. Bordure s'échappe
13. Le Czar dit « D'accord »

APPENDICES

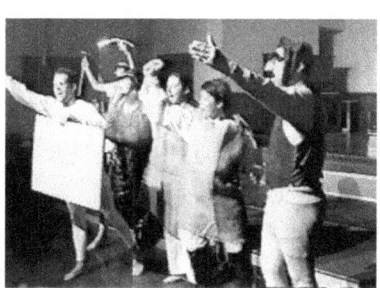

Fig. 14. "Père Ubu." Actors direct the audience in singing "The De-braining Song." John Gonsoulin, Emily Christianson, Ashlee Sanders, Diana Devy, Sarah Boucher, Josh Hopkins. Wesley Foundation, University of Tennessee, Knoxville, TN. Photo by Les Essif.

14. « Il n'y a qu'un parti à prendre, Père Ubu: LA GUERRE! »
15. Mére Ubu trouve le trésor
16. « C'est brutal sur le champ de bataille! »
17. Père Ubu est un lâche bougre
18. Une apparition surnaturelle. « Torsion du nez, arrachement des cheveux! »
19. Bougrelas chasse les Ubu: « Tiens, an-douille, fri-pouille, pas-ta-fa-zouille! »
20. En route: « Ah! quel délice de revoir bientôt la douce France! »

The Casting Chart for Ubu

UBU ROI: distribution

T$_1$A/B: *Le cul sur un trône*
PU: Jean
MU: Diana
Ours/Maître d'hôtel: Josh

T$_1$C: *Le veau!* —TOUS
PU, MU, Ours: les mêmes
Bordure: Sarah
Soldat 1: Ashlee/Marionnette (Marion)
Soldat 2: Emilie/Marion

T$_1$D: *Ce n'est pas moi!*
PU, MU, Ours: les mêmes
Messager: l'Ours/Josh

T1E: *Vive le PU!* — TOUS
PU, MU, Ours, Bordure, Soldats: les mêmes qu'au T1C

T2A: *Je suis reine!!!* — TOUS
PU, MU, Ours, Bordure: les mêmes
Venceslas: Ours/Josh
Reine/Bougrelas/ (et Bordure): Sarah/Marion
Soldat 1: Ashlee/Marion
Soldat 2: Emilie/Marion

T2B: *Vive Dieu!*
PU, Ours, Reine/Bougrelas/ Bordure: mêmes
Voix de Venceslas: Ours/Josh
Soldat 1: Ashlee
Soldat 2: Emilie

T2C: *Je ne lâcherai pas un sou!*
PU, MU, Ours, Bordure: mêmes

T2D: *Vive le PU! (les impôts)*
PU, MU, Ours, Bordure: mêmes
Peuple: Ashlee/Marion, Emilie/Marion

T3A: *Bordure ne sera pas duc!*
PU: Ashlee
MU: Emilie
Ours: Josh

T3B: *A la trappe!* — TOUS
PU, MU, Ours: mêmes
Greffier (et tambour): Ours/Josh
Nobles, Magistrats, Paysans: Sarah (Stanislas?), Jean, Diana

T3C: *Bordure s'échappe*
PU, MU, [Ours?]: mêmes
Bordure: Sarah

APPENDICES

T3D: *le Czar dit oui*
Bordure: Sarah
Czar: Ours/Josh
L'Interprète: Jean

T3E: *La guerre!* — TOUS
PU, MU, Ours: mêmes
Messager: Ours/Josh
Soldats/Palotin 1: Jean
Soldat/Palotin 2: Diana

T4A: *le trésor*
MU: Emilie
[Ours?]: Josh
Bougrelas: Sarah
Polonais/Tous: Diana/Marion

T4B: *Grande bataille* – TOUS
PU: Ashlee
Ours/Envoyé/Journaliste: Josh
Bordure/Soldat Russe: Sarah/Marion
Armée Ubu: 1) (Rensky) Jean/Marion; 2) Diana/Marion

T4C: *Lâche bougre!*
PU, Ours: mêmes
Cotice: Sarah
Pile: Jean

T5A: *Une apparition surnaturelle*
MU: Emilie
PU: Diana
[Ours?]: Josh

T5B: *Tiens, Pastafazouille!*
PU, MU: mêmes
Bougrelas: Sarah
Armée de Bougrelas: Jean, Ashlee
[Ours?]: Josh

T5C: *PU a raison*
PU, MU: les mêmes

T5D: *En route!*—TOUS
PU: Emilie, Diana, Josh
MU: Jean, Ashlee, Sarah

Rôles principaux de chaque acteur:
Josh: Ours, Venceslas, Messager, Journaliste, Envoyé, etc.
Jean: PU (1,2)
Diana: MU (1,2); PU (5)
Ashlee: PU (3,4)
Sarah: Bordure, Bougrelas/Reine
Emilie: MU (3,4,5)

NB:
1. Quelques rôles risquent de changer au cours de nos répétitions
2. Prévoyons l'emploi de marionnettes
3. L'Ours peut devenir un PORC

Proposed Names for the Theatre Company and Titles for Play

Compagnie
Compagnie de la Merdre
Troupe des Gloutons
Les Traveling Ubu (name chosen)
Compagnie de la Mangeaille
Les Mangeurs de Merdre
Compagnie de l'Andouille
Les Polonais Dansant

Titre
Vive le Père Ubu!
Vive le Père Ubu! Vive l'andouille!
Père Ubu: Roi de Nulle Part (title chosen)
Ubu Roi?
La Couronne et l'andouille
Père Ubu: il a faim
Père Ubu: le bon vivant qui voulait être roi de Pologne
Père Ubu, l'andouille et la guerre!

APPENDICES

First (Introductory) Scene of "Jeanne d'Arc: un certain je ne sais quoi!"

For the introductory scene to "Jeanne" (1997), the actors stripped down to the black body suits that represented the more or less neutral ground to which their costume pieces and props would be added as they assumed their role(s) inside the story. Together, and mostly in English, they staged a collective and performative synopsis of the story (see fig. 1). After one of the actors introduced the theme of Joan of Arc, each of the other actors took turns representing the first six of the seven stages of the young saint's life and rehearsing the audience in the key phrase that provided the title to each of these scenes/stages. The synopsis of each of the scenes included additional key phrases in French that were acted out (given a pre-performance rendering) by the same actors who would be playing the roles in the comprehensive performance of the scene that would follow the introduction. As usual, for the final version of the performance, some of this text and the accompanying stage directions were modified or cut. (See chapter 2, "Introducing the 'Systems' of Style, Costume, Prop, and Music, and the Styles of Jeanne d'Arc," and figs. 1–8 for related photo illustrations.)

Jeanne: L'Intro
    [Tous prononcent les phrases-clées – Jeu très accéléré]

1. Tous les acteurs "déshabillés"sont autour de Jeanne-absente sur le bûcher [musique de Ph Glass]
2. Pancarte: « *Brûlez l'hérétique!* »
3. Tous appliqueront un accent français en parlant anglais, sauf Tim.
4. *Tim.* Burn the heretic? Why would you want to do that to poor little Jeanne d'Arc? ... Just because she played soldier and enjoyed wearing pants? ... You know the story, do you? Do you know it well enough to help us play it out? We're a little short on personnel, especially the hordes of those Froggie common people who are very important to her story. Ah come on now, you'll make a great bunch of commoner/peasant/rustic/provincial Froggies. Yes you willllll. We'll give you a quick refresher course and then you'll feel better about it. Take a look at your program. Turn to the back page and you'll see the synopsis. Then, below that, you'll see the tableaux that represent the stages of Jeanne's life.

5. First you have TABLEAU 1 AT DOMRÉMY. Note the title of the tableau: (*tous les acteurs le prononce avec le public*) « Une fille, ça tisse, ça lave et ça reste à la maison! »

A very pious girl, Jeanne hears voices from heaven:

« *Je serai bonne et sage enfant et j'irai souvent à l'église, Monseigneur. Promis!* »

But then the voices ask poor little innocent Jeannette to save France by leading the king's army against the British and having the king crowned at Reims.

« *Pitié! Pitié, Messire! Je ne suis qu'une pauvre petite fille, je suis heureuse.* »

Consequently, there is trouble with her father, who is sure that all she wants is to "run with the soldiers." ... Ohh! The father, that's me!

« *Petite salope! [gifle] – Je n'ai rien fait de mal, mon père* »

And, in the end, her mother is really no help either:

« *Une fille ça tisse, ça lave et ça reste à la maison.* »

6. *Lourdes*: Now we move to TABLEAU 2 AT VAUCOULEURS. The title is (All – too – ge-zer!): « *Un certain je ne sais quoi* ».

Directed by her voices, Jeanne leaves home and goes to visit the principal lord of the region, Capitaine Beaudricourt. She needs horses and an escort (aside: and men's clothing) so she can make the trip to see the king. At first, Beaudricourt is willing to strike a deal ... for a, let's say, "price":

« *Oui, d'accord, mais ça va te coûter très cher!* » (*with lust in his eyes*)

But when she tells him of her divine mission, his "spirit" (*entre guillemets*) is, as we French might say, "dégonflée" (*l'indexe qui s'affaisse*).

« *Mille millions de tonnerres, je ne te fais donc pas peur?* »

But Jeannette is guided by her heavenly voices. Beaudricourt is putty in her hands.

« *Vous ne me ferez pas de mal, Messire?* »

7. *Pat.* Next up: TABLEAU 3, CHINON, CHEZ LE DAUPHIN. The title: (*la main portée à l'oreille*): « *Un coup de Pucelle* ». Charles, who is a bit insecure, spends his time making big decisions like whether he can afford new hats for his mistress and his queen. Ah, là là. A propos ... We need two volunteers to play this role. Would you mind? Come on, you get to wear a great hat. Allez, allez! (*On choisit deux membres du public pour jouer vite fait les rôles des reines*).

« *Un nouveau chapeau! ... un nouveau chapeau! ... un nouveau chapeau!...* »

(*les "reines" sont réinstallées dans la salle et on leur dit:*) ... « *Merci bien! A tout à l'heure* »

APPENDICES

Stéphanie. When news of the Pucelle's mission reaches court, two of the Dauphin's corrupt counselors, the Archbishop and La Trémouille, take action. They do not want Charles to rally the French peuple by allowing an audience with this girl.

« *Une fille de paysan chez le roi! ... —J'aime pas ça!* »

Pat. But Charles's mother-in-law, la reine Yolande, who, unlike the others, is not on the British payroll, thinks otherwise:

« *Déjà dans le peuple, on ne parle plus que d'elle ... Cette fille a quelque chose d'extraordinaire – un certain ... je ne sais quoi!* »

Stéphanie. Charles tries to trick Jeanne by placing Gilles, a page, on his throne. But Jeanne is not fooled. You might say she has "divine" taste. (*jeu muet*)

Pat. It does not take long for Jeanne to convince Charles of her certain « *je ne sais quoi* ».

« *Je donne le commandement de mon armée royale à la Pucelle ici présente* »

« *Vive la Pucelle et vive la France!* »

7. *Elisabeth.* TABLEAU 4: ORLEANS: title « *La Guerre, le Paradis et l'oignon* ». Jeanne goes right to work. In battle, a kind of lust for "camaraderie in conquest" is born within her.

« *A cheval maintenant, mon gars. A cheval!* » ... (*Ils enfourchent des chevaux imaginaires ... elle respire à fond*) ... « *C'est la guerre ... botte à botte avec un co-pain* »

10. *Flo.* TABLEAU 5: REIMS – LE SACRE (THE CORONATION): « *Vive le roi! Vive la Pucelle! Vive la Guerre!* »

Thanks to Jeanne, the Dauphin is finally crowned at Reims. But Jeanne wants more for France. Some believe that she has allowed God to go to her head.

« *Je réponds d'eux tous! Quand on essaie de me brûler, ils viendront me délivrer tous* »

She is soon caught by the English and turned over to the Church to be tried as a heretic.

11. *Bijou.* TABLEAU 6: ROUEN/PROCES (THE TRIAL): « *Une culotte à une fille?* »

Though he collaborates with the English, Bishop Cauchon seems to want to save Jeanne's soul:

« *Ton roi t'abandonne, Jeanne! Pourquoi t'obstiner à le défendre?* »

The Inquisitor, on the other hand, was quite hateful:

« *Plus notre ennemi est petit et fragile, plus il est abominable.* »

Warwick, the English officer, and our narrator for this tableau, pulled the strings for the Church trial:

« *Go with Cauchon, Jeanne* »

But all the men of the Church were particularly upset with Jeanne's reluctance to wear a dress:

« *C'est le diable ... c'est le diable ... c'est le diable!* »

Jeanne abjures, then retracts; she's excommunicated from the Church and turned over to the British for burning. And this is where we were at the beginning ... Ze End. « *A mort la sorcière! ... Brûlez l'hérétique! ... A mort! à mort! à mort!* »

So much for the previews. « *Que le spectacle commence!* » (*la musique commence et les acteurs de la première scène se précipitent sur leur place*)

Jeanne d'Arc: Tableau 7, the Conclusion

This scene is one of the most complex, coherent, and powerful I have (collaboratively) re-created and directed. With very little text and with precisely articulated action, gestures, and images, it neatly and uniquely synthesizes the contradictory forces at work in the play.

JEANNE, TABLEAU 7, VERSION 2

Dieu/Bûcher

Personnages: Jeanne (toute petite), Mère, Inquisiteur/Gilles, Soldat anglais/Père/Beaudricourt, Promoteur/Charles/Yolande/(La Hire), Warwick/Archevêque/La Hire, Cauchon/Frère, Trémouille/Boudousse/Ladvenu, La Foule et Le Peuple-Public (notre public).

> *Tout cela est rapide et brutal, comme un assassinat/opération de police. Toute la foule saute sur elle et du chaos il en sort une toute petite Jeannette du peuple-public. Jeanne n'arrive pas à avoir son pantalon qu'elle a réclamé à la fin de Tableau 6. On la tient devant le peuple-public. Les CRS/flics font reculer la foule:* « *Reculez! ... Circulez! ... Dégagez!* »

APPENDICES

Musique de Philippe Glass? Lumière clignotante/stroboscopique.

Tous les acteurs « déshabillés » (sans costumes), sauf Jeanne et sa mère.

Jeanne: Laissez-moi! ... Sales rosbifs! ... Laissez-moi ... Maman! Papa! *(On incite le peuple-public. Pancartes: « A mort la sorcière! ... Brûlez l'hérétique! ... A mort! à mort! à mort! ». Et puis, on élève Jeanne sur le bûcher en forme de « croix »).*
Ladvenu: Courage, Jeanne. Nous prions tous pour toi!
Jeanne: Une croix! Une croix par pitié!
Promoteur: Pas de croix pour une sorcière!
Inquisiteur: Qu'elle se taise, vite!
La Foule: Vite! Vite! Vite!
Jeanne: Une croix par pitié!
Inquisiteur: Allez, mets le feu, toi, vite! Que la fumée l'entoure, qu'on ne la voie plus! ... Il faut faire vite!
La Foule: Vite! Vite! Vite!
 (Tout ceci est rapide, bousculé, improvisé, honteux, comme une opération de police.)
Jeanne: Une croix par pitié!
Soldat anglais: *(Il se dégage doucement de la foule et lui tend une croix. Plutôt sérieux qu'angoissé)* They're burning a saint.
Inquisiteur: *(situé dans la salle, debout et les bras croisés, n'osant pas regarder Jeanne, il parle aux spectateurs)* Elle regarde droit devant elle? ... *(Jeanne sourit)* et il y a presqu'un sourire? ... Je ne le vaincrai jamais!
La Foule: Mon Dieu, pardonnez-nous!
Jeanne: Mon Dieu, pardonnez-leur tous. Ils ont brûlé une sainte!
Mère: *(s'étant tenu un peu à l'écart de la foule pendant toute l'action précédante, elle avance lentement vers le bûcher et glisse le bâton de Jeanne sous ses bras croisés. Puis, elle s'approche de l'Inquisiteur et dit:)* Ca reste à la maison. *(musique)*

– NOIR –

APPENDIX G:
SAMPLE PROMOTIONAL MATERIALS AND METHODS

Sample Promotional Letter to Potential Spectators

28 February 2000

Dear Students and Teachers of French, Francophones, Francophiles, and Theatrophiles:

Ça y est! The theatre company LES TRAVELLING UBU, of the UTK Department of Modern Foreign Languages, will be performing *Père Ubu: Roi de nulle part* at the *Wesley Center* (on campus, near the International House and Hodges Library, at 1718 Melrose Pl.) at the following times: *Wednesday, April 12 at 4:30 p.m., Thursday, April 13 at 8:00 p.m., and Friday, April 24 at 4:30 p.m.* Running time is approximately one hour.

This year, we will again have the pleasure of performing the play "on the road" at Powell High School (Wednesday, April 19), at Austin-East High School (Tuesday, April 25), and at Cleveland State Community College (Thursday, April 27). Students from other area high schools and middle schools will travel to Powell and Austin-East to see the show. Thank you Saralee Peccolo-Taylor, Korey Dugger, Diane Changas, and Catherine Smith for your interest and your organizational efforts.

Our play is based on Alfred Jarry's *Ubu Roi*, a late-nineteenth-century "absurdist" type play. It's the story of the gluttonous, greedy, ignorant, deceitful Père Ubu, who, coaxed by his "charming" wife (Mère Ubu!), slaughters the royal family and takes over the throne of Poland ("Nulle Part"). He immediately massacres the Polish hierarchy and squeezes his subjects for every *rixdale* they've got. But then, on fait la GUERRE, and the legitimate successor to the throne, Bougrelas, defeats the Ubu couple, who flee toward another "nulle part" (France).

Our *re-created* version of this play will be presented primarily in French, with some English narration. As always, our goal is to find the best combination of image, action, narration, dialogue, sound, and audience participation to tell our story to French and theatre aficionados at

APPENDICES

all levels of competence in French. The actors will "rehearse" the audience in the performance of chants and songs in French.

General admission tickets are *$3.00 each*. We regret that this year we are unable to offer advance ticket sales. Tickets will be available at the door, but we encourage you to arrive early to assure a seat.

We are looking forward to your participation in this event. Please spread the word.

INFORMATION: [Name], tel: [...]; e-mail: [...]

Theatrically yours,
Les Essif et Les Travelling Ubu

Sample Press Release

PRESS RELEASE

Please announce the following theatrical performance:

The theatrical company *Les Travelling Ubu* (of UTK Dept. of Modern Foreign Languages and Literatures) will perform a freely adapted version of the late-nineteenth-century play by Alfred Jarry, *Ubu Roi*. The title of our version of the play is *Père Ubu: Roi de nulle part*. It will be presented in French, with English narration.

Performances will be at the *Wesley Center* (UTK campus, 1718 Melrose Pl.) at the following times:

Wednesday, April 12 at 4:30 p.m.; Thursday, April 13 at 8:00 p.m., and Friday, April 14 at 4:30 p.m.

Information: [my name and contact information here]

Instructions and Suggestions for Activist Promotion

UBU: LA PUBLICITE: extraits du spectacle joués devant un public préliminaire
(Du jeudi 6 avril jusqu'au mardi 11 avril)
Costume: un chapeau (et peut-être un autre élément) et un objet

1. Frappez à la porte de la salle de classe et, avant d'y entrer, énoncez le titre de la pièce d'une façon stylisée.
2. Entrez (comme il faut, *dans votre rôle*) et assumez vos places "en scène." NB: Faites très attention à la façon dont vous vous placez dans la salle. Restez dans votre rôle et n'en sortez pas!
3. Un acteur fait le narrateur (à l'impro) et explique très vite en français ou franglais l'action qui va se passer.
4. Jouez votre "clip" (2–3 répliques, 30 secondes au max). Au besoin vous pouvez varier ou modifier les répliques du texte.
5. On affiche le poster en annonçant de nouveau le titre de la pièce.
6. Sortez en file indienne *tout en restant dans votre rôle*.

NB:
- Chaque acteur doit *s'inscrire* pour au moins 8–10 interventions!
- Nous répéterons ces "clips" mercredi et jeudi prochain.
- Pour mieux profiter de votre temps, arrangez-vous pour visiter la fin d'un cours et le début d'un autre

Possibilités de "clips":

(Notez bien qu'il pourrait être nécessaire de modifier légèrement le texte pour qu'il soit compréhensible en fonction de la situation)

A. Diane, Jean, Josh. T1A: « Ah! MU, vous me faites injure…Eh! pauvre malheureux…A ta place, ce cul…sur un trône » (L'Ours singeant les actions – et quelques paroles – des autres)
B. Mêmes. T1B: « Tiens, j'ai faim. Je vais mordre dans…[et puis, on modifie la réplique de MU, accompagnée de l'Ours]: « Ahh, le veau, le veau…au secours »
C. Sarah, Josh, (Diane): T1C: « Capitaine Bordure, je suis décidé de vous faire… Vous allez tuer Venceslas?…Il a deviné…Pourquoi pas? »
D. Jean, Josh, Sarah: T1E: « Oh, là. Attendez un peu…Oui, nous le jurons, Vive le PU! »
E. Jean, Diana, Josh, Sarah: T2A: « Vas-y tue le roi…J'ai faim! »
F. Jean, Sarah, (marionette?): T2B: « Oh! ce PU! le coquin…laissez-moi m'en aller »
G. Sarah, Josh: T2B: « Et par qui grand Dieu…nous aurons notre vengeance »

APPENDICES   233

H. Jean, Diane, (Sarah?) (Josh?): T2C: « Non, je ne veux rien distribuer…je ne lâcherai pas un sou ».
I. Jean, Diane, (Josh, Emilie, Ashlee?): T2D: « Tenez, voilà pour vous [coupez "Ca ne m'amusait guère..c'est la MU qui a voulu"])…Oui, vive le PU »
J. Ashlee, Emilie: T3A: « Tu as grand tort, PU…te mettre en morceau »
K. Ashlee, Josh, (Emilie?), (et un noble), et les étudiants-spectateurs de la classe: T3B: « Amenez le premier noble…Quelle basse férocité! »
L. Ashlee, Emilie, Sarah: T3C: [Bordure s'échappe]
M. Josh, Jean, Sarah: T3D: [Le Czar dit d'accord]
N. Ashlee, Emilie, Josh: T3E: « Donne-moi ma cuirasse…Tue bien le Czar »
O. Emilie, Sarah, (Diana?Jean?): T4A: « Où est donc ce trésor? [on coupe, jusqu'à] Voilà! voilà l'or…Vive Bougrelas! »
P. Josh, Ashlee, Jean, (Diana?): T4B: « Il y a la guerre entre…Vive le PU, notre grand maître »
Q. Sarah, Josh: T4B: « Oh, que la guerre est brutale…On massacre tout le monde ».
R. Diana, Emilie: T5A: « Ah! C'est trop fort…Ca te va-t-il, andouille? »
S. Sarah, Diana, Emilie: T5B: « En avant, mes amis!…dans ma culotte »

"The Traffic Accident" *(L'accident de route)*

The following exercise, "The Traffic Accident," is a dramatic game that also functions as a promotional exercise in the form of an improvisational theatrical intervention, one that I used for the actors involved in two of my early re-created projects. While it goes a long way toward training the actors in the art of improvisation (in the foreign language) with an audience, and it provides the "audience" with a more active role in the action of the performance, it has two clear disadvantages as a promotional activity: it is unrelated to the story of the play that the actors will perform, and because of the considerable amount of time it requires to perform, it reaches a limited pool of potential spectators.

My actors spent about ninety minutes of class time planning a theatrical scene, a hypothetical accident involving a vehicle and a pedestrian, to stage for the unsuspecting students of another French class. I divided the actors into groups of three or four actors each, and I instructed each group to develop the scenario of an accident involving some or all of the following characters: driver(s), victim(s), witness(es), police officer(s), ambulance attendant(s). Each actor in the group would assume one of these roles with the understanding that the group would assign, on an ad hoc basis, at least two of the roles to one or more of the students in the host class. Each actor develops an inventory of possible actions and utterances for each character. My actors had three minutes in which to play out the action. Only the instructors of the host classes would have advance notice of our visit. The major objectives of this exercise for my actors were to convey as concretely as possible the idea of the action they were performing and to involve the students of the host class in some way in the action itself. This assignment served as my actors' first confrontation with an audience under circumstances that would compel them to work closely with the "audience" and to be highly cognizant of the reception of their actions. They also had to be creative enough to develop a flexible relation to the French verbal text instead of being enslaved by it. It was definitely an exercise in which they could detach themselves from language as simply language— that is, as a conventional communication tool. While they were not entirely unconscious of their French text, with rehearsals of the exercise they became able to improvise more creatively in French. Because of the versatility of this exercise and its independence from the central theatrical project, I've used it as an improvisational activity in other intermediate language classes.

APPENDIX H:
AUDIENCE SURVEY

To economize space, I have removed the empty lines between the questions for responses.

In the Macbett project (1998), the survey also included a separate question about our use of marionettes: "What did you think about the use of the marionettes? Were the marionette-characters easy to identify? Do you feel they were an artistically effective addition to the play?"

Questionnaire

AUDIENCE FEEDBACK: *PERE UBU: ROI DE NULLE PART*

Your responses to the following questions will help us plan future productions. Please make any comments you can and deposit in the box provided in the theatre, or mail to: [director's name and address].

1) Did you understand the play? Did the performance enable you to easily follow our Ubu story? Or were some of the characters and some parts of the action difficult to figure out? What about the marionettes?
2) To what extent did you feel engaged in the play? Were you comfortable with the narrators and their requests to repeat phrases and sing along? Did the use of English commentary help you to follow the action and understand the French, or do you feel it might have hindered in some way your appreciation of the performance? Did you find it useful to have the plot summary and French phrases listed in the program?
4) How did you hear about the play (mailing list, word of mouth, poster, news release, language teacher, class visit by actors)?
5) Overall, did you enjoy the play? Did you find it amusing, creative, well-acted, or thought-provoking? Why or why not? What improvements would you suggest?

APPENDIX I:
INSTRUCTIONS FOR FINAL UNDERGRADUATE AND GRADUATE WRITTEN ASSIGNMENTS

Final Written Assignment for Undergraduates

Révisez vos notes (surtout dans votre journal), les textes et les documents distribués dans le cours. Regardez aussi la vidéo de notre spectacle. Et puis:

1. 4–5 pages: Ecrivez d'un point de vue critique, analytique et précis (exemples spécifiques) sur l'évolution de notre projet: du premier germe du spectacle (en passant par le stade des répétitions) au spectacle joué devant un public. Surprises? Doutes? Prises de conscience, découvertes ou révélations sur le sens et sur la portée de votre jeu, de votre contribution personnelle ainsi que le sens et la portée du projet global?
2. 3–4 pages, un sujet au choix:
A) Faites une petite analyse « sémiotique » (voir le questionnaire distribué pour l'analyse du *Bacchae*) de *l'un* des "systèmes signifiants" de notre spectacle: les objets ou les costumes et leur emploi? L'aménagement et l'emploi de l'espace? Le déplacement et le groupement des personnages? L'interprétation des acteurs? Le son, la voix, la musique?

OU:

B) Si vous préférez, vous pouvez également essayer d'analyser les méthodes sémiotiques que nous avons employées pour élaborer un certain thème (l'amour, l'hypocrisie, le non-sens de la vie, etc.).

A votre avis, quels sont les choix (de costume, d'objet, de jeu d'acteur, etc) que nous avons faits? Quels sont les effets de ces choix sur la réception du spectateur? Vous pouvez, bien sûr, parler de ce que vous croyez être un mauvais choix: comment est-ce que nous aurions pu mieux (et d'une façon plus cohérente) communiquer une certaine idée, sentiment ou sens des « histoires » que nous avons racontés?

APPENDICES

Final Written Research Assignment for Graduate Students

1. 10–12 pages.
2. Consultez les bibliographies et lisez les textes indiqués dans la bibliographie (une marque=importante; double marque=obligatoire). Et puis, faites vos propres recherches sur le sujet qui vous intéresse particulièrement.
3. Relisez les textes dramatiques d'un point de vue de metteur en scène, c'est-à-dire en pensant toujours à la mise en scène du texte au rapport entre texte et mise en scène.
4. Pensez surtout au rapport entre le personnage et l'espace dans les textes. Pensez aussi à l'idée du couple et les rapports de force entre les deux (ou les trois) individus.
5. Vous pouvez également essayer d'analyser les méthodes sémiotiques dont le dramaturge et/ou le metteur en scène se servent pour élaborer un certain thème (l'amour, l'hypocrisie, le non-sens de la vie, etc.).
6. Enfin, une fois que vous aurez déterminé la "construction" d'un certain phénomène textuel, il faudrait expliquer/analyser la façon dont ce phénomène se traduit théâtralement sur la scène dans notre spectacle final ou bien la façon dont ce phénomène aurait pu se traduire. Vous jouerez donc le rôle du « dramaturg » (voir « dramaturge »/« dramaturgie » dans le *Dictionnaire*) post-mise-en-scène de notre spectacle. L'idéal serait que votre travail contribue à la créativité de notre spectacle.
7. Vous pouvez continuer à mettre à l'essai quelques-unes de vos idées dans votre journal.

Works Cited

Abirached, Robert. "Une abstraction qui marche." *La crise du personnage dans le théâtre moderne*. Paris: Gallimard, 1994. 187-195.

———. *La crise du personnage dans le théâtre moderne*. Paris: Gallimard, 1994.

Artaud, Antonin. "La Recherche de la fécalité." *Oeuvres complètes*. Vol. 13. Paris: Gallimard, 1974. 81–87.

———. *The Theater and Its Double*. Trans. Mary Caroline Richards. New York: Grove Press, 1958.

Bakhtin, Mikhail. *Rabelais and His World*. Trans. Helene Iswolsky. Cambridge: MIT Press, 1965.

Barson, John. *La Grammaire à l'oeuvre*. 5th ed. New York: Harcourt Brace, 1996.

Barthes, Roland. "Le Théâtre de Baudelaire." *Essais critiques*. Paris: Seuil, 1964. 41–48.

Beckett, Samuel. *Endgame*. New York: Grove Weidenfeld, 1958.

Béhar, Henri. *Jarry Dramaturge*. Paris: Nizet, 1980.

Boal, Augusto. *Games for Actors and Non-actors*. 2nd ed. Trans. Adrian Jackson. London: Routledge, 2002.

———. *Jeux pour acteurs et non-acteurs*. Trans. Réine Mellac. Paris: La Découverte, 1991.

———. *The Rainbow of Desire: The Boal Method of Theatre and Therapy*. Trans. Adrian Jackson. London: Routledge, 1995.

———. *Theater of the Oppressed*. Trans. Charles A. and Maria-Odilia Leal McBride. New York: Urizen Books, 1979.

Brecht, Bertolt. *Brecht on Theatre: The Development of an Aesthetic*. Trans. John Willett. New York: Hill and Wang, 1964.

Bryant-Bertail, Sarah. *Space and Time in Epic Theater: The Brechtian Legacy*. New York: Camden House, 2000.

Chevaly, Maurice. *Petit précis d'expression corporelle d'art dramatique et de théâtre pour tous*. Marseille, France: Editions Autres Temps, 1998.

Clurman, Harold. *On Directing*. New York: Fireside, 1997.

Cohen, Robert. *Creative Play Direction*. 2nd ed. Englewood Cliffs, NJ: Prentice-Hall, 1984.

Cole, David. *The Theatrical Event: A Mythos, a Vocabulary, a Perspective*. Middletown, CN: Wesleyan UP, 1975.

Corvin, Michel. "Pour une analyse de la représentation." *Molière et ses metteurs en scène d'aujourd'hui*. Lyon, France: Presses Universitaires de Lyon, 1985. 9–30.

Dagnino, Nicole, and Nicole Zucca. *Exemples de lieux scéniques*. Paris: CNDP, 1985.

Davis, Ken. *Rehearsing the Audience: Ways to Develop Student Perceptions of Theatre*. Urbana, IL: ERIC, 1988.

Diva. Dir. Jean-Jacques Beineix. France, 1981.

Dort, Bernard. *La Représentation émanicipée*. Arles, France: Actes Sud, 1988.

Doubrovsky, Serge. *The New Criticism in France*. Chicago: U of Chicago P, 1973.

Eco, Umberto. "Interpreting Drama." *The Limits of Interpretation*. Bloomington, IN: Indiana UP, 1990. 101–10.

Edwards, Jango. "Clown and Mime Workshop." Périgueux, France, August 4–6, 1996.

Elam, Keir. *The Semiotics of Theatre and Drama*. London: Methuen, 1980.

Essif, Les. *Empty Figure on an Empty Stage: The Theatre of Samuel Beckett and His Generation*. Indiana UP, 2001.

———. "(Re-)Creating the Critique: In(tro)ducing the Semiotics of Theatre in the Foreign-Language Performance Project." *Theatre Topics* 12.2 (September 2002): 119–42.

———. "Teaching Literary-Dramatic Texts as Culture-in-Process in the Foreign-Language Theater Practicum: The Strategy of Combining Texts." *ADFL Bulletin* 29.3 (Spring 1998): 24–33.

———. "Way Off Broadway and Way Out of the Classroom: American Students De-, Re-, and Per-forming the French Dramatic Text." *ADFL Bulletin* 27.1 (Fall 1995): 32–37.

———. "A Workshop on the *Re-Creative* Approach to Performing and Teaching Theater: The Example of Jarry's *King Ubu*." *The Theater of Teaching and the Lessons of Theater*. Ed. Domnica Radulescu and Maria Stadter Fox. New York: Lexington Books, 2005. 15-26.

Esslin, Martin. *Theatre of the Absurd*. New York: Anchor Books, 1969.

Feldhendler, Daniel. "Expression dramaturgique: 'Quand le prof' de langue devient animateur en expression et en communication!" *Le Français dans le monde* 176 (April 1983): 45–52.

Ferran, Peter W. "New Measures for Brecht in America." *Theater* 25.2 (1994): 11–28.

Fischer-Lichte, Erika. *The Semiotics of Theater*. Trans. Jeremy Gaines and Doris L. Jones. Bloomington, IN: Indiana UP, 1992.

Frye, Northrop. "Literary and Linguistic Scholarship in a Post-literate World." *PMLA* 99 (1984): 990–95.

Garner, Stanton B., Jr. *Bodied Spaces: Phenomenology and Performance in Contemporary Drama*. Ithaca, NY: Cornell UP, 1994.

Genette, Gérard. *Palimpsestes: La littérature au second degré*. Paris: Seuil, 1982.

Gronbeck-Tedesco, John. *Acting through Exercises*. Mountain View, CA: Mayfield Publishing, 1992.

WORKS CITED

Haggstrom, Margaret A. "A Performative Approach to the Study of Theater: Bridging the Gap between Language and Literature Courses." *The French Review* 66.1 (1992): 7–19.

Hahlo, Richard, and Peter Reynolds. *Dramatic Events: How to Run a Successful Workshop for Theater, Education or Business.* New York: Palgrave MacMillan, 2000.

Hodge, Francis. *Play Directing: Analysis, Communication, and Style.* Boston: Allyn Bacon, 2000.

Ionesco, Eugène. *Macbett.* Paris: Gallimard (Folio), 1972.

Issacharoff, Michael. "Répétition et création." *Théâtre et création.* Ed. Emmanuel Jacquart. Paris: Honoré Champion, 1994. 47-58.

Jarry, Alfred. *Tout Ubu.* Paris: Librairie Générale Française, 1985.

Jones, Louisa E. *Sad Clowns and Pale Pierrots: Literature and the Popular Comic Arts in 19th-Century France.* Lexington, KY: French Forum Publishers, 1984.

Kattwinkel, Susan, ed. *Audience Participation: Essays on Inclusion in Performance.* Westport, CT: Praeger, 2003.

Kleiger-Stillman, Linda. *La Théâtralité dans l'oeuvre d'Alfred Jarry.* York, SC: French Literature Publications, 1980.

Kramsch, Claire. "Literary Texts in the Classroom: A Discourse." *Modern Language Journal* 69 (1985): 356–65.

———. *Context and Culture in Language Teaching.* Oxford: Oxford UP, 1993.

Le Bal. Dir. Ettore Scola. France/Italy/Algeria (La Troupe du Théâtre du Campagnol), 1982.

Le Retour de Martin Guerre. Dir. Daniel Vigne. France (Dussault), 1982.

Les Visiteurs. Dir. Jean-Marie Poire. France, 1993.

Lyons, Charles. "Character and Theatrical Space." *The Theatrical Space.* Ed. James Redmond. Cambridge: Cambridge UP, 1987. 27–44.

Mésavage. Ruth Matilde. *En cours de route.* 2nd ed. Boston: Heinle, 1992.

Monod, Richard, and Jean-Pierre Ryngaert. "Workshop on Dramatic Games and Pedagogy." Institut d'Etudes Théâtrales, Université de Paris III. Paris, France. October 1985–June 1986.

Pavis, Patrice. "Acting." Encyclopedia of Languages and Linguistics. Edinburgh: Pergamon Press, 1993. 16–21.

———. *L'Analyse des spectacles.* Paris: Nathan, 1996.

———. *Dictionnaire du théâtre.* Paris: Dunod, 1996.

———. "Du texte à la scène: un enfantement difficile." *Théâtre/Public* 79 (1988): 27–35.

———. *Languages of the Stage: Essays in the Semiology of the Theatre.* New York: Performing Arts Journal Publications, 1982.

———. *Theatre Dictionary.* Toronto: U of Toronto P, 1996.

———. *Voix et images de la scène: pour une sémiologie de la réception.* Lille, France: Presses Universitaires de Lille, 1985.

Pezin, Patrick. *Le livre des exercices à l'usage des acteurs.* Saussan, France: L'Entretemps, 1999.

Pierra, Gisèle. *Une esthétique théâtrale en langue étrangère.* Paris: L'Harmattan, 2001.

Pruner, Michel. *L'Analyse du texte de théâtre.* Paris: Dunod, 1998.

Rodgers, James W., and Wanda C. Rodgers. *Play Director's Survival Kit: A Complete Step-by-Step Guide to Producing Theater in Any School or Community Setting.* San Francisco: Jossey-Bass, 2002.

Ryngaert, Jean-Pierre. *Introduction à l'analyse du théâtre.* Paris: Dunod, 1993.

———. *Le jeu dramatique en milieu scolaire.* Bruxelles: De Boeck, 1991.

———. *Lire le théâtre contemporain.* Paris: Bordas, 1991.

Salaün-Gorrell, Isabelle. *Tête-à-tête.* Boston: Heinle, 1992.

Schechner, Richard. *The End of Humanism: Writings on Performance.* New York: Performing Arts Journal Publications, 1982.

Smith, Stephen M. *The Theatre Arts and the Teaching of Second Languages.* Reading, MA: Addison, 1984.

Spolin, Viola. *Theater Games for Rehearsal.* Evanston, IL: Northwestern UP, 1985.

States, Bert O. *Great Reckonings in Little Rooms: On the Phenomenology of Theatre.* Berkeley: U of California P, 1985.

———. "Performance as Metaphor." *Theatre Journal* 48.1 (March 1996): 1–26.

Steele, Ross, Susan St. Onge, and Ronald St. Onge. *La civilisation française en évolution I: Institutions et culture avant la Ve République.* Boston: Heinle and Heinle, 1996.

———. *La civilisation française en évolution II: Institutions et culture de la Ve République.* Boston: Heinle and Heinle, 1997.

Swaffar, Janet K. "Curricular Issues and Language Research: The Shifting Interaction." *ADFL Bulletin* 20.3 (1989): 54–60.

Turner, Victor. *From Ritual to Theatre: The Human Seriousness of Play.* New York: PAJ Publications, 1982.

Ubersfeld, Anne. *L'Ecole du spectateur.* Paris: Editions Sociales, 1981.

———. *Lire le théâtre 1.* Paris: Editions Sociales, 1982.

———. *Reading Theatre.* Trans. Frank Collins. Toronto: U of Toronto P, 1999.

Valette, Jean-Paul, and Rebecca Valette. *A votre tour!* Lexington: Heath, 1995.

Wasiolek, Edward. Introduction. *The New Criticism in France.* By Serge Doubrovsky. Chicago: U of Chicago P, 1973. 1–34.

Waterson, Karolyn. "Every Classroom's a Stage: Theatrical Contributions to Language and Literature Teaching." Dalhousie University, Department of French. Nova Scotia, NB, Canada, 1989.

Worthen, W. B. "Disciplines of the Text/Sites of Performance." *The Drama Review* 39.1 (Spring 1995): 13–28.

Notes

1 Bert O. States speaks of theatre as "presentation" and "transformation" (a term States borrows from Richard Schechner) in the following manner: "In theatrical presentation something is always transformed; it is simultaneously 'not itself' and 'not not itself'.... As audience, we go to theatre to witness a transformation of the things of reality (or fantasy) and presumably the actor performs in order to undergo a transformation, or to become twice-*not*ted self" ("Performance as Metaphor" 21).

2 Of the slew of books written in the 1980s, the one that comes closest to foreign-language play production is Stephen Smith's *The Theatre Arts and the Teaching of Second Languages*. Despite the book's title, however, it is based on the case of an English-as-a-second-language production. So the language issues it covers do not broach the overarching problem of getting student-actors to perform for a large number of anglophone spectators with weak comprehension skills in the foreign-language play. Though the text is quite useful for its theories and practical exercises, it offers a rather traditional approach to the process of production, borrowing mostly from manuals on theatre production for theatre faculty and other professional practitioners. Good manuals for English-language play production include Harold Clurman's *On Directing*, James W. Rodgers and Wanda C. Rodgers's *Play Director's Survival Kit*, Robert Cohen's *Creative Play Direction*, and Francis Hodge's *Play Directing*.

3 See, for example, Karolyn Waterson's account of "theatrical contributions to language and literature teaching." She uses the term "word professionals" for teachers of language and literature, and extends its use to directors and actors as well (1–2).

4 Another way of putting the argument is that students should feel they are *producing* a "text" rather than *interpreting* a "work." In an article addressing the much debated definition of "text," the "textuality of performance"(14), and the distinctions between the (written) dramatic text and the theatrical production of that text, W. B. Worthen revisits the *work versus text* dichotomy advanced by Roland Barthes. Worthen finds that Barthes's "sense of text is self-consciously performative" (15) because, while the *work* is "the vehicle for authorized cultural reproduction, a 'signified' approached through interpretation," the *text* is the "field of production rather than interpretation," and, as Barthes described it, the field of the signifier (15).

5 See, for example, Mésavage. At the end of each theme-based chapter there is a section titled "Mini-théâtre" with scenes relating to everyday life situations to play out. In *A votre tour!* Jean-Paul and Rebecca M. Valette include exercises

in role playing, elementary script development, and performances of everyday situations. Likewise, Isabelle Salaün-Gorrell includes a section titled "Mise en scène" in each chapter of *Tête-à-tête*. In addition to these intermediate basic-language texts, for advanced undergraduate courses I personally use two excellent textbooks that provide well-developed end-of-chapter performance-based exercises to round out their methodologies. The text that I use for my advanced grammar course, John Barson's *La Grammaire à l'oeuvre*, encourages the students to rehearse the chapter's grammar through the group creation of a *sketch*; and in the two-volume *La civilisation française en évolution* by Ross Steele, Susan St. Onge, and Ronald St. Onge, in a section titled *Mise-en-scène*, each chapter provides performance activities to interrogate, reinvent, and rehearse French and francophone history and culture.

6 In response to this interpretational limitation of semiotics, theatre studies has seen the development of phenomenological approaches to drama and performance. See, for example, Bert O. States's *Great Reckonings*, Stanton B. Garner, Jr.'s *Bodied Spaces*, and my own *Empty Figure*.

7 "The term 'performance' is, of course, derived from Old English [sic] *parfournir*, literally 'to furnish completely or thoroughly.' To perform is thus to bring something about, to consummate something, or to '*carry out*' a play, order, or project. But in '*carrying out*,' I hold, something new may be generated. The performance transforms itself" (79). Note Turner's use of "transform" here, and also note that *Webster's Third New International Dictionary* identifies the origin of *parfournir* as Old French and not Old English.

8 See, for example, Serge Doubrovsky's study of the Barthes-Picard controversy in his *The New Criticism in France*. In the introduction to this study, Edward Wasiolek explains that the Barthes-Picard feud was not simply "a feud between the historian and the critic," but that "both the American New Critics and the historians of literature against whom they argued believed in the existence of an *objective text*, which could be elucidated by critical process" (9; my emphasis).

9 Genette developed an elaborate theory of intertextuality involving terms such as "paratextuality," "transtextuality," "architextuality," and "hypertextuality" (see esp. *Palimpsestes* 7–19).

10 The indicative-subjunctive paradigm is a part of Turner's widely adopted theory of liminality in cultural development. He speaks, for instance, of the "subjunctive antistructure of the liminal process" (82).

11 Our century's most articulate metaphysician of theatre, Antonin Artaud, shared this interest in poietic cultural renewal with the Marxists and the anthropologists. "Masterpieces of the past are good for the past; they are not good for us," says Artaud, because they are "fixed in forms that no longer respond to the needs of the time" (74–75).

12 "Classic" does not necessarily imply that the text must be part of the canon. Since my thesis largely challenges the "authority" of any text, it is, of course, up to the teacher-director to decide which text she believes has a creative principle that is worthy of re-creation.

13 This and all further translations of French text are mine, unless otherwise noted.

NOTES

14 Assuming that this advance on-campus promotion of the project takes place at least two to three months before the semester project begins, I also contact French faculty at area high schools and community colleges and provide them with advance notice of the upcoming French play performance. See appendix G: "Sample Promotional Materials and Methods."

15 I prefer to translate "l'être" by "the living" instead of the more literal "being."

16 Richard Hahlo and Peter Reynolds, *Dramatic Events*, and Augusto Boal, *Jeux pour acteurs et non-acteurs*. I use the French translation of Boal's original Portuguese text, but there is also an English translation: *Games for Actors and Non-Actors*, trans. Adrian Jackson (London: Routledge, 1992).

17 In the 1997 Joan of Arc project, my students re-created a scene in which young Joan attempts to explain to her father her vision of the Archangel. They offered titles such as "*Tête contre tête*" ("Head against Head"), "*Caresses maternelles*" ("Maternal Caress"), and "*Jeanne déterminée*" ("A Determined Joan").

18 At the invitation of Professor Domnica Radulescu, the symposium director, I had the pleasure of presenting this re-creative exercise as a workshop on October 19, 2001 at the National Symposium on Theatre in Academe at Washington and Lee University. The participants and audience consisted of a mixed group of about fifty theatre practitioners, academics, and students representing English, theatre, classics, and foreign-language departments from American and foreign universities. Following the presentation, for the remaining two days of the symposium and several months thereafter, I received a number of comments from symposium participants, most of which were quite positive though some did betray at least a mild measure of scepticism about the potential benefits of my re-creative approach. One email message I received was both representative and impressive in the way that it interprets the writer's personal struggle between critical caution and the inquisitive desire to explore new ground. On December 5, 2001, Elizabeth Combier, a member of the Spanish faculty of North Georgia College and State University, wrote: "I have been thinking for months now about your approach to theatre. Rarely has anything struck me as so unique as this idea of yours to reduce a theatrical text into a language that students choose. I admit that I was very resistant during our symposium, but tried to keep an open mind. I believe it is not only a new way of thinking, but that it is a very valid and useful approach to theatrical texts. I don't know when I arrived at this conclusion, but I have definitely decided to employ your approach to the next play that I direct. I decided in fact to do a play that I had already directed (with the original text) in order to compare the results.... I just wanted to let you know that you have made a difference in my thinking and I'm glad." Subsequently, at the October 2004 symposium, Elizabeth delivered a paper on her own experiences and experiments in doing re-creative theatre with her students of Spanish. I was delighted.

19 This preliminary information is available in Jarry's *Tout Ubu*. See Michel Pruner's *L'Analyse du texte de théâtre* for a classification of those parts of a dramatic text that he divides into "*le paratexte*" (paratext), which covers titles and prefaces, and "*texte*," which in turn is divided into "*didascalies*" (didascalia) and "*dialogue*" (dialogue). The didascalia is that part of the text that is not dialogue. There are

many sub-types of didascalia. The list of characters, for example, is classified as the "*didascalies initiales*" (initial didascalia).

20 See Nicole Dagnino's and Nicole Zucca's *Exemples de lieux scéniques* for an enlightening discussion of the history of theatrical spaces.

21 The following texts, in French and in English, are good sources for ideas on basic warm-up exercises as well as for interactive dramatic activities (see appendix B, "Sample Interactive Dramatic Games and Exercises") that are appropriate to the nature of the class:

1. Patrick Pezin's *Le livre des exercices à l'usage des acteurs*. See especially the first two chapters: "L'Entraînement" (19–42) and "Approche de la biomécanique" (47–80), which presents biomechanical exercises from a seminar by Nicolas Karpov.
2. Maurice Chevaly's *Petit précis d'expression corporelle d'art dramatique et de théâtre pour tous*. See especially the "Exercices préparatoires" (13–19) and the "Exercices de base individuels et collectifs" (20–40), which are largely drawn from the Hindu Hatha-Yoga tradition.
4. In Gisèle Pierra's *Une esthétique théâtrale en langue étrangère*, the chapter "Journal de bord" (75–106) describes warm-up exercises Pierra used in a foreign-language (French) theatrical workshop that met weekly over the course of a semester.
3. In English, in addition to Richard Hahlo's and Peter Reynolds's *Dramatic Events* and Augusto Boal's *Games for Actors and Non-Actors* (in English translation), see Viola Spolin's *Theater Games for Rehearsal* and John Gronbeck-Tedesco's *Acting through Exercises* for a variety of ideas for warm-up exercises.

Since every instructor-director, every group, and every project is different, some exercises will fit certain instructors, groups, and projects better than others. And, inevitably, each instructor will adapt and personalize the exercises she adopts from other practitioners. These exercises often improve as they get borrowed and adapted.

22 For a history of the French use of the term *jeux dramatiques*, see Maurice Chevaly, *Petits précis*, 79–82. In French, the term "interactif" is generally used in the technical sense rather than in the sense of activity between or among individuals.

23 I usually connect this idea of the belly and the predominance of scatological references in the work to Mikhail Bakhtin's theory that the popular cultures of medieval and Renaissance Europe had a deep and immodest interest in the "*bas corporel*," the lower body of the human individual. See his *Rabelais*, and also Louisa E. Jones's *Sad Clowns* for more on this topic.

24 There are excellent "how to" texts in French to help readers read drama more as an intermediate performance document on its way to the stage than as a finished literary text. One of the most astute, if difficult, among these is Anne Ubersfeld's *Lire le théâtre*, recently translated into English (*Reading Theatre*). (One will find her *L'Ecole du spectateur [Lire le théâtre 2]*, a manual on the semiotic reception of performance, more accessible.) A less detailed, yet thorough and easily comprehensible text is *L'Analyse du théâtre* by Michel Pruner. These manuals

guide students through the specifics of space, time, rhythm, props, language, and action as these "systems" apply to various types of dramatic texts, from the Ancients to contemporary drama. Two texts by Jean-Pierre Ryngaert are also very useful for understanding the performance objectives of the text: *Lire le théâtre contemporain* and *Introduction à l'analyse du théâtre*.

25 See, for example, Charles Lyons's essay "Character and Theatrical Space," where he astutely points out that "the dramatic image of character within space and time is irreducible and that it is impossible to separate the image of theatrical space from the image of character" (28).

26 In spring 2003, when I altered the project to include the reading and performative analysis of three complete texts instead of one (*Dom Juan, Ubu Roi, Fin de partie*), I provided an additional set of guidelines for *Dom Juan* and *Fin de partie*. A good portion of these guidelines were similar to those provided for *Ubu*. However, I added other criteria for analysis, asking students to compare one text with another – their structures, actions, space, characters, and language, as well as their realism and their "theatricality": the theatricality and realism (or non-realism) of the aforementioned categories (space, character, etc.).

27 "Le Théâtre de Baudelaire" 41; my translation. See also Michel Corvin's essay "Pour une analyse de la représentation," where he discusses the multiple effects of redundancy (*redondance*), the superposition of sign systems on the stage.

28 In recent years my student-actors have analyzed the University of Tennessee's Clarence Brown Theatre productions of George Tabori's *The Brecht File*, Wole Soyinka's *Bacchae*, and Sam Shepard's *Buried Child*.

29 Though some elements of this ceremony might seem politically incorrect, I've not noticed any objections, resistance, or uneasiness, even at my Bible-Belt state university,.

30 While it is not clear to me that Brecht ever explicitly advocated role sharing for performance before an audience, he did encourage this practice in his *Lehrstücke* (learning plays) for the critical benefit of the actors. In *The Measures Taken*, for instance, he advised that each of the four actors should play one of the Young Comrade's four main scenes (Ferran 14).

31 Patrice Pavis puts it this way: "[B]eyond all his deceptive manoeuvres, the actor is a bearer of signs, a source of information about the story being told (his place in the fictional universe), the psychological and gestural characterization of the characters, the relationship with stage space or the development of the performance. Seen in this light, he loses his mysterious aura and becomes part of the process of meaning and integration into the performance as a whole" ("Acting" 18).

32 Before contracting this space, I confirmed that the religious affiliation of the centre would in no way restrict or influence the content of our play.

33 The introductions and conclusions to my plays generally are largely developed – and often conceived – toward the end of the rehearsal period. For example, the first part of the first scene of the Ubu story was conceived and finalized in the final phase of rehearsals. Likewise, the introductory and concluding scenes of the Joan of Arc story were written less than two weeks before the first performance. See appendix F for the final written versions of these scenes: "First Scene of 'Père Ubu: Roi de nulle part," "First (Introductory) Scene of 'Jeanne d'Arc: Un certain je ne sais quoi!," "Jeanne d'Arc: Tableau 7, the Conclusion."

34 Given the radically metatheatrical nature of my projects, many of these approximate, self-produced simulations of sound effects survive into the performance.

35 In one early scene of the Ubu story, for example, Pa Ubu is supposed to enter on stage with an "unmentionable brush" (*balai innommable*), which has been translated to English as a "lavatory brush." One of the actors brought to rehearsal a primitive sort of toilet plunger – a clean one! – that we began to use to rehearse the scene. Eventually for the performance we modified it by spray-painting it gold.

36 My Candide project (1996) and my most recent "Human Bombing" (*Le Bombardement humain*) project (2005) produced the most elaborate lighting designs, which were achieved in collaboration with theatre graduate and undergraduate students specialized in lighting design. However, with a minimum of collaboration with the theatre department staff, we also managed a fairly complex lighting design for the Macbett project in 1998.

37 For "Human Bombing," the five actors all applied a dark grey paint to their lips and under their eyes.

38 This is, of course, a metatheatrical step ahead of the practice of Ariane Mnouchkine's Théâtre du Soleil, where, before the performance, the actors prepare themselves – applying makeup and stretching and bantering among themselves – in an area that is in full view of the spectators on their way to their seats.

39 Some colleagues ask the actors to remain for a minute or two of discussion with their class, but I discourage the actors from complying with this request. By remaining in their roles, focused on the function and mission of the promotional spot, they convey a sense of theatrical professionalism and they foster an air of mystery that, like an *amuse-gueule* (appetizer), piques the curiosity of the viewers. In my memo to colleagues informing them of the forthcoming class visits, I do mention that the actors will not remain to discuss the play.

40 While one group is performing their sketch, or at the conclusion of their sketch, another actor from the "audience" will enter the scene and attempt to break into the action in a number of different ways, such as imposing herself as a new character in the story, or claiming to be the long-lost narrator, or simply asking a question about the scene. The form and content of the intervention is entirely up to the actor who assumes the role.

41 I borrow this phrase from Ken Davis's book title, *Rehearsing the Audience: Ways to Develop Student Perceptions of Theatre*, but I use it in a different sense. For Davis, the sense of audience rehearsal is aligned with David Cole's meaning of the term: "What I mean by an audience rehearsal is an opportunity for those who will be the eventual spectators of a given production to increase their capacity for the kinds of perceptivity which that production will require of them" (82). Both Cole and Davis are primarily concerned with teaching theatre-going students to be more knowledgeable about the practice of specific theatrical conventions; they want to provide the educational background and analytical tools that they believe are necessary for a more comprehensive and profound understanding of a given play. As the reader will see in this section, in my projects, I consider

the "rehearsal" of the audience to mean something more performative, direct, engaging, and immediate.

42 In the recent past I attended a professional conference where a distinguished artistic director of a high-profile community theatre gave a keynote presentation on the topic of professionalism in the staging of plays on university campuses in the U.S. The upshot of his argument was that campus faculty who are not primarily trained in the practice of theatre – faculty in English and foreign languages, for example – run the risk of trivializing or even disgracing theatrical art by producing amateurish sorts of play production. Needless to say, I took exception to this cavalier and sweeping dismissal of our work. Yet I do agree that non-professional practitioners who do theatre should be aware of *some* possible limits to the staying power of our productions.

43 With a little experience, during rehearsals the director will be able to get a feel for the approximate length that the production will have when everything finally comes together smoothly. The actors, on the other hand, are generally unable to project accurately the actual time of the performance based on their judgment of the rehearsals. They usually seem to think it will be too long.

44 Early in my experience with play production, like many of my colleagues in the business, I used videotapes of rehearsals as a tool to get my actors to recognize possible flaws in their performance work and to discuss corrective measures. I no longer rely on this practice because I suspect it draws the actors' attention to themselves as spectators (rather than spect-actors) of their own image thereby adversely affecting their first-degree self-awareness and their second-degree awareness of their commun(e)-ication with the onstage acting community (their fellow actors). In other words, by presenting the actors with the perspective of a viewer who is to some extent external to the first-degree stage community, it might jeopardize and/or diminish their sense of belonging first and foremost to the stage reality, their sense of projecting their image and force *from* the stage through the audience space. I confess that I'm not entirely sure that ultimately this decision will not prove to be counterproductive to my purposes, but my artistic and instructional intuition holds for the time being.

45 When my children were very young, around the ages of five and seven, they enjoyed watching video recordings of my plays. They loved doing impressions of the various characters and the distinctive mannerisms of each of the actors portraying their characters. Having observed the rehearsals and live performances as well as watching the tapes, they knew many of my early plays so well that they produced and performed their own "re-created" versions of the re-created plays for their parents and our friends.

46 See "Intertextualité" in Pavis's *Dictionnaire* (178). See also Bernard Dort's brief discussion of the director Roger Planchon's search for "totality" by "assembling" an assortment of scenes from different plays published as *La Petite Illustration* (176).

47 *Exercices* was not even written specifically as a play, though many of the text's "exercises," presented as monologue or dialogue, manifest a dramatic structure. Some even contain stage directions, and one in particular, titled "Comédie," is presented as a play. The work consists entirely of the same frivolous anecdote

recounted ninety-nine different ways. On a bus, the narrator meets a young man with a long neck who first gets upset with another passenger and then throws himself onto a seat that has become vacant. Two hours later, the narrator sees the same young man conversing with a friend who is advising him to raise the top button of his overcoat. (Riveting stuff, eh?) It's all about form, not content.

48 In this 1993 version of the Ubu story, the narrator – a role that we added to the original version, of course – was played alternately by four different actors.

49 I have translated the original French text to English. A brief synopsis of the two plays might be helpful here. *Dom Juan* is, of course, the story of a love-them-and-leave-them nobleman of the seventeenth century and his valet, Sganarelle, who tries to get him to mend his libertine and dissolute ways. Throughout the story, Dom Juan is warned of the inevitable punishment for his sins by a variety of characters: Sganarelle; Done Elvire, the wife he has just loved and left; his father; and, believe it or not, the Statue of the Commander whom he killed in a duel six months prior to the action of the play. His refusal to repent for his debauchery and to acknowledge the supernatural power of the Church leads to his supernatural demise when the Statue unleashes the force that casts him into the fiery abyss of hell. Cyrano, on the other hand, after proving simultaneously his vastly superior swordsmanship and his superhuman intellect in a duel with a viscount, is about to declare his unequalled love to his cousin Roxane, when she reveals her infatuation with Christian, the handsome new cadet in town. Dejected, the long-nosed Cyrano agrees to serve as a go-between for his love object's new love object (Christian) and soon discovers that despite his physical beauty, Christian has no talent for eloquence in dealing with women, an indispensable virtue when dealing with a *précieuse* such as Roxane. Cyrano happily offers to act as the eloquent poetic spirit behind Christian's seductive body. This perfect match (Cyrano and Christian) leads to a marriage between Roxane and Christian, a marriage that remains unconsummated when Christian and Cyrano are whisked off to war. Roxane is overwhelmed by the love letters she receives daily from the front, letters written by Cyrano in Christian's name. She is moved to visit Christian on the battlefield to declare that she now has realized that it is his soul (disclosed by the letters) that she loves and not his physical beauty. Consequently, encouraged by Christian, Cyrano resolves to reveal the truth about the identity of Christian's "soul." But in this neo-romantic work he doesn't get the chance. Christian is suddenly and fatally wounded by a bullet, and Cyrano, out of a brutal sense of honour, duty, and dramatic tension perhaps, assures Christian of Roxane's unchanged loved and re-resolves to forever withhold the truth of his authorship. The fifth and final act takes place fifteen years later in a convent where Roxane has secluded herself. Her "friend" and cousin Cyrano has visited her faithfully every Saturday evening to inform her of the local news. The Saturday of the action, Cyrano is mortally wounded by brigands. When he arrives late for his meeting with Roxane, delirious from the head wound and knowing this will be his last rendezvous with the woman he has adored all his life, his tongue slips and Roxane discovers the truth only moments before his death.

50 At the beginning of the *Dom Juan* sequence of act 3, for example, Sganarelle intimates to the audience, "Oh if I only had a master as faithful and devoted to

NOTES

love as Monsieur Cyrano." And la Duègne introduces the *Cyrano* part of the same act with: "No threats from heaven for Cyrano ... but he does suffer a great deal from heartache."

51 During the action of both original texts, none of the principal characters (or any other character, male or female, for that matter) has the opportunity to sexually consummate a relationship. Sexual possession between potential sexual partners is frustrated at every turn. Cyrano and Christian die virgins, the same fate that awaits Roxane, and the only specific sexual episode that forms a part of the Dom Juan story, the one between Juan and Elvire, predates the action of the play and is merely implied. During the actual time of the play, Juan never gets to engage in sex, though he constantly tries: with an unnamed, unaware newlywed, with the two credulous country girls, and finally, with a repentant Elvire.

52 Costuming and makeup too played a significant role in bringing the two plays together "poietically." Cyrano's Pinocchio nose was refracted in the feline nose for Dom Juan. Both (passionate) protagonists wore knee-length black boots and a black fedora hat. But while Dom Juan wore only a period shirt with breeches, Cyrano wore a breast plate over his shirt.

53 Richard Schechner believes that "the emphasis in making a performance text is on systems of relationships: *confrontations*, or otherwise, among words, gestures, performers, space, spectators, music, light – whatever happens on stage" (33; my emphasis). The combining of texts, I think, provides a more fundamental approach to reconstructing these systems of relationships.

54 The work begins with the tandem appearance of Glamiss and Candor, the generals who originally insurrected against King Duncan and who will be defeated by Macbett and Banco, who also appear in tandem.

55 In Shakespeare's text, "illness," meaning "wickedness" or "ruthlessness," is translated to French as "cruelty" (1.5.19).

56 According to Ubersfeld, naturalist theatre – whose goal it is to create a total illusion of a familiar, referential reality for the spectator – relies on "transparent" signs to create a transparent theatrical art (*L'Ecole* 45–47, 294–96). On the other hand, the bulk of "high culture" avant-garde theatre tends to employ opaque signs to produce an effect of *opacification*, one that calls self-reflexive attention to the creative, artistic (artificial) dimension of the performance: "When a sign becomes opaque, instead of expressing world it undertakes to express theatre" (*L'Ecole* 294). From this angle, opacification means, more or less, to render enigmatic, and, in a sense, to confuse creatively. There are, of course, varying degrees of opacity and transparency within theatrical sign systems and in the amalgamation of these systems.

57 We borrowed from Beckett's *Endgame* the phrase "something is taking its course," a notion that is quite relevant to the regenerative, integrative processes of this project.

58 See my *Empty Figure on an Empty Stage*, especially chapter 2.

www.ingramcontent.com/pod-product-compliance
Lightning Source LLC
Chambersburg PA
CBHW060947230426
43665CB00015B/2094